Small Business Computer Systems

Small Business Computer Systems

Alan Clark

HODDER AND STOUGHTON
LONDON SYDNEY AUCKLAND TORONTO

British Library Cataloguing in Publication Data

Clark, Alan
    Small business computer systems.
    1. Small business—Data processing
    I. Title
    658'.022'0285   HF5548.2

ISBN 0 340 40642 9

First published 1987

Copyright © 1988 Alan Clark

All rights reserved. No part of this publication may be reproduced or transmitted in any form or by any means, electronic, or mechanical, including photocopy, recording, or any information storage and retrieval system, without permission in writing from the publisher or under licence from the Copyright Licensing Agency limited. Details of such licences (for reprographic reproduction) may be obtained from the Copyright licensing Agency Limited, of 33–34 Alfred Place, London, WC1E 7DP.

Typeset by Latimer Trend & Company Ltd, Plymouth
Printed in Great Britain
for Hodder and Stoughton Educational
a division of Hodder and Stoughton Ltd, Mill Road
Dunton Green, Sevenoaks, Kent by The Eastern Press Ltd, London and Reading.

CONTENTS

Introduction   About this book

Section A   The skills of the computer practitioner

1	Say what you mean and mean what you say	1
2	The business of computing	16
3	Training in computer systems	24

Section B   Systems analysis

4	*Caveat emptor* – The buyer beware!	33
5	The feasibility study	41
6	Designing the system	47
7	Evaluating proposals	60
8	Going live	67
9	Running computer systems	76

Section C   Software needs

10	The Good Software Guide	89
11	Word processing	100
12	For the record	112
13	Spreadsheets and their uses	126
14	Using graphics	137
15	Integrated software	146
16	The money programs	153

Section D   Other considerations

17	Operating systems	167
18	Hard choices	175
19	Join the professionals	190

Appendix A   Case study   197

Appendix B   Some useful addresses   200

Outline solutions to study questions   201

Index   209

To Edward Ilett, the teacher who opened up so many new horizons for me.

Acknowledgements

The following people have played an important part in inspiring me, developing my interests, and giving me advice, encouragement and constructive criticism:
Graham Batty, Rev. Roger Bidnell, Harry Clark, Brenda Clark, Norman Cowley, Rev. John Dover, Ann Duffin, Rev. Chris Gale, Campbell Grant, Ray Heasley, Joan Heasley, Edward Ilett, Pete Loewenstein, Diane Pill, Dizzy Prentice, Glyn Price, Chris Sibson, Roger Smith, Howard Toon and Bob Tristram.
To these friends, I express my sincere thanks. Those who have commented on my draft texts share no responsibility for any errors and shortcomings which remain.

INTRODUCTION – ABOUT THIS BOOK

The business of computing calls for a wide range of skills, which can best be developed by practice. This book therefore concentrates on the application of ideas and techniques to realistic and familiar situations.

The computer professional needs careful preparation and a disciplined approach to work. In such a fast-changing area, it is more important for students to develop skills than to memorise facts about current techniques and equipment. For this reason, this book does not emphasise the rote learning of facts. In many circumstances, the computer practitioner can bring any and all available resources to bear on a problem. These resources include books, magazines and experience of similar situations, as well as appropriate software used to analyse and present a solution. Students must develop their ability to compare new situations with those encountered previously and to use knowledge gained and facts recorded to solve the current problem.

To help in developing these skills, many of the exercises in this book will entail much detailed searching out of material. The true worth of a tool (such as a piece of software, or a technique) is best appreciated in its use. While a general introduction is given to various subject areas, the power of the tools introduced can be appreciated more fully when seen in a familiar situation. Through working on the assignments within this book, the reader should build up a body of knowledge and resources, both of which have their part to play in the shaping of a suitable computer practitioner.

Computing is a fast-changing world. This book therefore makes no attempt to recommend particular models of computer or particular programs to buy. What is described is general in nature and aimed at enabling the reader to evaluate the products available. A wide range of examples is quoted from differing situations and readers can then apply the general principles to their own circumstances.

A Research Machines Nimbus microcomputer in use

TOPIC AREAS COVERED

The development of skills is particularly emphasised in the first three chapters of the book. The concentration here is on the skills of a computer practitioner in communication, in relating computing to business methods and in the training needs within the industry. This is followed by a look at the processes which have to be carried out in order to introduce a computerised system to a company, from an initial study, through the design of possible solutions to the installation and running of that system.

The third section of the text is devoted to examining the types of programs which are currently on sale. The study of these products will give the reader a wide-ranging impression of the uses to which computers are now being put in small and not-so-small businesses.

In the closing chapters, two important areas which underlie a computer system are examined: namely the operating system and the equipment used. These technical issues are only tackled in the light of what we want to *do* with our computer. Many readers are perhaps daunted by the prospect of wading through page after page of technical detail in a computer book before getting to the point of what computers can be used for. The approach of this book is from the other end, details of equipment are only introduced where absolutely necessary.

We conclude with a chapter on professional behaviour. A consideration of such matters should form an important aspect of any introduction to the computing industry.

APPLICATION OF THE MATERIAL

Reading this book takes a considerable effort and commitment. The reader must pick relevant situations from his or her own experience and apply the techniques and theoretical work to these situations. Computing, with its many varied disciplines, is held together by a common thread: namely all the skills needed are best acquired through doing. In several cases, exercises can only be carried out using appropriate computing resources. The exercises also require the reader to play a number of different roles and should be attempted in detail to gain the maximum benefit.

The exercises provided are of three kinds:

> **Tasks** are included at points within the text as a stimulus to further thought. They are aimed at provoking the reader into thinking further about what he or she is reading. The material for the tasks is either directly in the text or is gathered by thinking through what the text is saying. Tasks might be a useful basis for a discussion. There is usually no one 'right' answer, and no such answers are provided.
>
> **Study questions** appear at the end of most chapters. These form a useful review of some of the material within the chapter and also follow through some topics in more detail than the flow of the chapter's text allows. Outline answers to the study questions are provided.
>
> **Assignments** are included at the end of the chapters. These are in-depth exercises calling for considerable research of material and an emphasis on presentation.

Tasks and study questions aim to ensure that the basic ideas have been understood, since basic knowledge of the subject areas is assumed by the more detailed assignments.

When this book is used as part of a course of study, the assignments can be used as part of the assessment strategy. This book is designed to give the background to a wide range of topics with which the modern computer practitioner should be familiar. Further detail on particular topic areas can be filled in by reading appropriate books or magazines. The reader is encouraged (perhaps even inspired) to pursue particular subjects of interest in more depth than space here will allow.

SECTION A

THE SKILLS OF THE COMPUTER PRACTITIONER

1 SAY WHAT YOU MEAN AND MEAN WHAT YOU SAY

1.1 COMMUNICATION IN A BUSINESS

A computer practitioner, like any business professional, is called upon to communicate ideas to all sorts of other people. This will include submitting reports, explaining ideas and contributing to meetings, as well as being involved to some extent in the specialist areas of demonstrating and training. The best ideas can be misunderstood or incorrectly implemented if they are not properly explained.

What is to be communicated?

Computer practitioners need skills in communicating many different types of information. This can include the statement of facts, the objective explaining of options or the presentation of opinions. Each of these types of communication calls for different approaches and different forms of presentation can be used. Whether information is to be communicated in a written or oral form, or in a combination of both, the first priority should be a consideration of the target audience for which it is intended.

The computer practitioner might be asked to **outline the facts**, for example, when explaining a new system or piece of hardware. The audience will expect considerable objectivity when a situation is being explained. This puts the responsibility on the presenter to muster as many relevant facts as possible and to present them in a systematic way.

In other circumstances, what may be required is to compare several possible courses of action. Here information must be collected both about the costs and the benefits of each of the possibilities. It might well be that part of the process of presenting options is to identify clearly what options are available.

In different circumstances, a computer professional might be called upon, as an expert, to **give opinions** about a situation. This might include the statement of a preference from a range of options or of an opinion of the relevance and importance of facts presented.

In all three cases, there is a temptation to bias the presentation of information in a particular direction. It is particularly tempting to present opinions as facts. It is sometimes difficult or impossible to distinguish the two. The concern which the computer practitioner shows about this is a matter of professional conscience.

The form in which information is presented has a crucial bearing upon the degree to which it is understood, remembered and acted upon. In many situations, the form of presentation is determined by the person or persons requiring the information, but in some circumstances, the choice of medium is left to the presenter. With any form of communication, it is clearly important that facts and ideas have been carefully gathered and prepared. We shall return to these skills, which are similar and related whatever the form of presentation. Firstly, however, we examine three common forms of business communication: written reports, talks and meetings.

1.2. WRITTEN REPORTS

A REPORT ON THE PRESENTATION OF BUSINESS REPORTS FOR COMPUTING STUDENTS

by
Alan Clark
20th September 1987

CONTENTS

	i
Terms of reference	i
Procedure	i
Findings	i
1 Using sections	iii
2 The sections to include	iv
3 Do we need all the sections?	iv
4 Why do we have standards?	v
5 The appearance of a report	v
6 Types of reports	vi
7 Using an appropriate style	vi
8 Using more than just words	vi
Conclusions	vii
Recommendations	vii
Summary	vii
Glossary	vii
Acknowledgements	viii
References and bibliography	viii
Appendix	
Index	

Terms of reference

A report is required outlining the way in which information might be presented in the form of a written report. The report is to be read by students who will be responsible for drawing up reports as computer practitioners. The information should itself be presented in the recommended format.

Procedure

A number of books on the subject were examined (see Bibliography). Computer literature was consulted to determine the range of styles used by authors, both for independent publications and for manufacturers' literature. A wide range of reports written by students over a period of five years was examined to determine effective and ineffective means of communication.

Findings

1. Using sections

Writing a report involves presenting a number of ideas. It is not appropriate to present all the information without breaking it down into a number of parts. The use of sections helps the reader to follow the development of ideas and to distinguish the detail from the overall structure. Using section headings also breaks up the body of the text and gives the report a more pleasant appearance.

2. The sections to include

Different books give a different set of headings which can be used within a report. It is much more important to remember to include all the relevant detail than it is to stick rigidly to the headings. The use of a standard set of headings does, however, aid the writer to remember what areas to cover.

2.1 *Title*   A title page should give the **name of the report**, possibly with a more detailed subtitle. The title page should also give the name of the author or authors, and the date of preparation.

2.2 *Contents*   A contents page is provided so that the reader knows immediately **what is contained** within the report. This can also be useful when referring back to the document to find specific information in the future.

2.3 *Terms of reference*   This section should state **what the report is about** in its simplest terms. This can be stated as an initial sentence or paragraph. Depending on the context, this might be followed by a more- or less-detailed description of the reasons for and the circumstances behind the preparation of the report.

The terms of reference should also state **for whom the report has been written,** in order to avoid confusion in other readers who might find the content or style inappropriate. If it is considered useful, the writer might also explain the format and approach of the report (first, we look at this, then we do that . . .).

2.4 *Procedure* This section should explain **how the writer went about preparing the report.** It could include a statement of the situations which have been observed and recorded, the people or categories of people who have been interviewed, the literature which has been read, the visits which have been made and so on.

This section will not attempt to describe what was discovered in any of these instances, but will summarise what sources of information have been considered.

It might also be important to include details of those who have been involved or consulted in producing conclusions and recommendations.

2.5 *Findings* This section is sometimes described as the **main body** of the report. As this part can be quite long, it is important for it to be divided into sections. These sections, which should be clearly headed, should be in a logical order. One common way of ordering sections is chronological. (This is a particularly useful technique when giving descriptions.) Another approach is to allow one section to build on the previous section, in order to develop ideas. This can be helpful when more difficult concepts or descriptions cannot be comprehended until more basic information is understood.

The length of a report is often determined by the amount of detail which is included in the findings, as this section can account for half of the length of the report or more. It is important to remember that the findings should be **relevant,** so the writer should ask 'Does the reader (as stated in the terms of reference) need to know that?'

2.6 *Conclusions* This section should draw out the **main points** which arise from the previous section. There is no need to repeat the detail of findings, but simply to state why they justify the conclusions. In other words, this section should show why the facts discovered and presented are important and significant for the reader.

New evidence should not be introduced here.

2.7 *Recommendations* Quite simply this section states **what should be done** in the light of the facts that have been presented. Recommendations should be realistic, in the sense that the person or persons for whom the report has been prepared can do something or get something done about them. The points should be clearly laid out (numbering is particularly useful) and should be in a relevant order (for example in descending order of importance).

ii

2.8 *Summary* A summary of a report should convey, in much less detail, the **material included** in all the other sections. It should be self-contained, so that it can be read separately from the main body of the report, either to help a person to determine whether the contents of the report are relevant, or as a brief reminder of the main points for somebody who read the report some time ago. Indeed, the best summaries can be published separately from the main report for circulation to a wider audience than that for which the report was intended, as an abstract of its contents.

2.9 *Glossary* This section should include the definitions of any technical words used within the report, either specialist words or words which are used within this particular report to have a specific meaning.

2.10 *Acknowledgements* This section should list the **sources** of information and help whom the author has consulted, by way of a thank you.

2.11 *References and bibliography* This should be a formal list of **published material** either consulted or quoted in the report. It is helpful to number the sources of quotations so that readers can refer to them if necessary. Such a list could be in order of use within the report, or in alphabetical order according to writer's names.

2.12 *Appendices* **Detailed information** might be included in a separate section, as it would break the flow of a report to include a mass of detail in the 'Findings' section. Where wading through such detail would be unhelpful, particularly on a first reading, such material can be placed in an appendix, with an appropriate reference in the main body of the text. Such detail could include diagrams, descriptions of procedures and tables of statistics.

2.13 *Index* An index can be useful in a larger report to enable a reader to look up **key concepts.** The process of indexing will involve the selection of words or ideas within the text which are to be included and then their incorporation into an alphabetical list. An index is most useful for somebody who has already read the whole report, is familiar with the contents in broad terms, but who wishes to refer back to a particular point.

3. *Do we need all the sections?*

The standard headings and recommendations on preparing reports are meant for **guidance only.** For any set of standards, there will be those who will be able to suggest situations in which rigid adherence to them would be inappropriate.

There may be circumstances (such as in this report) in which more than one section can be contained within a single page of the report. In many cases, however, the clarity of a substantial report is improved by commencing each section on a new page.

Sometimes, it will not be necessary to include all the sections stated. A report might be prepared as a briefing paper to inform the reader of a set of circumstances or to fill in background information. In this case, it would be of no use to include recommendations, as the only action required is for the reader to assimilate the information. Similarly, some reports which are produced as a matter of routine, such as monthly sales reports, would not contain a Procedure section, as this would not vary from month to month.

In each of these situations, the writer must judge, or ask, what is required.

4. Why do we have standards?

Many organisations will have standard formats for reports, which may include standard headings, agreed page layouts and even standard covers and titles. Such an approach will have a number of advantages. Primarily, the reader will feel at ease with the format and will know the order in which ideas will be developed. This is helpful for looking-up particular points.

The use of standards for all kinds of reports will also help to ensure that none of the relevant areas is missed. This will be of particular help to a trainee or a new employee, who will find it easier to gauge what is expected of a report.

A standard approach helps to achieve one of the main aims of a report, namely to communicate the information required without recourse to the original author. The use of standards is particularly apt when employing a computer to prepare a report.

5. The appearance of a report

The best planned report will fail to have impact if it is not read. Thus, achieving a high standard of presentation is a critical part of writing a report. The use of house standards ensures a certain minimum level of presentation, but there are many techniques which can be used to aid readability.

Sections of a report should be clearly labelled and may be numbered. The importance of different headings and subheadings can be emphasised in a number of ways. The numbering of sections and subsections, as in this document, gives a clear pattern. This hierarchy can be further emphasised by the use of different character types, such as **bold characters** and underlining (see Appendix). Such printing techniques have the advantage over section numbering that they do not even have to be read for the section layout to be obvious.

An additional technique which can be used to effect is to indent paragraphs. This can be extended to the use of indentation within indentation. This not only gives an immediate visual reinforcement of the structure, but it breaks up the regular rectangular shape on the page and is more pleasing to the eye.

iv

Paragraphs should be well used to break up separate points and a series of related points can be made by using numbered paragraphs.

Many of the facilities of word processing are provided to help improve the presentation of a report. Most obviously, word processing enables a report to be typed without errors, however little training or experience in typing a user has. The ease with which a report can be redrafted (compared to manual techniques), is also an encouragement to aim for the highest standards. Facilities such as page headings and page numbering provided by many word processors also enhance the appearance of a document. Additional features of word processing, such as spelling checkers and page indexers, can also be of great benefit in writing a report.

In preparing reports, it might also be possible to use tools such as a database (for the creation of an index) and a spreadsheet (for the preparation of tables).

6. Types of report

The style as well as the content of a report will reflect the purpose for which it is written. Two important factors to consider in this context are 'Who has requested the report?' and 'How is it to be used?'

The nature of the request for the report will normally set a context for the background knowledge to be assumed in the reader, the choice of an appropriate length and the main purpose or purposes of the report. Thus a report to the computer resources manager about the functioning of printers would enable him or her to evaluate previous purchasing policy, to assess current maintenance needs and to plan future acquisitions. Such a report would have a very limited readership and should be exact in its analysis.

The use to which a report is to be put will be another important influence on its style. Often, the wider the circulation of a document is, the more general the language and the content has to be. Thus the annual report of an organisation should make very few assumptions about its readership, as they will have such a vastly differing knowledge and experience.

7. Using an appropriate style

The aim for a writer of any report is to make the reading of the report as simple as possible for the audience. This should include an appropriate style of writing. Facts and details should be presented concisely and accurately. (Facts should always be double checked.)

A writer should remember also that facts or opinions which the reader will not find easy to accept, for whatever reason, should be carefully and tactfully presented.

8. *Using more than just words*

Another useful technique is to include a simple illustration as a title page. Not only is this pleasing to look at, but it makes an impact, makes the report memorable and makes it easy to identify at a later date. Cover illustrations should relate as closely as possible to the circumstances or content of the report.

Photographs and line drawings can be included within the text, where appropriate, to aid the reader. There are two main types of illustration. Firstly, there are those which are an integral part of reading the report, and are referred to within the text. Secondly, there are those which, whilst not being irrelevant, are not essential for following the development of the material. The main purpose of such illustrations is to break up large quantities of text and to act as a reminder to a reader who browses through the report at a later date.

Tables of figures, graphs, histograms and even flowcharts can be used to emphasise or reinforce points. When these include a substantial element of detail, however, they are best included in an appendix. Much graphics work can be prepared using computer technology.

Conclusions

Standard section headings are available for reports, and are a useful guide to the areas to be covered.

The appearance of a report is crucial to its effectiveness.

The use of sections and subsections aids the comprehension of a report.

Many organisations establish their own house standards for reports.

Recommendations

1 All computer practitioners should learn how to present reports in an appropriate manner, so that they are read and acted upon.

2 Suggested standard headings should be used as a guideline rather than rigid rules, though some organisations impose house standards for all their reports.

3 This report should be read by everybody responsible for drawing up reports.

Summary

By examining a variety of circumstances in which reports are required, this report looks at the purpose of a report and the intention with which it is produced. It also explains how a report is prepared and, by giving a set of recommended section headings, how a report is presented in the most appropriate form.

Glossary

A database is a computer program used to record a series of items or records, which can then be analysed in various ways (depending upon the program used).

A spreadsheet is a computer program which can be used to analyse and manipulate tables of figures held as rows and columns.

Acknowledgements

I am indebted both to the students (who are too numerous to mention by name) whose work I have read and to the authors of the books listed below for their suggestions.

References and bibliography

Introducing Systems Analysis and Design vol. 1 Barry Lee (NCC 1978)
Writing Technical Reports Bruce Cooper (Pelican 1964)
People in Touch John Pearce, Alan Cooper, Peter Leggott and Cyril Sprenger (Edward Arnold 1978)

Appendix

Features of word processing which can be helpful in presenting reports

Feature	Use
Bold characters	Emphasis on words or phrases, particularly stressing key words or ideas (useful for subsequent reading of the report).
Underlining	Emphasis on words or phrases, often to accentuate the relative importance of part of a sentence.
Capital letters	Emphasis on words or phrases, particularly used to highlight a heading.
Italic characters	Emphasis on words or phrases, sometimes words with special meaning, or well-known phrases from foreign languages.
Superscript	For references to additional notes elsewhere (to footnotes, an appendix or a bibliography).

Index

Acknowledgements	iii, vii
Appearance	iv, v
Appendices	iii
Conclusions	ii, vii
Findings	i, ii
Glossary	iii, vii
Illustration	iii
Index	iv
Procedure	i, ii
Recommendations	ii, vii
Reference, terms of	i
References	iii, vi
Reports, types of	v ff
Sections	i ff
Standards	iv
Summary	iii, vii

viii

1.3. A TALK ABOUT TALKS – OUTLINE NOTES PREPARED FOR A LECTURE ABOUT ORAL PRESENTATIONS

Introduction

(a) Situations in which talks are given – presentation of a system or idea.
(b) A 'standard' structure for talks, including choice of content.
(c) Aids to the listener's understanding.
(d) Language and style.

Reasons for talks

Talks can be descriptive, outlining a situation; analytical; and informative. The style of a talk should reflect the fact that audiences can have very different levels of experience; one could be giving a talk to superiors or those lower down an organisation. Members of the audience may be experts in the particular field you are talking about or could be novices, while being well informed about their own specialist areas. The hardest situation is where the audience is very mixed.

Structure

The structure of a talk has to be made **more obvious** from the content than in a report; a report has structure emphasised by presentation. Major points in a talk should be emphasised by repetition, as the listener does not have the advantage that the reader has of being able to re-read difficult sections.

Example   Listen to a politician speaking. Many use the simple device of introducing a series of related topics with the same phrase. Neil Kinnock has said, 'I warn you not to be old . . . I warn you not to be ill . . .'. Such structures seem to work best in threes.

Standard structure, then, should include:

(a) a very brief introduction – welcome, thanks etc.,
(b) tell them what you are going to tell them,
(c) tell them,
(d) tell them what you have told them,
(e) closing remarks – recap on the purpose of the talk.

In making the main points:

(a) state clearly what they are as you make them,
(b) make it clear when you have completed a point,
(c) summarise the points as you complete them and relate them to the next point,
(d) use illustrations and visual aids to reinforce the points.

Aids to the listener's understanding

Stories, **accounts** and **case studies** can be used to aid the audiences' understanding. These can directly illustrate the point being made, but make sure that the main point of the story is the point being made in the talk, otherwise the listener is confused. Relating a description is easier to follow and this allows time for the main points to sink in.

Example   When giving a talk about different types of computer software, the three main concepts being covered might be word processing, database and spreadsheets. At the conclusion of the description of each type of software, an account could be given of how such software is used in an actual working situation. This reinforces the main points and relates the theory to practical experiences with which the audience might be familiar.

Questions and **discussion** can also be an effective technique. An opportunity can be allowed at the end for members of the audience to ask questions. (This, of course, can lead to very positive or very negative developments.) Depending on the context, questions could be asked of the audience. This can break up the tedium of one voice being heard all the time, but can be threatening to the listeners: 'Has anybody experienced this? You, at the back, have you?'

What are sometimes called 'buzz groups' can be used, where the audience breaks for a moment or two into groups of two or three, without leaving their seats, to discuss a particular point. The results of the discussions may or may not be reported back: 'Now break up into little groups, just where you are, and decide when you feel 'buzz groups' might be useful. . . . Now what did you conclude?'

Practical demonstrations, particularly using computers, can help illustrate the talk and provide variety.

Visual aids can be very effective in supporting the spoken content of a talk. Equipment that can be used include videos, films and overhead projectors. It is important that the equipment used does not break the flow of the talk. You should make sure:

(a) that there is not so much equipment that it is distracting,
(b) that the equipment works properly beforehand and the screen has been well set up and can be seen,
(c) that you can get proper access to operate it (and that you can work it),
(d) and that you switch off the equipment when you are finished with it, so that material that is finished with does not distract from later points.

Feedback from an audience is useful to evaluate how it has gone, and is particularly useful so that future talks can be revised in the light of the comments.

The language and style of a talk

The English used in a talk should be kept simple. Sentence structure has to be less complex than in written English: 'No talk is effective (**drop voice**) if it cannot be heard. (**Raise voice**) Is that agreed at the back?'

The voice must be lively, but not deliberately over-affected, so don't ham it up too much. It is useful to raise or lower the pitch, to speed up, and say something quickly, and to slow down, or even pause for effect.

The interest of an audience can be increased by looking at them. This is known as eye contact. While avoiding mannerisms (such as **throwing chalk up and down in the hand**), the body can be used to emphasise points. This can include facial expressions, deliberate use of the hands and even movement of the whole body (such as walking **across the room**).

Summary

(a) Talks are used in a variety of situations with a variety of audiences.
(b) All talks must have a structure, to aid both the presenter and the audience.
(c) Talks can be broken up by lightening theory with anecdotes, demonstrations, discussion and questions.
(d) The 'performance' of the person giving the talk can aid or hinder the effectiveness of the presentation.

Conclusion

Thanks for coming along, I hope this will be helpful in your various situations. Now, tell me what you thought of that!

1.4. MAKING EFFECTIVE USE OF MEETINGS – EXTRACTS FROM A REPORT BY THE WORKING PARTY ON MEETING ORGANISATION

Terms of reference

The working party was established to provide detailed guidelines as to the types of meetings which can be held, the ways that they are organised and how their deliberations are reported.

Procedure

The working party held a number of meetings over a period of a month. Members of the group read and discussed the report *The presentation of business reports for computing students*. The main headings recommended in that report were used, but it was found that not all the sections were needed.

Findings

There are three main types of meetings which can be established to aid the smooth running of an organisation, a group or a team. These are **committees**, **working parties** and **executives**.

(a) a **committee** is a group which meets regularly to carry out specific duties. Some committees have responsibilities for the entire running of an organisation, but more usually some duties and powers are delegated to other committees and subcommittees. These then report back to the main body. While a company is run by a board of directors, and a local authority by an elected council, they will often consider reports from other groups for ultimate decision-making.

(b) A **working party** is a group set up by a committee to investigate and report on a specific item or area for which there might not be time for a detailed discussion in its normal meetings. Membership of a working party will consist primarily of members of the committee establishing it. Extra people might be added, though, to bring additional specialist knowledge into the working party. Both the membership and the terms of reference for a working party should be clearly established by the committee setting it up.

(c) An **executive** of a committee can be established to look after the day-to-day running of an organisation. It will usually function only in accordance with the policy laid down by the full committee. When action is required by an executive on which the policy of the committee is unclear, the executive will report the matter back to the main committee for discussion and decision. In cases where action is necessary before the next committee meeting, the executive will act accordingly and report its action back to the committee to be 'ratified'.

Any organisation ought to keep **minutes** which are a record of what happened at a meeting. Minutes must record the business transacted and the decisions reached. There should also be a list of those who were present at the meeting and were responsible for the decision. In the case of particularly important votes, it might be necessary, on the request of some members, to record the votes for and against. It will depend on the circumstances how much detail of discussions is recorded. Some minutes might simply state the decisions reached, others might include the main points made about each topic. A working party, whose purpose is to produce a report, should keep some kind of minutes, but what is most important is to keep a record of the various views put forward for their inclusion in the report.

The business to be discussed at a meeting should be stated in an **agenda**. This enables members to ensure that topics of importance to them are covered. For more formal meetings, agendas should be circulated in advance, usually with the minutes of the previous meeting. In the case of companies governed by the Companies Act (1985), there must be two weeks' notice by law. At less formal meetings, perhaps particularly at working parties, an agenda can be agreed at the start of a meeting.

All meetings should have somebody to **chair** them. This person needs to ensure that all members of the meeting are able to make their points, but that nobody gets an unfair amount of time. Part of the work in chairing a meeting also includes ensuring that the discussion does not go off at a tangent and that it moves on to other points when necessary.

A working party may well proceed by holding one or two initial discussions to outline the main areas to be covered and to sound out opinions on these areas. One or two members might then be asked to draft a report for the next meeting, based on their understanding of the views of the working party. Future meetings would then redraft and rephrase the report until it accurately reflected the views of the majority of the working party. The numbering of the points of the report helps speakers to refer to specific items of concern. In some cases, where a few members of the working party differ in their views, they may add a 'minority report', outlining their disagreements.

Recommendations

An organisation should choose the appropriate forms of meetings for the tasks in hand. Meetings should be well prepared, used appropriately and the results recorded accurately.

1.5. A WORD ABOUT ENGLISH

It is important for the writer of technical material to pay particular attention to the language used. Correct grammar is important when attempting to communicate something precisely. Poor phrasing can distract the reader from the purpose for which the material is written.

There is a tendency which technologists have, which to some extent we all fall into, which is a pity, to use sentences which, when one analyses them, if one has the opportunity, have so many subordinate clauses with convoluted and tortuous phraseology, and yet which could be more simply expressed, if only the writer thought about it, by a series of short snappy sentences. A good writer should avoid such bad English, and such over-long phrases as 'at this moment in time' (meaning 'now') and 'define what is meant by' (meaning 'define'). Two important tools in writing are a dictionary (for spelling and meaning) and a thesaurus (for word ideas).

Many writers of reports and business letters in particular tend to use complicated phrasing and old-fashioned words which are little used in everyday language (such as 'esteemed' and 'undermentioned'). The use of foreign-language phrases, such as *'per se'* and *'ultra vires'*, add little to the reader's understanding.

Technical writing often includes the monotonous repetition of technical words, which may or may not be explained, and the overuse of certain ill-defined terms, such as 'situation'. A well written report should explain all new or technical terms clearly and avoid their overuse. In addition, any argument or explanation is easier to follow if it is stated in short sentences. Ideas should be developed in paragraphs, with one idea to one paragraph.

1.6. VISUAL AIDS

Illustrations can be used as visual aids in reports, when giving talks and in presentations to committees or working parties. When giving a talk, either an overhead projector or a slide projector can be used. A disadvantage of the use of slides is that the room has to be darkened, whereas an overhead projector can be used in normal light. A further visual form which is developing is the use of large screens for the projection of video pictures or computer screen output.

Visual forms of presenting information include tables, diagrams (which are often better explained orally), graphs, histograms, pie and bar charts and flowcharts, and even cartoons. Where possible, the use of colour enhances the effectiveness of visual presentation considerably.

The documents to be used in a new administrative system could perhaps first be introduced using an overhead projector. Statistics are more readily digestible in a pictorial rather than a tabular form. A series of points in a talk can more easily be followed or remembered if they are displayed on a screen.

1.7. TEAMWORK

A very important aspect of work in the computer field, as in many other business areas, in an ability to work as part of a team. The computer professional must be able to relate to other people and to work together with them. When other people are dependent directly on an individual's piece of work, this can bring extra responsibility and pressure.

A group discussion can help in working out precisely what is required in a particular situation. When a group works well, it can produce solutions to problems which may not have been thought of by any of the individuals alone. This can often be enhanced by 'brainstorming', where members of the group try to 'bounce' ideas off one another, in the hope of producing a 'spark' of inspiration.

Working on a large task together will involve the splitting-up of the major task into a number of smaller tasks on which individuals can work and then report back to the larger group. This can be difficult, as it is not always clear how much is involved in each part of the work before it is done. This can lead to bitterness about the unequal sharing of the load. For the sake of clarity it is worthwhile keeping notes of group meetings. A group might also need to keep a record of any queries which have to be sorted out with a superior, so that the most effective use can be made of evaluation meetings.

When individual parts of a piece of work have been completed, they should be read by all the other members of the group. This can stimulate additional ideas, can check the consistency of the report as a whole, and can iron out errors and spelling mistakes. This process of checking can be made less arduous by the use of computer technology. Checks can also be made that the whole report will be presented in a set style. When a verbal report is required, this should be rehearsed by the whole group.

Preparing a piece of work as part of a team can be one of the most difficult and frustrating parts of a job. Frequently, however, it is one of the most satisfying and rewarding experiences.

1.8. ASSIGNMENTS

There are no formal assignments for this chapter. The various communications skills which are described here should be applied by computer practitioners in their own area of interest. The assignments in the rest of the book draw on these skills and their application to the various topics. Computer practitioners can be called upon to submit reports, give talks, attend and contribute to meetings, write memoranda to colleagues and write technical letters (for example to a customer about a piece of hardware or software). At other times they will be asked to contribute to the writing of technical manuals, as well as communicating using the telephone and electronic mail.

All these skills are developed through practice; the assignments in this book ground this practice in the computer field.

2 THE BUSINESS OF COMPUTING

2.1 THE NEED FOR INFORMATION

Information is the life-blood of an organisation. People working in a business require information in order to take decisions about what to do. A manufacturer might need to decide whether to change the colour of a product. An organisation might have to choose a new employee. A restaurant might have to choose a supplier of vegetables. Hundreds of decisions, large and small, have to be made on a day-to-day basis.

To run smoothly, an organisation will need clearly defined methods of decision-making, whether decisions are made by committees or by individuals with particular responsibilities. Within any organisation, incorrect decisions *will* be made. This often worries decision-makers, and some are reluctant to take decisions for fear of taking a wrong one. Most decisions have to be made based on incomplete information, as future trends, for example, cannot be predicted entirely accurately. Decision-makers should bear in mind that when a decision has to be made (and judging when a decision is called for is a decision in itself!) then it should be made on the best information available *at that time*. It is in its efficiency in providing good information that the computer becomes a useful business tool.

TASK

Make a list of reasons why a decision which seemed correct at the time might prove wrong at a later date.

The study of computers in business concentrates on the appropriateness of computers as tools for manipulating data, and as aids to decision-making, rather than on the technicalities of the equipment's operation. Thus the primary consideration in understanding small business computer systems is to ask the question 'Why use computers?' rather than 'How do they work?'

2.2 WHAT IS GOOD INFORMATION?

A distinction is made between **data** and **information**. **Data** is the term used to describe raw facts which are collected, such as the hours a person worked, the number of customers arriving in an hour or a price per kilogram. Data is collected in a number of ways, such as the completion of forms and surveys or direct input to a computer. **Information** is the result of processing the data into a report, a summary or some other analysis of those facts. The term **data processing** is used to describe the use of computers (or other devices) to collate, sort and summarise facts into information. Information is then used as the basis of decision-making.

In the main, what makes information 'good' is that it is helpful in decision-making. A manager is only interested in having information which is relevant and which might mean that action must be taken.

Level of detail

Information should be **at an appropriate level of detail**. In order for somebody to make a decision, he or she should be presented with just the right amount of information – more detail than is necessary can simply confuse. For example, to decide the amount of ice cream to make for the coming week, the production manager will want to know how much has been sold this week, including the amounts of each flavour. It is not likely that it will be relevant to know which shops have sold how much of each flavour. The distribution manager, on the other hand, will want to know the breakdown of the sales in order to plan deliveries. Thus, the extent to which information should be summarised and the format in which it ought to be presented will depend on the position within the company of the person who will be using the information. Different people have different information needs.

Accuracy

Information should be **accurate**; good decisions are rarely made when they are based on bad or inaccurate information. Computers are a great help in producing accurate information, provided that the original data is accurate. Computers are much less prone than humans are to making mistakes in calculating, sorting and reproducing lists. Errors in processing occur much less frequently with computers than they do with humans.

Timing

Information should be **timely**. Ideally, information should be produced from up-to-date data. The processing speed of a computer allows for the quick production of information from data. It is a data processing management judgement whether the data held is up-to-date and sufficiently accurate. If decisions are based on out-of-date information, then it is unlikely that the conclusions that are reached will be the best that could be reached at that particular time. It needs coordination between management decision-makers and data processing staff to produce up-to-date information when a decision is to be made.

Targeting

Information should be **targeted**. Information must not only be available, it must be available to the right people. It is important that reports or summaries which will form the basis of a decision should be given to those who can interpret their meaning and can act upon them. Information is relatively less useful to somebody who cannot do anything about a problem.

TASK

Compare the information presented in a half-hour news bulletin on television with a news summary of five minutes or less. Outline the extent to which the information can be said to be:

(a) at an appropriate level of detail,
(b) accurate,
(c) timely,
(d) targeted.

2.3. INFORMATION FLOW

A well-organised company will ensure that there is a smooth flow of information between different sections. This is normally achieved by a combination of meetings, memos, informal discussions and reports. This communication can be aided in several ways by computers.

The work of a department can be helped by informed discussion within the department of issues presented in good reports and summaries. Links between departments can become strained because departments do not know what other departments are doing. Often, the extra effort of keeping others informed can prove too much when departments are concentrating on doing their own job properly. The use of computer information systems can reduce the effort needed to produce information for other people in an appropriate and useful way.

The introduction of a computerised system may also force an organisation to analyse its information requirements and to approach communication in a more disciplined way. The use of a single computer to provide for the information needs of several parts of the company can begin to automate information flow. The move towards linking the flow of information within an organisation is referred to as 'integration' or a bringing together. ('Integration' literally means 'making whole'.)

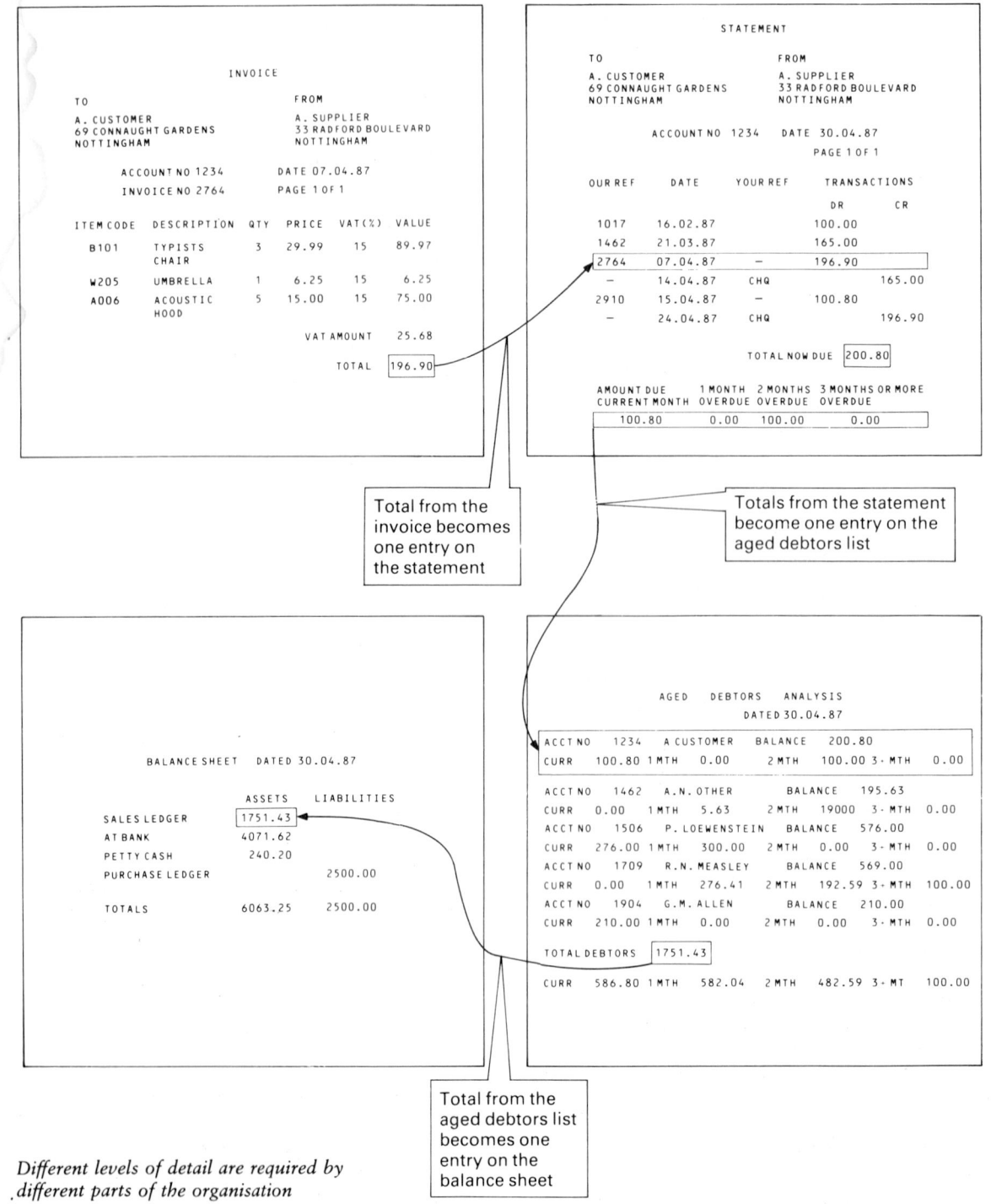

Different levels of detail are required by different parts of the organisation

```
┌─────────────────────┐                    ┌─────────────────────┐     An example of
│ SALES SECTION       │                    │ DESPATCH SECTION    │     information flow—
│ accepts requests    │                    │ sends goods to      │     stock control for a
│ for goods from      │                    │ customers as directed│    wholesaler
│ customers; informs  │                    │ by Stock Control Section│
│ Stock Control Section│                   └─────────────────────┘
└─────────────────────┘
            │                ┌──────────────────┐         ▲
            │                │ STOCK CONTROL    │         │
            └───────────────▶│ SECTION          │─────────┘
                             │ records current  │
            ┌───────────────▶│ levels of stock  │─────────┐
            │                └──────────────────┘         │
            │                                             ▼
┌─────────────────────┐                    ┌─────────────────────┐
│ RECEIVING SECTION   │                    │ ORDERING SECTION    │
│ accepts delivery of │                    │ orders goods from   │
│ goods from suppliers;│                   │ suppliers as        │
│ informs Stock       │                    │ directed by Stock   │
│ Control Section     │                    │ Control Section     │
└─────────────────────┘                    └─────────────────────┘
```

TASK

For an organisation with several departments, write down the benefits of using computers for information flow:

(a) within departments,
(b) between departments.

2.4 DECISIONS, DECISIONS!

The choices necessary within any organisation fall into two loose categories. There are short-term and long-term decisions.

Short-term decisions are those which have to be made about particular situations. Should goods be ordered from a particular supplier? What price should be charged for a specific job? Such decisions are made against a background of overall company policy, and the action to be taken will normally be within guidelines which have been agreed. However, it is not possible to lay down guidelines for every possible eventuality. At various levels of responsibility within an organisation, therefore, individuals or teams will have discretion to make decisions which they think are appropriate.

Long-term decisions usually affect the overall direction of the company and are therefore usually about policy. Decisions of this type may involve setting the maximum credit level that customers may enjoy or choosing whether to market a new product and if so which. These strategy decisions are frequently made at the higher levels of an organisation. Long-term decisions can have an effect on the way that short-term decisions are made and can often form the basis for a review or rethink of procedures.

TASK

Write lists of the short-term and the long-term decisions involved in running a sports team.

2.5. DIFFERENT TYPES OF TASK

A distinction is also drawn between what are called **active** and **reactive** tasks. In a management role, a person should set objectives, whether these be production targets, profit targets or targets for a level of service.

Active tasks are those tasks which are carried out in working towards the objectives of the job. **Reactive tasks** are those which are carried out in response to other people, such as dealing with memos, answering telephone calls and so on. There is a danger that management will be drawn into purely reactive tasks, allowing little space for active tasks. A disciplined approach to the production and use of reports can help in making effective use of a manager's time.

TASK

Write down a list of fifteen or more things which you did yesterday. Divide them into separate lists of active and reactive tasks.

2.6 DIFFERENT TYPES OF REPORT

Exception reports

Exception reports are based on the idea that routine decisions can be automated. Transactions falling outside the category of 'routine' will require some special attention.

The principle behind exception reports is that those with responsibilities for decision-making need only have situations reported to them where they are required to make a decision about what is to be done. For all other cases, normal procedures are laid down and can be followed through without the need for further decisions. Management then proceeds on the basis that 'no news is good news', so that the vast majority of business transactions, deemed to be 'normal', are not reported in detail.

The exception principle ensures that information is presented briefly. It is better for the ordering department to be presented with a list of the ten items which should be ordered than it is for it to be given a complete list of the current stock level for all nine hundred items.

Similarly, many organisations operate a system whereby expenditure over a certain limit must be authorised by a senior manager. This again works on the notion that the manager is then only called upon to be involved in major decisions.

No automated system, and indeed no manual system, can be designed to cover every possible circumstance. Indeed, when designing computer systems, much effort can be wasted in designing complex (and often interesting) ways round peculiar combinations of circumstances.

The story is told of the effort that went into the design of the inbuilt calendar of a computer so that it would cope with the complicated rules about leap years. The last year in a century is not a leap year, unless it is divisible by 400. (Thus 1900 and 2100 are not leap years, but 2000 is.) Though the problem may be interesting in its own right, time and money would have been saved by deciding that the computer could be told by the operator what to do. After all, the problem only occurs once every hundred years!

The use of carefully designed systems of exception reporting in a computerised system will mean that many of the reactive tasks that a person carries out will be properly organised and constrained. For example, those responsible for ensuring that the organisation will not run out of supplies need not worry if they are confident that the computer system will report all those items with very low stock. These will be the items that will have to be dealt with when the report is produced. It is part of the computer professional's job to instil confidence about such systems in managers and other workers.

TASK

Write a list of the benefits of the exception reporting principle for the hard-pressed manager.

Regular reports

Regular reports are prepared at fixed intervals, their production being designed as an integral part of a computerised or manual administration system. These regular reports will include summaries of past performance, analyses of trends and forecasts for the future. Thus the policy of buying in stock can be evaluated by working out, for example, the total value of stock at a particular time and the number of items which are out of stock. Similarly, regular reports can be produced on sales of products, or on the performance of an individual section or region. A pricing policy can be reviewed in the light of an analysis of costs produced at the end of an accounting period. This might take into account the wages bill for the month, which perhaps cannot be predicted because bonus payments are made based on production figures.

Many reports will be produced on a monthly cycle, to fit in with a regular calendar of meetings for making decisions, which can then be based on up-to-date information. In order to exercise control over an organisation's affairs, those responsible want a number of types of feedback about the current performance.

One form of monitoring is to take a 'snapshot' of the current state of affairs. Information is therefore produced about the position at a particular time; this may be done on a regular basis. Many other decisions will be based on changes in figures produced and so reports might include statistics for last month, three months ago and a year ago, for example. Decisions can then be based on the trends in the statistics.

Reports should be produced as frequently as they are needed in order to take decisions. In a manual system, both the cost and the delay before reports can be ready might mean that they are produced less frequently than would be desirable in management terms. The cost of report production within the regular processing cycle is far lower in a computerised system.

On-demand reports

On-demand reports are produced in order to meet a specific need. The times when information will be required for decision-making cannot be entirely predicted. Unforeseen circumstances mean that some reports will be needed as requested. On-demand reports are also known as *ad hoc* reports.

The design of a business information system has to strike a balance between the inclusion of regular reporting within the processing cycle and the provision for on-demand reports. Regular reports provide a stimulus for action from management on a reactive basis. On-demand reports are initiated by managers in an active way. Too much emphasis on regular reports may mean that managers are swamped with paperwork and reports lose their impact. Too much reliance on on-demand reporting may mean that those who have a problem to solve do not know they have a problem.

2.7. COMPUTERS AS A DECISION-MAKING TOOL IN BUSINESS

Managers can use computers effectively to help them to do what they are already doing, but better. Sometimes, difficult decisions have to be made, and perhaps the evidence shows that a choice between two options is very close. The capacity of a computer to analyse large amounts of data and to produce reports quickly can be of considerable help in making such marginal decisions.

Computers are now used by an increasing number of people. The earliest computers were designed and used to perform large scale 'number crunching' arithmetic. Many early installations were in the military and scientific field. Computing has gone through many changes since then as the philosophy moves towards 'one per desk', with office workers having computing power literally at their fingertips. Progress has often been measured in 'generations' of computer hardware, but there has been just as big a change in the nature of computer applications.

The earliest computers could only be operated by those with sufficient knowledge of electronics to keep the equipment functioning. Programming involved setting switches and revolved around numbers. The boom in mainframe computers in the 1960s led to a clear distinction between the programmer on the one hand and the operator on the other. One programming manual of that era suggests that it is never desirable for a programmer to run his own programs! Equipment has developed so much now that the processing power can be put

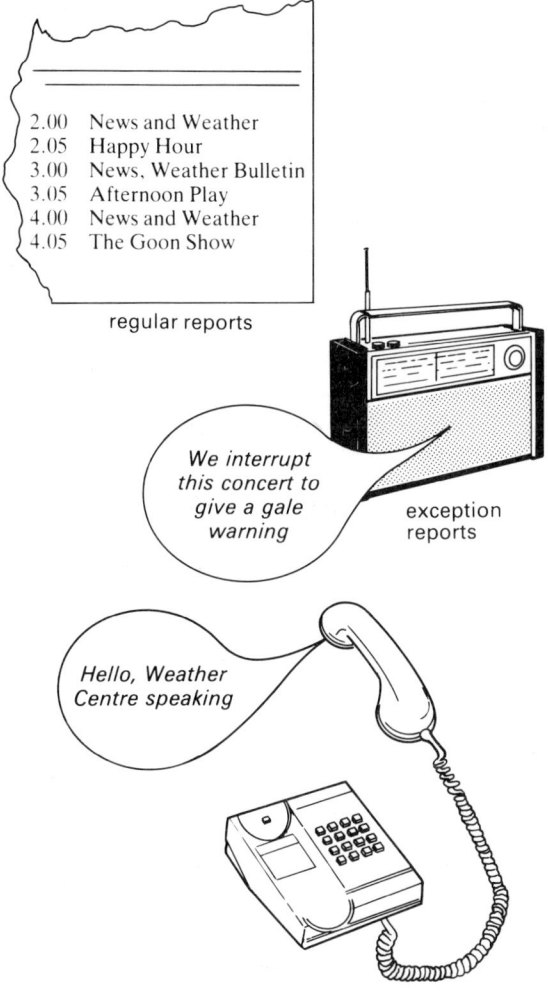

Three ways of getting a report on the weather

in the hands of the decision-makers. Easy-to-use software (which many describe as being **user friendly**) is seen as being just as important a feature of a system's design as good hardware.

TASK

Write a list of the information needs in running a house. Outline the structures of decision-making. List any ways that a computer could help in this. (Lots of computer programs have been sold to 'do your home accounts', but do *you* know anybody who actually uses such a program?)

Decisions about the type and style of provision of computer processing power are based on what is best for the organisation, rather than simply what is technically possible. Many systems now provide computing power in individual departments or sections, in a style called 'distributed processing', rather than concentrating all the resources in a 'computer department'. This can mean more independence for the various parts of an organisation. Similarly, the organisation might be best served by ensuring that data is captured into the computer system as close as possible to the point of origin of that data.

Decisions on the design of computer systems are as much to do with appropriate styles of business organisations as they are to do with technical feasibility.

TASK

A manager once told his staff: 'Don't come to me with a problem unless you bring me two solutions', the idea being to aid thinking about solutions to the problem. Suggest ways in which this principle might apply to an accounts clerk who reports directly to the owner of a small business. Describe ways that a computer could be useful in this process.

2.8. THE SKILLS NEEDED IN BUSINESS COMPUTING

With the widespread use of computers in businesses large and small, there is an increasing demand from companies for people within them to have a broad range of knowledge about computers and their uses. Such people must relate to fellow-workers and customers at all levels of influence and expertise.

There are four common myths concerning what computing is about.

Myth 1

This is that work in computing depends on a high level of mathematics. In education, this link is emphasised because much computing in schools is taught as part of mathematics, by mathematics teachers. *Using* computers requires very little mathematical knowledge. The main advantage of having studied mathematics is that it encourages a disciplined and structured approach to tasks. Such skills can, however, be developed in very different ways. Some people claim that Latin is a better qualification for computing than mathematics!

Myth 2

This claims that computing is about programming. A competent and regular computer user may not need *any* programming knowledge. The study of small business computer applications need make no direct reference to the specialism that is programming. Where the study of programs is necessary, it is often in terms of judging how well designed a program is from the *user's* point of view.

Myth 3

This myth states that the study of computing is the study of hardware. The educated computer user can leave detailed knowledge about electronics to the experts in that area, in the same way that most television users know little about how the picture appears on the screen. The computer professional should know how to reduce the chance of breakdowns, how to minimise their effect and how to get equipment repaired, but needs little engineering skill.

Myth 4

Myth 4 is that computers are for the experts. Because of the mystique that surrounded the use of mainframe computers for many years and the way that computers have been portrayed in science fiction and detective films, many people think that computing is something for the experts. With the modern generation of software, this need no longer be the case.

The skills that are useful for a career which involves the use of computing are much more broadly based on business awareness.

Teamwork and integrity

Computing calls upon people to work together as a team. Good teamwork requires a balancing of the interests of team members and allocating work among members on an equitable and co-operative basis, rather than on competitive grounds. These are qualities particularly vital for work in a small business.

Computing involves a considerable amount of evaluation and judgement and therefore calls for a great deal of integrity. The presentation of a finished system has a lot of influence on its usefulness and durability and the polishing of a finished product is important. The computer practitioner must take great pains to ensure the preparation of a product that meets the requirements of the person requesting it. This is more important than including all the features possible to show off the equipment to the full. Many computer 'experts' are prone to the arrogance of believing, often wrongly, that they know exactly what is required without asking. The industry is better served by the meticulous than the misdirected genius.

Skills of communication are important for the computer practitioner: reports have to be written, meetings need to be held, bids have to be made for money. Computer practitioners are also frequently faced with helping people to overcome fears they have about new technology. This is often because people fear the unknown. This can call for a good deal of skill in terms of personal discussions. Frequently, other people have to be trained to use computing equipment effectively. This can involve work with other staff who have their own specialised knowledge and skills; the computer practitioner may need to relate to a wide range of people. Many of these skills are developed through years of practice.

2.9. STUDY QUESTIONS

1 Your domestic consumption of electricity will be recorded within a computer information system. Suggest circumstances in which information about your consumption will appear on exception reports, regular reports and on-demand reports.

2 Many employees within companies feel that they are not told enough about what is going on. Like mushrooms, they say, they are kept in the dark! Suggest reasons why communication from the top breaks down.

3 Many managers feel frustrated in that they are not sufficiently in touch with the 'grass roots' of the organisation. Suggest reasons why communication from the bottom up breaks down.

2.10. ASSIGNMENTS

1 Write a report entitled *The changing face of computing*, describing the way in which the use of computers has broadened in the last 50 years. The development of hardware should *not* be the main emphasis of the report, as it should be about the development of applications. The report should include illustrations and should show an awareness of the range of uses of computers.

2 Imagine that you are the manager of a small ice cream firm, which produces its own ice cream and sells it from a fleet of eight ice cream vans. Describe the information needs of:

   (a) the production manager,
   (b) the accounts clerk,
   (c) each van driver,
   (d) yourself,
   (e) the owner of the firm.

3 TRAINING IN COMPUTER SYSTEMS

Even when the hardware has been chosen correctly, and adequate software has been acquired, a computer system will only be as good as its liveware! 'Liveware' is the name which has been coined to describe the personnel involved in a computer system, though the term is used more as a joke than a serious jargon term. A computer system can only function at its best when staff are well used. Staff resistance to change can be a major brake on progress, but of equal concern can be the presence of willing but badly informed users.

Good computer practitioners will recognise that training is vital and they should be able both to learn skills and to teach them to others.

3.1 WHO NEEDS TRAINING?

In the early years of computing, the term 'operator' was used for the person who physically operated the equipment. Loading cards, changing paper in the printer and swapping tapes were all part of this process. This was not considered to be as sophisticated a role as that of the programmer, who wrote instructions, but rarely had direct contact with a computer. Punch operators were used to prepare data from input forms. The people who filled in the forms also rarely got near the computer, merely writing data ready for input and handling the output of the processing.

These roles have changed dramatically in recent years. Programmers work through terminals. Those responsible for the origination of data often enter it directly, and in many cases, get results immediately. Thus while the term 'operator' still has its technical meaning for larger installations, there are many other people who are required to use computers in their work. These people have to be trained to perform their job efficiently.

3.2. INFORMAL TRAINING – 'SITTING BY NELLIE'

Many computer skills have been passed on from one person to another by an informal means of the learner sitting and watching a competent user. This has frequently proved to be an effective way to learn how a particular job is done. However, this approach of 'sitting by Nellie' (to see how she does the job) is very dependent on the abilities of 'Nellie', not just as a user of the system, but also as a teacher of skills. A person who is being shown the ropes will obviously be limited by the depth of understanding of the person passing on the skills.

A person using a computer system will want to know how to start it up and shut it down. It is surprising how many systems are left running all day and all night for fear of switching them off. A good user will find it essential to log jobs done and perform elementary job control. When an error occurs at any stage of a process, a user will have to know what to do in computer or administrative

The changing view of business computer users—the use of computers is a fact of modern office life (left), and not just the preserve of the expert few (right)

terms. Equipment also has to be regularly maintained and the environment has to be kept clean.

3.3. INITIAL TRAINING

Managers need to know what benefits can be obtained with the use of a computer system. In the main, they will want to know what a system can do rather than to be able to use all the individual elements of a system. Increasingly, of course, managers are able to perform enquiries on a computer system. It is desirable that they are trained to gain the maximum benefit from this. It is also vital for managers to be trained in the interpretation and use of computer-generated reports, whether they are regularly and automatically provided by the system, or are produced by request.

When a computerised system is being devised, it is an important part of the analyst's job to determine which tasks are to be performed by whom. This will then be reflected in the training when the system is introduced.

3.4. ONGOING TRAINING

Whatever the quality of the initial training of users, there will inevitably be a turnover of staff using a system. Thus most staff who are involved with a computer system will come into contact with the 'sitting by Nellie' process from both ends – as trainer and as trainee.

One of the various skills needed by a computer practitioner is an ability to train others, whether at a formal or informal level. Many systems fall down in their operation, not being put to best use because the training of users has been inadequate. This is frequently revealed in the attitudes of users to manuals. If asked whether they have read the manual, many would reply that they can do all they want to with the system. This is often a thin disguise for a lack of exploration of a program's advanced facilities, whether it be word processing, a financial package or any other software. Many users carry out tasks in a longwinded way because 'it works'.

TASK
Make a list of shortcomings of the attitude that 'I can do all I want to with the computer'.

3.5. WHAT IS THE STARTING POINT?

Before starting to train people it is important to determine their level of competence. What experience have they had with other systems before? How frequently will they be using the system in the future? The answers to these questions might determine, for example, the importance of keyboard competence, as well as the requirements for support materials to remind users about facilities. A frequent user will probably be able to remember most commands without reference to written material. An infrequent user needs to know where material is and how it is organised in order to look things up when necessary.

An irregular user desires to know in some detail what a system is capable of doing. For all but the most frequently used facilities, however, a knowledge of how particular things are achieved can be left at the level of knowing where to look things up in a manual or quick reference guide.

TASK
Describe some of the feelings of embarrassment which people have when they are on training courses.

3.6. WHAT TYPES OF TRAINING ARE THERE?

Training has two main strands. The first aims at giving people an overall awareness about the use of computers. The second is the training of people in specific skills to be able to use a particular package or system. These two clearly interact, as understanding the overall capabilities of computing will help a learner to place the particular training in context.

Computer awareness

Other than at a very elementary level, the training of personnel in overall computer awareness is usually left to people who spend a large proportion of their time on such work. There are many courses and sources of this kind of training either on a full-time or a part-time basis. Such courses are sometimes described as computer education to distinguish them from computer training, which is the term used for teaching specific skills. Computer education courses are provided by a wide range of local colleges, such as technical colleges and polytechnics, as well as by private tuition colleges. Other courses are provided on a correspondence basis, for example through the Open University.

Some large organisations have their own training departments, which might provide an element of computer education. Training officers are sometimes appointed with responsibility for overseeing staff training, ensuring that all staff get the right mix of help in their development.

Computer skills training

In the specific skills area, however, many different computer personnel get involved in the communication business. The hardware designer may be called on to write manuals. The software designer, too, has to communicate how something functions. A consultant who has helped a client to pick a system of hardware and software is often also asked to get involved in explaining how the system is used.

TASK

Make a list of the qualities that you think make a person good at training others in computer skills. Outline how you would assess these skills in an individual.

3.7 WHAT ARE THE METHODS OF TRAINING?

Books

Many **books** have been published on computers, as can be seen in many high street shops which sell computers. Bookselling brings important extra business for such shops. For an organisation, a good book is a cheap way to train personnel. Books are written about many of the major packages available and appear fairly soon after the software is released. Even at £30, a book is a cheap form of training and can be used by several different people. Books allow readers to acquire knowledge at their own speed. Unsupported by a personal approach, however, books tend to fail to hold a trainee's attention. Books are often not available for software other than standard packages. At times, the availability of books about popular packages can be another argument in favour of choosing those packages.

Audio visual aids

The term **audio visual aids** is used to describe both audio and video tapes and their supporting written materials. The best of these training materials use professional actors, frequently well-known ones (such as John Cleese). This approach attracts the attention of the audience, who then remember the information more effectively. These materials are usually available for hire or purchase. They therefore share the advantages with books that they can be re-used and that they can be used at a convenient time. With books, they share the drawback that a limited range of topics is covered.

Formal courses

Formal courses provide a means of imparting a well-defined list of learning objectives to a group. As part of such a course, trainees may get more or less 'hands on' experience at the keyboard. In contrast with the other methods of training mentioned so far, a 'live' lecturer can respond as a course progresses and can adapt material according to the audience. The quality of a course will depend on the lecturer's ability to communicate. Many demonstrations appear to be given by people who may be very technically able and know the software and hardware inside out, but who cannot communicate the detail to an uninitiated audience. This approach to presentation is one of the things that has given computing a bad name in some circles; first impressions are very important!

Computer-aided training

Computer-aided training is a rapidly developing field. The early history of learning equipment was marked by the swift rise and even swifter fall of the teaching machines of the 1960s. These failed because the materials prepared for them were not general enough and could not be used in a wide variety of situations. Some of their supporters also made the mistake of not distinguishing between education and skills training.

Nowadays, however, when a potential user of a package is to be trained in its use, it now seems quite natural for the training to use computers, as these are the machines which the person is being trained to use.

Computer training packages are usually specially written programs which simulate parts of a package and use sample data. One of the most popular and effective subjects for computer-based training packages is the development of keyboard skills. Such programs are successful because they use the computer as a tool for setting fairly routine exercises and for monitoring mistakes, scores and times. The structure of such a course is fairly simple to comprehend and so the user can have a good overview of the work ahead.

Where laser discs are available, a learner can interact with a video film through a computer. Thus a whole series of pictures can be shown to demonstrate principles and to ask questions. This recent innovation has led to some imaginative developments.

Computer training packages can be exciting, because they give immediate results. The trainee can therefore see measurable progress quickly. Training packages can be used on the actual equipment on site and are re-usable. Thus several people can be devloping their skills at their own pace over the same period.

Computer training packages suffer from a similar drawback to books, in that they are only available (or suitable) for a limited range of software packages or other subjects.

3.8 HOW ARE TRAINING MATERIALS DESIGNED?

Consider training early

Often it is only when a system nears or reaches completion that thoughts turn to the people who are actually going to use the system.

This attitude is clearly undesirable. The day-to-day user is an important person to consult in the design of a computer-based system. Ease of use is as important in computer software terms as it would be in design of a car or a video recorder. The technical brilliance of a system will be overlooked if the user finds it difficult to benefit from this.

Consideration of how actual users are to be trained in using the system should start early in the life cycle of the system's development. While training needs might not directly influence the design of a system, adequate consideration should be given to training users of the system produced.

Most computer practitioners who are involved in the development of a system will be called upon to make some contribution to developing training materials. Taking training seriously should also help in designing better systems.

Forms of training

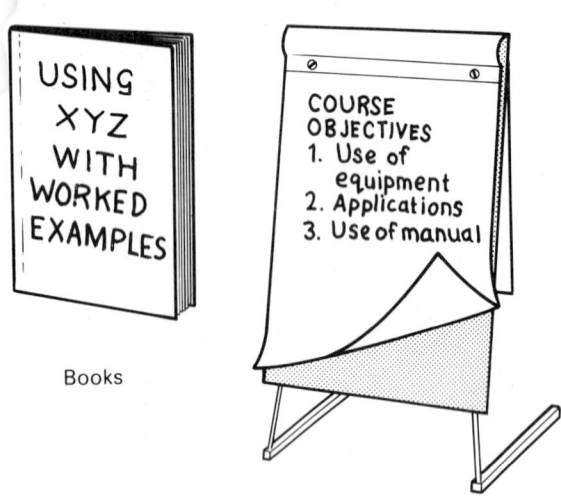

Books

Formal courses

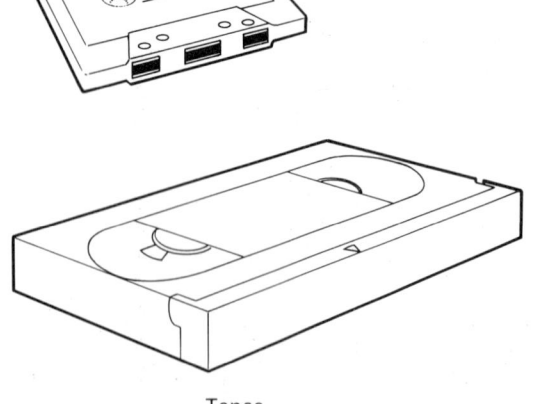

Tapes

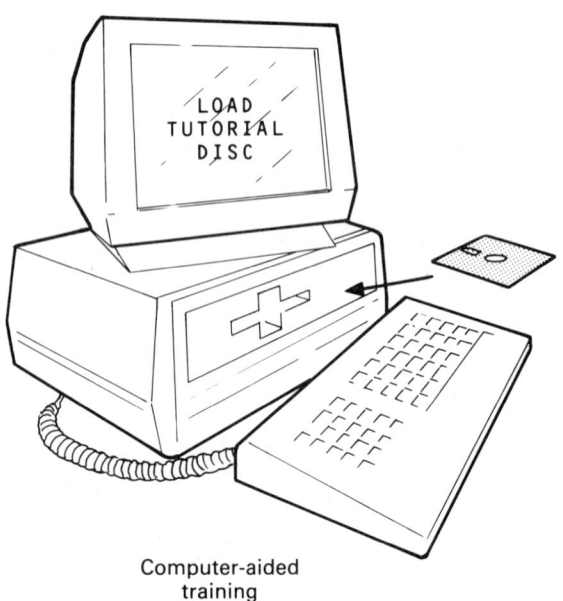

Computer-aided training

Consider the structure

As with all material, training resources are not written for their own sake, but to serve a specific purpose. This can affect the style of writing. The level of detail, the use of language and the speed of covering new ground must be considered. In designing materials, it can be a useful exercise to write down all the topic areas on one sheet of paper, in the order in which they come to mind. Topics can then be grouped if they are related or are similar in complexity. This can be done by bracketing them, or marking them in the same colour. Once the number of broad topic areas has been reduced to a manageable number, these can then be numbered in the order that the ideas are to be developed. Detailed writing of materials should then be done in the order chosen.

It may well be useful within written notes to summarise the learning in a particular section. One way in which this can be done is to build up a list of 'commands covered so far' which accumulates at the end of each section. This idea can be particularly effective if the new material within a summary appears in a different print style. Word processing can help in preparing such summary sheets.

Consider the reader

As well as being broken up into sections, training materials should have a clear introduction. Detail which would interrupt the flow of learning and which may not be essential to the competent use of the package can be left to an appendix. A contents list and/or an index are useful in guiding differing levels of reader through training materials. Good training materials should allow firstly for readers who start from very different levels of competence and experience, and secondly for regular users seeking to refresh their memories. Thus, a person who has previously read the whole document should be able to dip into the material to check up on one or two facts.

It is important to use **examples** in training materials. Firstly, this illustrates the concepts which have been described, and may reflect a similar situation to that experienced by the reader. Secondly, it gives a chance for a recap on the details to reinforce learning.

Frequently a **summary of commands** on a single sheet can act as a reminder of all the facilities available. This is often designed in a way that it can only be used after reading the main manual, and may contain page references to the manual. Such a resource is sometimes called a **quick reference guide**.

TASK

Make a list of books and manuals about software which you have read or used. Try to include in your list both supplier's manuals and commercially published books on the same packages. Give each a grade from 1 to 10 (1 being the lowest score and 10 the highest) as to how much of it you have actually read and another grade for how much you enjoyed reading it. Then give each book a grade for the number of examples and illustrations it has. Compare your three grades for each book or manual. Suggest reasons why the grades are or are not similar.

TASK

Take a manual for a package which you have not used. Draw up a table showing the order in which topics are covered. By using the list of contents and the index, plan out a course of reading. (The manual will almost certainly not be suitable for reading from cover to cover.)

3.9. WHAT SUPPORTING MATERIALS ARE REQUIRED?

A trainee reading written materials will normally appreciate suggestions of ideas to try. These should be designed to illustrate a range of recently covered concepts and are as important a part of good documentation as formal definition and description. Good, interesting exercises will back up the learning of theoretical ideas. In some cases, examples and exercises can be supplied on magnetic disc.

Where this is practicable, a trainee should have a system formally demonstrated and so the preparation of formal demonstrations should be one skill developed by the computer practitioner.

Demonstrations

These are of two main types. The use of particular facilities can be illustrated in a demonstration, from which it is anticipated that the learner will remember what to do. This technique is usually most effective when immediately followed by a practical session where examples are used to stress again the ideas already learnt.

A demonstration can also be used to motivate the learner. A wide range of uses should be illustrated in order to encourage a learner to use a package to the maximum. When preparing such demonstrations, it is important to strike a balance in the amount of detail, so that the audience is not overwhelmed; naturally, this would be counter-productive.

3.10. WHAT ARE THE SOURCES OF FORMAL COURSES?

Whether called upon to provide training themselves or not, computer practitioners are often called upon to give advice to clients about sources of training.

The two main external sources of training are the system supplier and specialist training agencies.

System suppliers

As part of a complete package, suppliers of hardware and software might provide training in their use. Alternatively, training might be offered at an additional cost. In either case, training is neither free nor cheap.

Many large suppliers employ a considerable number of training staff, perhaps 200 full-time staff in Britain. A supplier will clearly have considerable expertise in the particular system, and few trainers (or authors) have more detailed knowledge. If the training is negotiated as part of the whole purchase, then considerable advantages can be gained. Often training can be provided on the customer's own premises, at a mutually convenient time and pace. It can also be arranged on the customer's own equipment or on identical equipment loaned in advance of delivery.

Purchasers should be aware, however, that the primary interest of suppliers will be in sales and they might consider training merely as a necessary evil. This can be particularly true with smaller companies. Training by a supplier might (perhaps unwittingly) contain less criticism of machine or program and might consequently point out fewer 'tricks of the trade' for overcoming difficulties in their use.

With keen competition for sales, some dealers hire specialist training agencies to supply training and this may now be sold as part of a standard package.

TASK

Describe the advantage of negotiating the arrangements for a course before the purchase of the hardware and software.

Specialist training agencies

There are many advertisements in the computer press offering the services of training agencies. These organisations advertise courses ranging from general appreciation to detailed courses on particular hardware or software. They are generally respected for the quality of their training and for their independence.

Most have excellent facilities and are well equipped with both computer hardware and the very latest in other educational equipment. Much use is made of overhead projectors, demonstration programs, handouts and exercises. Training agencies can often provide courses directly tailored to an individual company's needs.

Charges for courses differ widely. Unfortunately, the price of a course is not a reliable guide to the quality of the training.

TASK

Imagine that you need to go on a course about a particular software area or on a particular package of your choice. Using various computer papers and magazines, draw up a list of courses available. Contrast the courses in terms of length, price, venue, equipment used, and any other factors which you consider important.

3.11. HOW IS THE RIGHT TRAINING CHOSEN?

Apart from the obvious criterion of cost, the following questions might usefully be asked when choosing between potential trainers:

(a) What are the qualifications and experience of the staff (particularly the staff who would be working on **this** contract)?
(b) Does the company generally provide one-off training or do customers return and make further use of them?
(c) How much of the work is lecture based and how much is hands on?
(d) Can the course be tailored to the particular situation? How could this be achieved?

3.12. WHERE WILL THE TRAINING BE DONE?

Training either from a supplier or from a specialist agency can be organised either at the normal place of work **on site** or at the trainers' premises **off site**.

On-site training

This brings with it the familiarity of a working environment and often staff on the course will know each other in advance. It helps to reduce the embarrassment which people feel when they make mistakes. Large-scale on-site training can, however, tie up scarce equipment resources at a crucial phase of the development of a system.

Off-site training

This may be popular with some staff, as it will create a break in working routine and a chance for a few days away from home. With others it will be just as unpopular. Accommodation and travel costs can also be a considerable extra expense.

3.13. THE HIDDEN AGENDA OF TRAINING

All training is designed for a particular purpose, but at times there is additional learning which is achieved on the way.

Training forms an important part in converting from one system to another. Indeed, people may talk about the conversion from a manual system to a computer system without considering the changes in the people, who are a vital part of that manual system.

Most computer trainers are involved in breaking down fear of new technology. With senior management particularly, this has to be dealt with sensitively. People who are respected for their expertise in one area often find it difficult when their lack of knowledge in other areas is exposed.

Training can also be a major means of providing motivation for users. This could mean overcoming the reluctance to change or it could mean teaching concepts which are not specific to the package being taught. For example, a course on one particular spreadsheet might put considerable emphasis on the concepts behind financial planning as well as on the details of commands. Indeed, this might benefit participants more in the long run. It would be difficult, however, to say directly to managers that they are to be trained in financial planning, which they are supposed to be doing already.

3.14. CASE STUDIES

1 *Working with dBaseII* by Mario de Pace (Granada 1984) is a good example of a beginner's text for a popular package. Throughout the book, one main example is built up — a simple one of cataloguing books. This is an example with which all readers should be familiar. Each new idea introduced is illustrated with the book example.

Once the concepts of data description and data manipulation have been explored in the first part of the book, the second part builds on the knowledge by introducing the ideas needed to use dBase II as a programming language.

When training users of a database, there are few problems in understanding the purpose of the package or of the basic elements of the program. In many cases, people who are using and manipulating a database may not need to design their own record structure. Thus, readers need only go as far through the book as their application requires. Most database users will want to access and change data, whether or not they wish to establish their own record structures. If they are only accessing data, users only have to read the first part of the book.

2   The documentation provided with 'View', a word processor by Acornsoft for the BBC microcomputer consists of two books. One is called 'Into View' and is an introductory text which outlines the purposes of word processing as well as building up the command repertoire of the reader. There are 13 chapters in under 50 pages, which means that only a few new commands are taught in each chapter. Indeed, some chapters are only two pages long. This ensures that the reader's confidence is quickly built up.

At the end of each chapter is a section titled 'New Commands in this Section', which only lists the commands covered, but is a useful recap. A technical appendix of some additional 25 pages includes command summary pages. These are cross-referenced to other pages of the appendix explaining commands in a formal definition, in contrast with the more descriptive approach of the earlier text.

The other document is called 'View Guide'. This is ring bound so that it can be kept open at any page. There is both a contents page and an index and throughout the text commands are explained in groups of similar facilities. This is often not the order in which they were introduced in the 'Into View' book.

Thus the View documentation contains three elements. There is a step-wise introduction, a formal reference section and a quick reference guide.

3.15. WHERE TO FIND OUT MORE

Both the weekly computer press and monthly magazines include articles, advertising and special features on training from time to time. These give an indication both of the skills training that is on the market and of typical prices of courses.

3.16. STUDY QUESTIONS

1   Why do you think that the early computer learning packages had very limited success?
2   Why are many manuals which are written as reference documents unsuitable for training?

3.17. ASSIGNMENTS

1   Write advertisements, suitable for inclusion in a monthly computing magazine describing, for a package of your choice, some materials for training which you might prepare:

(a) as a book,
(b) as a series of video films,
(c) as a residential course,
(d) as a computer-based training package.

2   Describe a series of tasks that a trainee ought to be capable of carrying out to ensure that he or she could be described as a competent user of a package of your choice.
3   For a package which you use regularly, plan out a course of training showing the topics in the order that you would cover them. Highlight the need for any written materials which would be necessary and any other supporting material.

SECTION B

SYSTEMS ANALYSIS

4 CAVEAT EMPTOR—THE BUYER BEWARE!

4.1. COMPUTER HORROR STORIES

The popular press and some television programmes make frequent reference to tales of woe about 'computer errors', yet we hear little or nothing of 'car errors' or 'cooker errors'! We do not imply that it is the car's fault or the cooker's fault when we make a mistake in using it, so why do we blame the computer?

To many people, computers are 'the latest thing', and because they are new, their coverage in the media can be on a trivial level. This trend is rapidly changing, with serious articles about computers and their applications appearing weekly in the better quality daily newspapers. Shocking though it may seem, however, there does lie a good deal of truth behind some horror stories in the press. It is extremely rare, however, that it is the computer which is at fault, virtually all 'computer errors' are in fact human errors.

All computer systems will involve ordinary people as part of the application, whether that person has contact with the system as part of a job, or as a member of the public. The patience of the general public is (justifiably) limited with computers which do not meet their needs. Thus, there are serious problems when a gas bill for £0.00 is sent out, and even greater ones if the customer is sent a final demand saying 'send us a cheque for £0.00, or your supply will be cut off'. Many owners of small businesses, too, will have heard tales of woe about the computerisation of small firms.

4.2. FRUSTRATIONS WITH COMPUTERS

There are perhaps four main reasons why small businesses find themselves in trouble and frustrated with computerised systems.

Frustration 1

The first frustration is caused by taking computerisation on board without thinking why. It is important that a firm should have clear aims in the process of computerisation. It is not sufficient, for example, simply to have vague notions that computers are 'the thing of the future'. (For a start, computers are the thing of the present, anyway.) To have clear aims in view can be a great help at the low points in the process when nothing seems to be going right. If some progress towards the end result can be measured, then morale can be lifted.

Also, when the aims of computerisation are unclear, frustration can be built up because there is nothing against which to measure progress. In this case failure can be more imaginary than real. Thus it is important to identify the aims of computerisation.

Frustration 2

A second frustration for the computer novice, which can be financially crippling, comes about through misjudging the scale of a project. This might be because the buyer does not understand the timescale of the computerisation process (it cannot happen tomorrow), or the amount of work involved, or the eventual cost. These problems are compounded when the firm outgrows the system within a year or two. If there is not room for growth within the system, the process must start all over again.

It is also tempting to try to computerise all the processes within the company at once. If the sales ledger, the stock control and the purchase ledger *can* be linked, they do not *have* to be. A serious and detailed assessment has to be made both of the costs and of the benefits. It is important to measure the scale of the project.

Frustration 3

This comes about because of a lack of technical competence by the purchaser. As with many technical subjects, computing uses technical words as a concise and precise form of communication. Many people use the word 'jargon' as a term of abuse, as if all technical words should be completely banished. This attitude should not be necessary. Technical vocabulary is essential for expressing technical ideas, but when it is used, it must be explained. Computing has suffered more than most disciplines from so-called 'professionals' who try to use jargon to impress or confuse, or both.

New users, floundering in a sea of technicalities, lose a grip on what they do and do not need to know. In particular, the technical language used can distract a purchaser of a business computer system from the details of business use, which is what business people actually understand. Some purchasers are so distracted by the apparent technical capabilities of sales staff and their equipment that they forget basic business sense. They rush the process without deciding on clear contracts and finding out precisely what is being offered for the money. Thus it is important to discover which technicalities are relevant and have to be understood and which are not.

Frustration 4

It is important to be realistic about the capabilities and interests of the staff. It is they who will be using the new system on a day-to-day basis. Will they be able to use it properly? Are they motivated to do so? Systems can go seriously wrong because staff are not clear about what they are supposed to do, and how they are supposed to use the system.

4.3. THE STAGES OF SYSTEMS ANALYSIS

The process of establishing clearly the aims of computerisation and of seeing this process through to its conclusion is known as **systems analysis**. This discipline has been in existence from the early days of the valve computers and its roots go back to the disciplines of organisation and methods (O & M) and work study. In broad outline, the established stages of traditional systems analysis

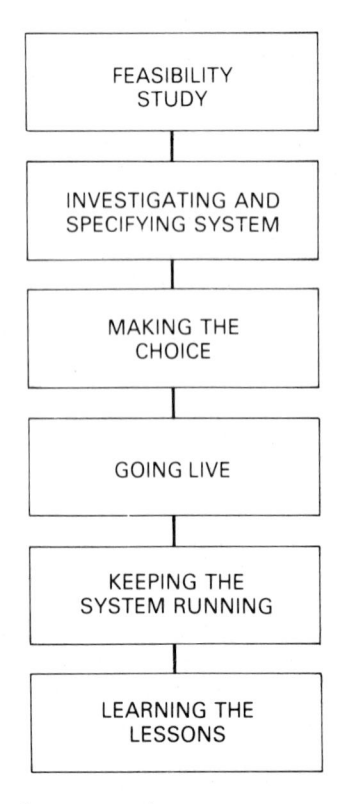

```
┌──────────────────────┐
│  FEASIBILITY         │
│  STUDY               │
└──────────┬───────────┘
           │
┌──────────┴───────────┐
│  INVESTIGATING AND   │
│  SPECIFYING SYSTEM   │
└──────────┬───────────┘
           │
┌──────────┴───────────┐
│  MAKING THE          │
│  CHOICE              │
└──────────┬───────────┘
           │
┌──────────┴───────────┐
│  GOING LIVE          │
└──────────┬───────────┘
           │
┌──────────┴───────────┐
│  KEEPING THE         │
│  SYSTEM RUNNING      │
└──────────┬───────────┘
           │
┌──────────┴───────────┐
│  LEARNING THE        │
│  LESSONS             │
└──────────────────────┘
```

The stages of systems analysis

apply equally to small business microcomputer systems as they do to large business mainframe systems. Understanding these stages in the work of a systems analyst is therefore important. This chapter takes a broad overview of these stages as they apply in businesses large and small. Later chapters will develop the ideas in detail as they relate to small businesses.

Carrying out a feasibility study

The purpose of a **feasibility study** is to establish in principle whether it is worthwhile designing and implementing a computerised solution to a business problem. Such a decision will almost certainly have to be made at the top level of an organisation. This is because computerisation will have an impact on the company's organisation, on financial arrangements, on the company's personnel, on its customers, its public image and so on. It is *not* a purely technical decision.

The decision as to whether to design and cost in detail one or more possible computerised solutions will be taken by people who are not primarily in the computer business, usually directors. They will want to be presented with information on which they can base a sound judgement, including a report outlining the arguments for and against computerising the particular process. The technical feasibility of the project will be one important consideration, but so also will be the estimated cost, the timescale, the impact on the organisation, whether there are solutions other than computerisation and so on. It might be decided that substantial benefits could be gained simply by improving the manual system, and so that course of action will be followed.

On the basis of a report drawn up at this stage, a decision will be made whether to commit money to the drawing up of detailed requirements. Computing has to compete for limited finance with all the other possible developments that may be useful or even essential for the business. These might range from the staff canteen to advertising. The costs and benefits for the organisation of each of these functions have to be measured against each other.

The work of drawing up a feasibility report is described in more detail in chapter 5.

Investigating and specifying the system

Assuming the go-ahead has been given at the previous stage, it is then important to define precisely what the computer system is to do and how it will do it. Hence the current system is investigated to see how orders are processed, or wage packets are made up or how other processes are carried out. This will involve observing current practices, interviewing staff, looking at existing forms and documents and so on.

Once the basic facts have been brought together and recorded, it is the job of the systems analyst to break the processes down and adapt them into ones which can be implemented on a computer. This could involve cutting out processes or documents which already are or will become unnecessary, improving existing processes and developing new features of a system. It certainly will involve delicate judgement to balance the needs of the organisation, the staff and the customers. There is again a temptation to incorporate too many improvements at an initial stage.

Once this process is completed, a top-level decision is made to confirm that what has been suggested is what is required by the organisation. Such a decision can again only be made with realistic estimates of the cost. It is wise to present a number of alternatives to the directors. They might then choose one or more options for costing, from which a choice will be made.

Further details of this design stage are given in chapter 6.

Making the choice

A solution must now be chosen which satisfies the objectives of the system and the financial constraints put upon it. Once it has been clarified what, in detail, is to be done, a number of ways of achieving it can be considered. Tenders can be sought for hardware and software, maintenance and running costs. This might involve external suppliers, internal costing or a mixture of both. Formal evaluation methods may well be used, as different possible systems will do some of the tasks better than others. It is virtually guaranteed that no one system will be the cheapest to buy *and* the cheapest to run *and* the first which could be implemented *and* the simplest to understand.

Methods should be arranged for comparing tenders, preferably before they are received; it is never a case of comparing like with like.

The work involved in comparing possible solutions is the subject of chapter 7.

Going live

The systems analyst's job does not cease when a system has been chosen. At the point of getting the system operational, an organisation will need considerable support. Equipment will have to be tested to ensure that it is working properly. Problems with a new system will have to be identified and ironed out. Day-to-day users will have to be trained. Managers will have to be taught how to interpret the information that the new system provides. These and many others are tasks which a systems analyst might carry out directly or might ensure that others carry out. The impact of a system in its first few weeks is crucial to its future effectiveness.

Chapter 8 analyses in detail the work involved in getting a computer system 'up and running'.

Keeping the system running

Once a system is running, it is still not the end of the story. The system has to be kept running. This will not only involve making arrangements for repairs and maintenance to equipment and for ordering supplies, but also adapting the system as circumstances change. Change can be brought on by external factors such as alterations in taxation or other laws, or by internal factors within a company, such as departmental reorganisation. Even software has to be maintained. Making satisfactory arrangements for this should be in the mind of the systems analyst from the beginning of the process.

In chapter 9, the work in the day-to-day running of a computer system is described.

Learning the lessons

No system is ever perfect. No process ever runs entirely smoothly. There will be lessons to be learnt from each system which is implemented. Computer systems therefore have to be evaluated. A systems analyst will note ways in which the process could have been improved and will learn from the mistakes, so that next time ... well at least different mistakes will be made, not the same ones!

TASK

For each of the stages of systems analysis outlined above, estimate the financial cost involved in pulling out of the project. Suggest factors other than finance which might be important in considering whether to abandon a project.

4.4. THE TRADITIONAL JOB OF THE SYSTEMS ANALYST

All of these roles, from feasibility study to review have been traditionally labelled 'systems analysis'. In a typical large organisation, then, the systems analyst formed the link between the professional computing team, the rest of the organisation and suppliers. So, from the programmer's point of view, the systems analyst was the one who 'gave the orders', specifying precisely what a program was required to do. Experienced programmers would move on to become systems analysts. It is important to remember, however, that systems analysis requires a much wider range of skills and a systems analyst is not just 'a programmer who has grown up', as one student wrote.

A good systems analyst should not be making major policy decisions. He or she should be giving advice and submitting reports to enable managers to manage. In the same way that programmers might expect accurate and concise program specifications from a systems analyst, management should expect accurate and concise reports which crystallise the issues to be discussed.

A systems analyst will also need a good deal of tact, as the nature of the job is normally to bring about change. Staff fear change for a whole range of different reasons and can become very defensive and negative in their attitudes. Thus a systems analyst must have the seniority to be able to get answers to searching questions, but also the tact not to ask such questions unless it is absolutely necessary.

TASK

You have been employed as a computer consultant by a small petrol station which employs four full-time staff. While two of the staff are young and keen on new ideas, the administrative assistant and the storekeeper are somewhat older and don't want anything to do with this 'new-fangled gadgetry'. Describe what you would do to put their minds at ease.

4.5. THE CHANGING JOB OF SYSTEMS ANALYSIS

Many large organisations, as they became computerised in the sixties and seventies, built up teams of data processing staff. Such a team would include computer operators, keyboard operators, programmers and systems analysts. The roles of all these staff have changed considerably in organisations both large and small. With the introduction of sophisticated operating systems and real-time systems, the number of operators necessary has been reduced. Similarly the job of systems analysis has diversified.

One of the most obvious changes is that many small companies would not identify a single person or group of people as 'systems analysts'. In large companies, the varied aspects within systems analysis may have been broken down so that staff have more specific briefs. In smaller companies, on the other hand, the work might be given to staff as an addition to current duties. Thus training on a completed system might be carried out by the person responsible for all the organisation's training; those involved with finance might be involved from the beginning with financial implications of a project and so on.

It is also becoming rarer for a system to be designed and written from scratch. A company may have an existing computerised system which needs to be adapted and changed for a new situation. If the first computerisation project was performed well, there will be much existing documentation to refer to.

Additionally, there is much software available for sale which performs the most common business tasks. The task of systems analysis must take seriously how easy, quick and cheap it might be to use or adapt commercial packages. Thus, a systems analyst might have half a mind to the types of

A good systems analyst ...

is clear-thinking   is analytical

is persuasive   is tactful

has experience
— of business organisation
— of technology
— of people

expresses ideas clearly
— in reports
— in meetings
— in presentations

can work to standards

can work to deadlines

can obtain, interpret and select relevant material

has knowledge
— of business
— of technology
— of law

can motivate others

can plan work

software commercially available. It is a matter for further consideration in any report how far the needs of the organisation should be adapted to the capabilities of existing software.

TASK

Imagine that you are employed as a personnel officer in a medium-sized firm which is about to employ a systems analyst for the first time with a view to using computers for a wide range of tasks. The advertising budget is only sufficient to advertise in one of two publications. The first is a computer specialist magazine, which is mainly read by programmers and is almost 50% job advertisements. The other is a business journal read by a large number of experienced managers in large and small firms. Both have roughly equal circulation figures. Describe the advantages and disadvantages of using each publication and make recommendations about what should be done.

4.6. CONSULTING A CONSULTANT

An alternative to carrying out the task of systems analysis within an organisation is to call in a computer consultant. A large number of consultancy firms has grown up in the last decade, ranging in size from individuals to several dozen staff.

Reasons for calling in a consultant

Hiring a consultant gives a firm an opportunity to harness specialist skills for a limited period. Taking on full-time members of staff, which is the alternative, leaves a company with the question of what to do with them after the project's completion. Working with a consultancy will probably also mean that the consultant's time will be available when required, as the project moves through more intensive and less intensive phases.

The cost of a consultant

Consultants charge between £100 and £400 per day (1987 rates). Now this might sound expensive, but a firm would be paying to bring in somebody with a wide range of experience in the industry, someone who would have been involved with a large number of systems. Indeed, a consultant who has worked with several similar organisations can be chosen. This can enable the consultant to work efficiently in identifying the firm's needs by comparison with other similar systems and so will produce results quickly.

The cost of consultancy must also be contrasted with the costs of some potential disasters of computerisation. If things have gone wrong and the sales ledger has become dependent on a computer, but will not function correctly, the price of recovery will be high. In order to ensure that cash continues to be collected, invoices might have to be produced from other printouts, so staff might have large scale, tedious work to do; this may well involve costly overtime.

Costs might not just occur as a result of disaster, however. There can be much waste, for example, in entering all the details of the sales ledger into a computer and then discovering that it is in an inappropriate format, so that it cannot be used. A quick calculation of the wages that such wastefulness would involve will indicate that a consultancy fee may be money well spent.

Choosing a consultant

The next question is: How do we choose a consultant? or 'Who do we consult about choosing a consultant?' There are no hard and fast rules here. One consultant has suggested that his main source of clients is from the personal recommendation of satisfied customers. This would suggest that a good starting point is for a firm to use business contacts to give advice about how they computerised. Talking to a consultant's previous clients is important, as this might be one of the best ways to discover whether the consultant has some other vested interest. Truly objective advice can only come from a consultant who has no formal or financial links with any manufacturer, software house or supplier.

brochures from hardware suppliers

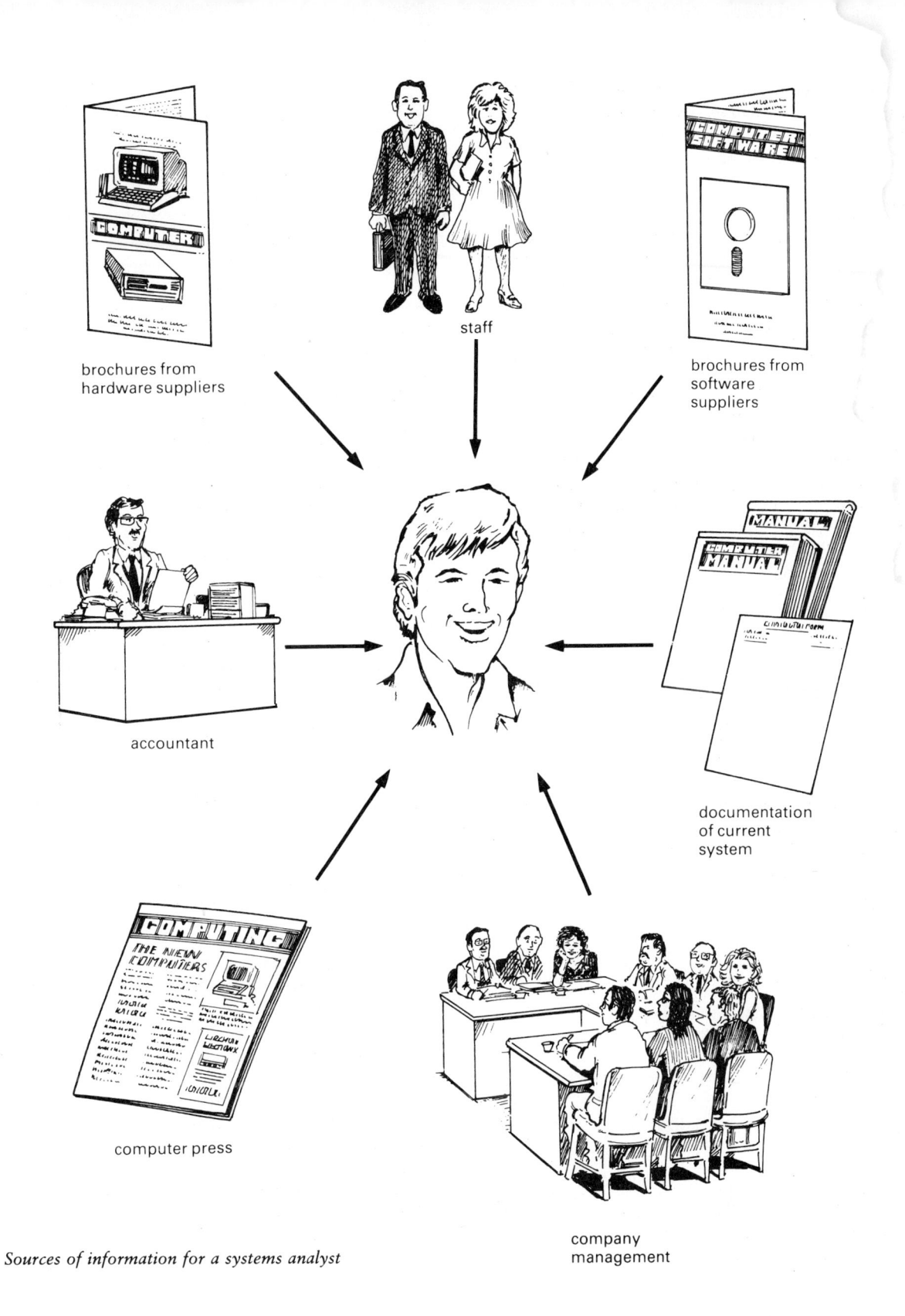

staff

brochures from software suppliers

accountant

documentation of current system

computer press

company management

Sources of information for a systems analyst

39

Bodies which will be able to provide advice directly, or can put organisations in touch with local consultants include the National Computing Centre, the British Computer Society, the British Institute of Management and the Small Firms Service (for details of where to find their addresses, see Appendix B). Another source of contacts could be a specialist trade body, such as those for the motor vehicle industry, tourism, catering and so on.

4.7. WHERE TO FIND OUT MORE

A number of the serious computing magazines, which concentrate on business applications, have regular features on companies of all sizes and their computer systems. In particular these examples often show the way in which firms went about the process, and give examples, both good and bad, of what can be done. The comments which experienced business people make about their own mistakes make informative reading.

Several magazines have regular features concentrating on a variety of different types of firm, examining in depth how particular firms have been computerised. Though the detail of the hardware and software chosen might not be relevant to a different situation, it is always useful to examine the reasons why people have made their particular choices. Descriptions like these might suggest aspects of a firm's situation to be looked at and the criteria for choice to be thought about.

A number of books which have been published as guides to the computerisation of small businesses include examples of how to computerise and how not to. These generally go through all the necessary stages of computerisation and illustrate good and bad points about the process, including simple down-to-earth advice from those at the sharp end of business. Such books have much grassroots advice in them and are very useful for browsing to get ideas.

Consultants can be contacted through local business advice centres, business contacts, the telephone directory and through business and computing exhibitions. An exhibition might be one of the few times when consultants are not rushed off their feet and have time for chatting, which might reveal their general approach. An organisation has to work closely with consultants, so they should be respected and liked by individuals within the organisation.

4.8. STUDY QUESTIONS

1. Suggest whose error it might be if:
   (a) a gas bill is sent for £0.00,
   (b) a final demand is sent for a gas bill of £0.00,
   (c) a large set of address labels is printed with the bottom half of one address and the top half of another address on each label,
   (d) a list of all customers with debts outstanding for more than three months does not include those which have been outstanding for over a year.

2. Draw up a list of the costs involved in employing a systems analyst.

3. In what ways do the issues raised in the process of systems analysis affect people outside the computer department?

4.9. ASSIGNMENTS

1. Describe the differences in the ways systems analysis might be carried out between that in a large company and that in a small company. Illustrate your answer with examples, real or fictional.

2. Design a letter to be sent to a number of computer consultants so that the answers received you could make an informed decision about which one to use. Draw up a list of six local firms which you might approach, giving reasons for their choice. Describe what you would be looking for in the replies.

3. Using an article from a magazine or newspaper which describes the process of computerisation within a firm, make a list of the things that they did right and a list of the things that they did wrong. Using this material, and other sources, write a brief report which could be given to a similar company, advising them how to go about the process.

5 THE FEASIBILITY STUDY

5.1. LOOK BEFORE YOU LEAP

All suggested computerisation projects have their benefits, but also their costs. In preparing a feasibility study, one is contrasting these two aspects in order to make a rational and informed decision.

Though it is extremely naive to leap straight into computerisation without weighing up the pros and cons, this does happen all too frequently. Some projects like this are successful, but in many other cases, those responsible are left to repent at their leisure.

5.2. COST–BENEFIT ANALYSIS

The discipline of cost–benefit analysis has been used in economics for several decades. It involves the drawing up on the one hand a list of the benefits of a project, a new product, a new service or whatever, and on the other a list of the costs which would be involved. Some costs and benefits will be measurable, whereas some will have to be estimated. Other benefits which cannot be measured, such as staff and customer goodwill, should also be given a monetary value to reflect their importance to the company. From such data, it is possible to compare estimated costs and the value of benefits. Other factors will also have to be considered, but this will then be against an informed background. It is with this kind of rigour in mind that a computer feasibility study should be drawn up.

5.3. EXPECTED BENEFITS

It is important to ask, in any situation where computerisation is suggested, what the justification for the process is. What are the expected benefits? There are a hundred and one possible ways in which an organisation could benefit from a computer; what must be identified are those benefits which are important. If the preparation of documents on a computer improves the company's public image, this benefit alone might justify the expense. On the other hand, if most of the computer output is for internal use, then this factor might be considerably less important.

Benefits of computerisation—some suggestions

▶ More clerical work can be completed with the same effort (or the same with less effort)

▶ Tedious work is done more accurately by the computer

▶ Clerical work is made less tedious, and so staff get more satisfaction and the work is done more accurately

▶ Resources can be centralised and so made more efficient

- Up-to-the-minute information can be available instantly at a number of different sites
- Previous performance can be analysed and future action can be planned from an analysis of trends
- Historical records can be kept in a more compact form, saving space and time
- Queries are answered more efficiently and effectively
- Work produced is neater, which will improve the company image
- Work produced is more polished (it is not too much of an effort to make that final revision), and so the customer gets a better service
- Management gets a more accurate feedback about activity
- There is more flexibility—troughs and peaks of work can be more easily dealt with
- The number and value of debts to the organisation is reduced—credit can be controlled
- The cost of purchases is reduced by bulk buying and timely buying—purchasing terms can be used creatively

When a list of expected benefits has been drawn up, and a project justified on this basis, the other unexpected benefits can come as a great bonus.

TASK

Make a list of reasons why people might go in for computerisation without having a clear idea of the benefits which they are expecting.

One way in which the potential benefits of computerisation can be broken down is to distinguish benefits for the whole organisation from those which are just for a part. An organisation will have set itself corporate objectives in terms of targets for its share of the market in a particular area, for diversifying its activity, for moving into new markets and so on. It could well be that the process of computerisation might assist in the achievement of these ends. Indeed, it is possible that the use of computers is seen as being essential to achieving some of these **strategic** objectives.

At the more detailed level, on the other hand, it might be considered important to streamline some areas of an organisation's activity in order to make it more efficient. There might be a desire for personnel to be 'better informed' or have a 'clearer overall picture'. Such improvements might be said to be **operational** ones, in contrast to the strategic ones.

Putting a figure on benefits

Some benefits are easy to put a figure on, but others might be difficult to rate in financial terms. Benefits such as improved company image or goodwill from staff, which are intangible, must be allocated some monetary value just as much as tangible ones in order to compare them on an equal footing.

The process of putting a value on benefits is primarily informed by experience. Help is needed from those who know the particular business as well as those who are familiar with computers. It is also useful to have the advice of people with experience of relating cost–benefit analysis to computers. This is not a task to give to a junior or inexperienced member of staff.

By discussion with people within an organisation, then, it is important to identify the benefits which it is hoped that computerisation might bring. In some cases, this might lead to disappointment if such benefits cannot be achieved or afforded, but it is probably better that expectations are made as realistic as possible as soon as possible.

The possible benefits of computerisation are many and varied. Their relative importance in various circumstances will be significantly different.

TASK

Describe the benefits that the introduction of a computer system might have for a petrol station owned and run by a family. Contrast this with how the benefits might differ if the scheme was for a chain of a dozen petrol stations within the same county.

TASK

Write down the ways in which you might personally benefit from having a computer. Make up a list of the benefits which you would derive, in order of importance *for you*.

5.4. THE NEED FOR COSTING

The costs of computerisation are generally more easily measurable than the benefits. At the feasibility stage, however, this might involve some careful estimation, as a system is only designed in broad outline at this stage. The advice of those experienced in this field will be particularly useful, as comparison with other systems is a good guide to costing.

It is important that a distinction is made between the **capital cost** and the **revenue cost** of projects.

Capital costs

The **capital cost** is the once-only investment needed in items such as equipment, software, work to buildings, the cost of initial training and so on. The acquisition of a computer can require a lot of capital over a relatively short period and means that the capital cannot be used for other things. Accountants can probably best advise whether capital should be used in this way; capital might be more wisely used elsewhere, though computerisation may itself produce a good return on the investment of the money.

Revenue costs

Revenue costs are those which come about in running a system from day to day. These costs include staffing, electricity, repairs and consumables such as paper and ribbons. It may well be that a major aim of computerisation is to reduce the revenue costs in the long term by increasing capital costs in the short term. Alternatively, the revenue costs might stay roughly the same, but more work is done.

The capital for investment in a computer system could, of course, be borrowed and paid back over a number of years. This could be preferable to the ever increasing and somewhat unpredictable revenue costs of manual systems.

A system can be justified either because it will pay for itself, or because the additional benefits are worth the extra cost.

TASK
List the various expenses that you have had with your own computer. Categorise each item of the expenditure as capital or revenue. (If you do not use one, then try to draw up estimates for what you consider would be a 'typical' business system.)

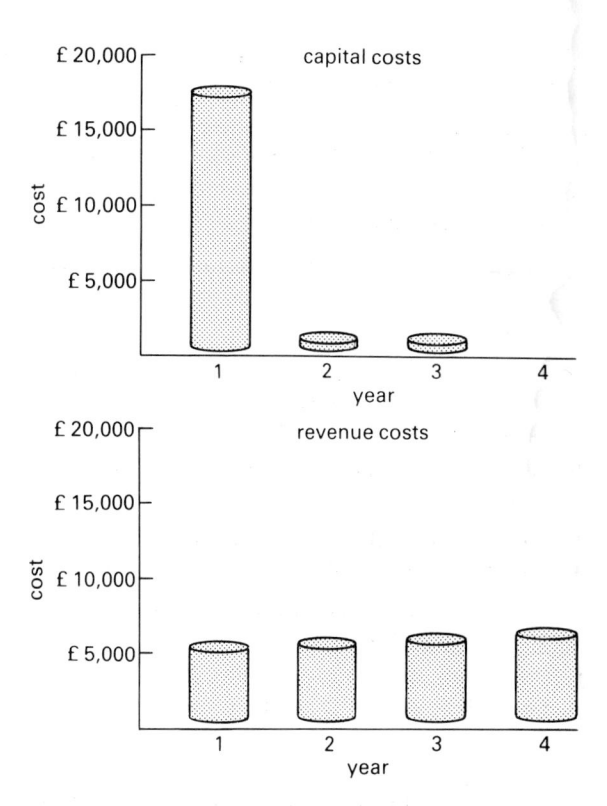

The difference between capital and revenue costs: the capital takes the form of initial outlay, the revenue is a recurring expense

5.5. HUMAN ASPECTS OF COMPUTERISATION

The pros and cons of computer systems cannot be measured in purely financial terms, though. The changes which are being contemplated will have their impact on people, not least on an organisation's staff.

The success of a computer system will depend on the ability of the staff who use it to exploit its features to the full. This will clearly mean that staff will have to be trained and this will have an impact on the scheme's budget. The capabilities of existing staff should also be taken into consideration when planning the scale and speed of computerisation. Computer personnel have to take the rest of the staff with them. A company may not have chosen staff for their computing skills and they are probably knowledgeable about all sorts of other things (including how to run the organisation). Indeed a firm may still not wish to recruit staff primarily for their computing skills; other personal qualities might continue to be more important.

Staff attitudes

Staff will differ considerably in their attitude to change. Some will resist change through fear of the unknown, others because they want a quiet life. Most staff will have attitudes to computerisation based on a whole mixture of experiences. It is part of the task of those bringing in a new system to talk with people about their concerns.

Other members of staff will be concerned about the effect of computers on jobs. Those with the more routine clerical jobs may fear that their role will disappear. Older members of staff may be encouraged to take early retirement. This would then be part of the cost of computerisation, of course. Younger members of staff might wish to use the opportunity as a way of career advancement. Many people will find their roles changed.

TASK
Make a list of possible things that people might say either directly against the introduction of computer technology or expressing their fears in a roundabout way.

Reducing fears

Throughout the whole process, starting with the feasibility study stage, the best way to reduce the fears of staff, particularly the panic caused by rumour, is to consult staff at all levels. This might be done through trade unions, staff associations or on a more informal level. Whatever form of consultation is chosen, it is important that there is seen to be consultation and that the voice of staff is listened to (and acted upon!).

The 'human' aspects of the system should be considered when drawing up the feasibility report. Key personnel who might be involved in the day-to-day use of the system should be included formally even at this preliminary stage.

While it is possible to impose a system on people without their goodwill, it is at best inefficient. To gain a benefit from goodwill, the cost has to be met.

TASK
From the list that you made earlier of comments against computer systems, write a dialogue between a person making the objections and yourself, giving your responses to the concerns.

5.6. THE BEST LAID PLANS OF MICE AND MEN ...

All the groundwork in preparing the path for computerisation is important, but it will go to waste if the project does not turn out to be technically feasible.

Some might say that anything can be computerised, as any suggested project, so long as it can be clearly defined, can be achieved by a set of computer instructions. This, however, is to miss the point that there are a wide variety of ways in which systems can be implemented and different possible systems will have remarkably different benefits. The point is not to determine what is possible, but what is worthwhile.

Real-time and batch processing systems

In some systems, files are immediately updated after each transaction so that the next transaction can be based on up-to-the-minute information. Such systems are called **real-time systems**. One example of this is an airline booking system. The provision of immediate updating, and the availability of that information in a large number of locations at the same time, are major reasons why airlines adopted the systems. In other firms, if the benefits were less, and the costs more, such a proposal might not be worth pursuing. On the other hand, a simple system where transactions are collected together for processing as a group might be worthwhile. Such systems are known as **batch processing systems**.

A company might wish to have large amounts of information available at a large number of locations, with the information only being updated periodically at a central location. Many banks have adopted this approach with automatic teller machines. Customers can only get their balance as it stood at midnight last night. The cost of making it possible to perform other functions might be considered (at a particular time) to outweigh the benefits.

In order to suggest technically feasible computer systems to replace existing systems, it will obviously be important to investigate the current system. The system will have to be examined in depth at later stages in the systems development life cycle. At the feasibility stage, what is needed is an appreciation of the style of current work and its scale. Bearing in mind the major suggested benefits of computerisation, a number of possible and practicable schemes can be drawn up. Estimates of the scale of the work will help in producing guidelines for costing the new schemes.

Draft proposals for a system can be put before crucial members of staff to see how they react to the suggested form of data entry, storage and use.

Don't put all your eggs in one basket

Once several proposed schemes have been suggested and costed, they can be compared and evaluated. Any organisation will have methods of deciding between bids for resources, though these may be more or less formal, depending on circumstances. Proposed computer schemes will have to stand alongside many other varied projects hoping to gain support. The clarity of the presentation of the feasibility report will have an effect on the way that the merits of a scheme are viewed.

5.7. MAKING COMPARISONS

Some companies will have very formalised and uniform methods of comparing projects, which can involve such accounting tools as net present values, estimates of inflation rates, interest rates and so on. Those responsible for producing the computer feasibility report would not be expected to apply all these techniques, but would be required to supply appropriate figures to the finance department. In this way, all potential projects within an organisation can be evaluated on an equal footing.

One important choice affecting the costing of a scheme is the decision *how* the project will be computerised. Will staff be taken on to write a system? Will it be contracted out? Will a ready-written system be acquired? The presentation of such choices is important at this stage. Many options should be considered.

Alongside this information, a timetable for the development of systems should be drawn up. The complexity and originality of a system will have a profound effect on the timescale within which the project can be completed. This will have implications for budgeting and these implications should be spelt out. A number of options should be presented, as the pacing of the process might be determined by the way in which other projects, such as opening a new factory, launching a new product or other schemes, might have already been programmed. Such plans, in a competitive business world, might only be known to a few people at the top of an organisation, but when these people read a computer feasibility report, a number of ideas might fall into place for possible coordination.

5.8 WHEN ALL'S SAID AND DONE, THERE'S A LOT MORE SAID THAN DONE

In summary, then, a feasibility study will set out to make a realistic assessment of the whys and wherefores of computerisation. From what is presented, it should be possible for those responsible to judge whether to proceed, based on understanding both the advantages and the drawbacks of any particular scheme.

If the go-ahead for a particular project is forthcoming, then the process moves on to the detailed investigation and design stage.

5.9. WHERE TO FIND OUT MORE

Textbooks and computer guides for small businesses offer advice about the benefits of computerisation. When a particular situation is examined, it is important to draw up a list which has specific benefits, rather than generalised (and therefore vague) hopes.

The costing of a projected system might use information from catalogues and advertising material, but will also be informed by the experience of the systems analyst. Browsing through a range of serious computing magazines, reading both advertisements and articles, will give an impression of current charges.

Understanding people's response to computerisation again calls for personal judgement, but again articles are frequently published on this issue. In magazine articles and in television and radio programmes, people often talk about their real hopes and fears.

5.10. STUDY QUESTIONS

1   What benefits might the staff of a company derive from the use of a computer?
2   How have real-time computer systems benefited airlines?
3   List the different information needs of:

   (a) a sales clerk,
   (b) a sales manager,
   (c) a company accountant

regarding sales of a new product.

5.11. ASSIGNMENTS

1   Imagine that you are responsible for the introduction of word processing to a typing pool which is currently using electric typewriters. What methods would you use to reduce the fears of the typists? You may assume that you have access to whatever means of communication you require.
2   It has been said that 'It is never the right time to buy a computer: you never know what development is just around the corner.' Do you agree with this statement? Justify your opinion in a formally presented report.
3   How, ideally, would you go about buying a computer system for home? How would this differ, if at all, from the way in which it should be done for a small business?

6 DESIGNING THE SYSTEM

Once the principle has been established that an organisation can benefit from the use of computers, the process of detailed design of that system has yet to be undertaken. At all stages of the process, it is important not to lose sight of the overall aims and the particular benefits which computerisation is expected to bring. The conclusions of the feasibility study should not be lost sight of, and indeed should be a guide to the rest of the process.

Often, computerisation of a business function takes place against the background of the existing use of computers for other things within the company. This will complicate the decisions to be made, as it introduces the possibility of incorporating the new function within an existing computer system. This may or may not be appropriate: only a detailed investigation will reveal this.

The process is somewhat simpler when a proposed computerisation project is to be the first within an organisation. In this case, it is unlikely that there will be sufficient expertise and experience among the current staff to tackle the project without help. Here a consultant may well be able to help.

TASK
Describe the ways in which the process of designing a new computerised system might be different in a firm which already had a computer compared with one which has not.

6.1. DETERMINING THE NEEDS

In order to determine the needs of the organisation, the current system has to be investigated. A detailed analysis of the way things are done within the organisation is needed, so that current good practice can be computerised, and current bad practice can be reorganised. It is the current information needs of the organisation that form the starting point for the future information needs.

It is particularly important that current practice is not only recorded accurately, but that, at appropriate points, it is also questioned as well. Thus questions have to be asked not only about what is done, but also why. An outsider can often bring a new light to bear on a situation, seeing things through fresh eyes, and might also be able to question current practice in a way which is less threatening to staff. If the analysis of current procedures is carried out within an organisation, it is a process which calls for much tact and diplomacy.

6.2. FACT FINDING

In order to draw up a detailed description of the system which is required, large amounts of information on the numbers and types of documents, the ways in which they are used, and by whom, must be brought together. There is a range of methods available for determining the details of the current system.

The questionnaire

The people currently using or affected by the process can be asked questions through a written questionnaire. This has the advantage that it can be carefully designed to ensure that all relevant areas are asked about. With many detailed questions, it is useful if people are able to answer them in their own time, at their own pace and in their own work situation, where all the information can be at hand.

One of the disadvantages of questionnaires is the difficulty of designing precise questions which can be understood without oral explanations. Another drawback is that there is possible wastefulness in several people filling in details of the same part of the process. (And what if their answers are different?) Questionnaires also have a notoriously low response rate and so a lot of chasing up may have to be done to ensure that they are all returned.

The face-to-face interview

Another method of fact collection is the interview. This must be approached with tact, so that the person being interviewed is not intimidated, as if on trial. The interviewer would clearly design a number of questions to be asked in advance and many of these would be put to most of the staff. A major advantage of the live interview is that the person who is requiring the information can probe deeper on particular points if answers are unclear or need further explanation.

In a discussion, some people might give more expansive spoken answers to questions than they could ably explain in writing. It is also possible for the interviewee to demonstrate how a task is carried out, rather than simply trying to describe it in words.

It is important that the interviewer makes careful notes of what each person said. Such notes can be made during or immediately after the interview. A number of important answers or remarks might have to be consulted two or three times when a new system is designed. It is important that they are remembered accurately.

Observation

Facts can also be collected by watching and recording what is going on in the organisation. Clerical processes can be observed, and the details recorded. Statistics can also be collected. In some instances this is easier for an external observer to do. For example, we may require an accurate figure for the number of telephone enquiries dealt with by a clerk in the average day, or the number of letters dealt with in an hour. This counting should be done by somebody else, otherwise the person is slowed down by spending time recording the information. This will lead to inaccurate figures and could mean that the current work does not get done in time.

Another approach is to follow a document through its life history, as it passes from department to department to see how information is collected, interpreted and used. In this way the information flow within the company can be observed. Problems with the system might also be seen in this way.

Quantitative surveys

It is also possible for somebody to go round the various parts of the organisation in order to count the number of each type of form processed, the number of records in each file, the number of different forms and so on. This must clearly be done without disturbing the day-to-day work. In some instances, this process can be used to get a 'snapshot' picture of the situation of a company at a 'typical' point on a 'typical' day.

TASK

Staff sometimes find the simple process of fact-finding threatening. Write a letter, as if from a trade union branch, outlining some of the fears of the staff.

6.3. DEFINING THE NEW SYSTEM

Having gathered the basic facts about the current data processing within an organisation, it is necessary to design a draft computerised system.

Such a design must incorporate as many improvements suggested in the fact-finding phase as practicable. People who operate the current system will be keen to talk about its shortcomings; they must be encouraged to suggest improvements.

A new design must pay great attention to the aims of computerisation which were identified at the feasibility stage. Management will be looking for these improvements within the new system.

6.4. USING STANDARD FORMS

A number of areas must be described to specify what a computerised system is to look like. This includes describing the input methods used, the files held, the output which is to be produced and the processes by which these relate. This is most frequently done by using a number of standard documents designed and issued by the National Computing Centre (NCC). This approach has the advantage that all the relevant aspects of the process are recorded; for each file or screen or form, the person filling in the document is reminded of the questions which need to be answered.

Documents are described by using a **clerical document description** (called a form S41), or by a **computer document description** (S43) (see pages 50 and 51). Some of the features of a form which need recording are its size, the number of copies which will be made, the number of pages (if, for example, it is a report), the departments to which copies are sent and the items of data which make up each record. In specifying the size of a report, it is useful to state the expected average and maximum sizes, and the factors which might affect this.

The NCC forms numbered S46 and S47 (see pages 52 and 53) are used to describe the output, the former is for **printer output**, the latter for **screen input/output** (called a 'display chart'). This form will show the layout of the fields with respect to each other and their size.

The details of a file can be specified using a **file specification** (S42) and a **record specification** (S44) (see pages 54 and 55). The file specification will include the file organisation method, the medium to be used, details of the key field, the size of each record (whether fixed or variable) and the number of records (again an average and a maximum). Other factors to be included are the growth rate of the file, the frequency of file back-up and arrangements for file reorganisation or maintenance.

The record specification will contain the details of each field, such as its size, its format and its range of possible values.

6.5. SYSTEMS DOCUMENTS

The relationship of various documents and reports can be illustrated in a number of ways.

Systems outline

A **systems outline** is intended to show in one page a summary of all the inputs, the processes which are involved, the outputs which are produced and the files which are referred to and are updated. Thus it shows what is done (as an overview), but not how it is done. Such a diagram is very important when attempting to get an overall picture of a system. Detailed descriptions are left to other documents.

Document flowcharts

A **document flowchart** shows in a diagrammatic way how a document, or the data from it, is processed through the company. This often

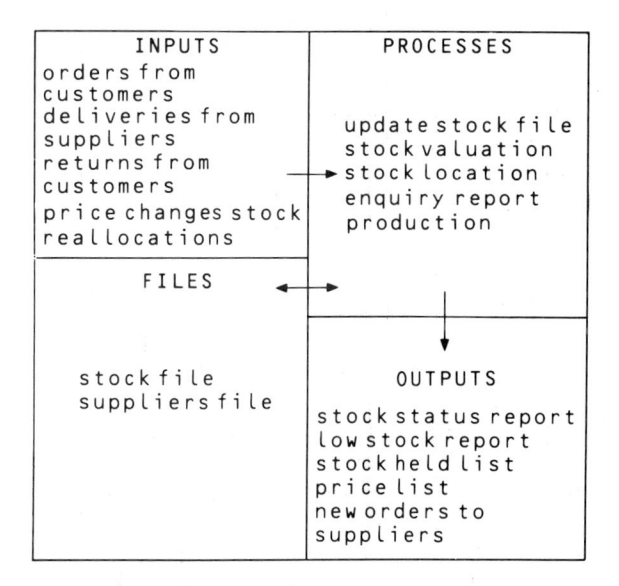

INPUTS	PROCESSES
orders from customers deliveries from suppliers returns from customers price changes stock reallocations	update stock file stock valuation stock location enquiry report production
FILES	
stock file suppliers file	OUTPUTS stock status report low stock report stock held list price list new orders to suppliers

A systems outline for a stock control system

Clerical Document Specification N.C.C	Document description		System	Document	Name	Sheet
	Stationery ref.	Size		Number of parts	Method of preparation	
	Filing sequence		Medium		Prepared/maintained by	
	Frequency of preparation/update		Retention period		Location	

VOLUME — Minimum | Maximum | Av/Abs | Growth rate/fluctuations

Users/recipients | Purpose | Frequency of use

Ref.	Item	Picture	Occurrence	Value range	Source of data

Notes

S 41

Author | Issue | Date

1969. The National Computing Centre Limited

Clerical document description (S41), published by NCC

Computer Document Specification NCC	Document title		System	Document		Name	Sheet	
	Stationery ref.		Width		Depth		Number of parts	
								Blank/pre-printed
	Pages	Average	Maximum		Growth rate % per or determining factor			
	Lines per page							
	OUTPUT ONLY	Page and line spacing/stepping						
		Ribbon type		Ribbon life		Printer speed	Lay-out chart ref.	Control loop Ref.
		Part No	Trim/ Burst	Distribution				Line	Channel
	MACHINE READABLE ONLY	Clear area — distance from edges				Reading method and font		
						Source		
	Level	Record Name			Size		Unit	Format	Occurrence

S 43
Author | Issue
| Date

Computer document description (S43), published by NCC

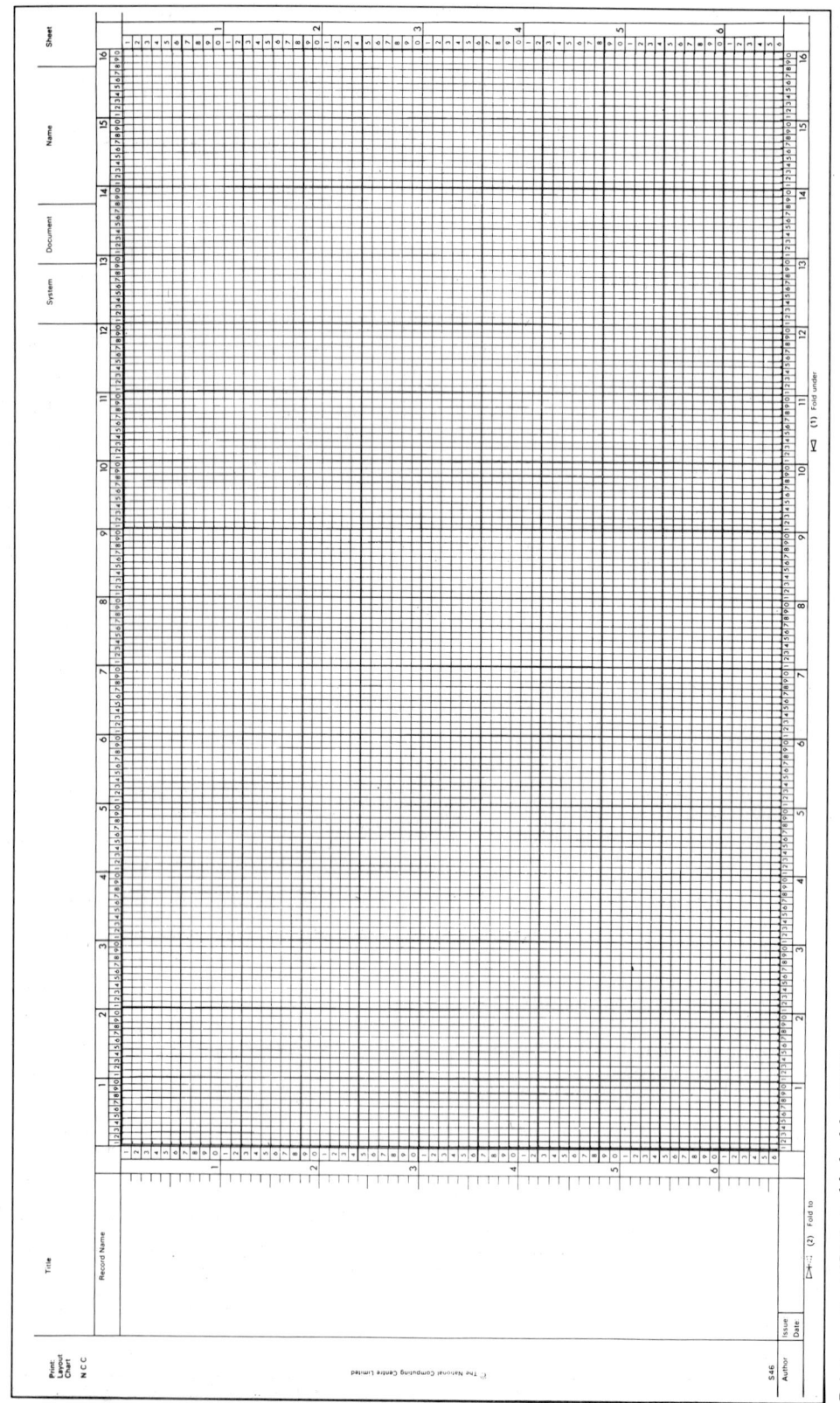

Printer output (S46), published by NCC

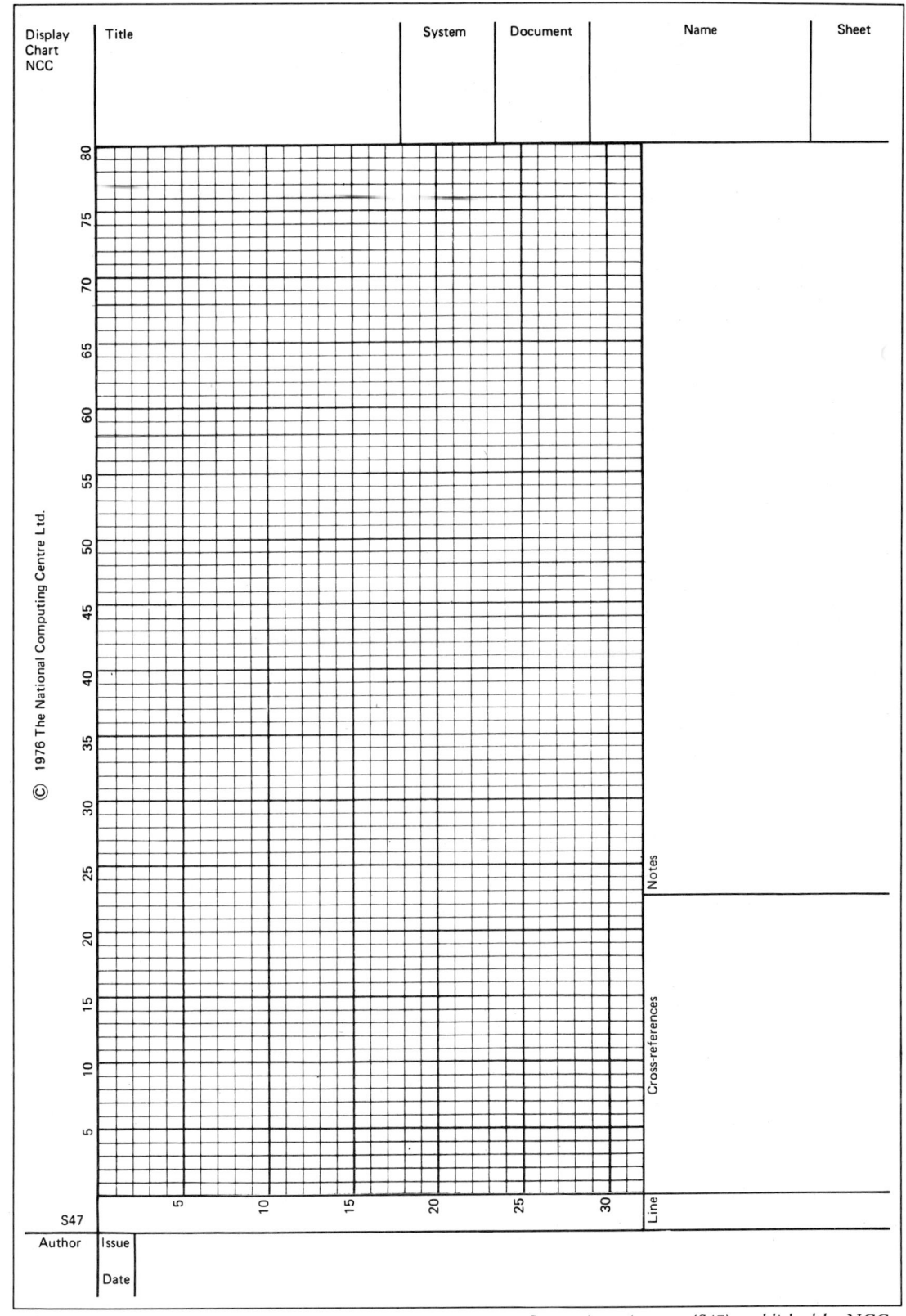

Screen input/output (S47), published by NCC

Computer File Specification

NCC

File description		System	Document	Name	Sheet

File type: Input ☐ Output ☐ Master ☐ Transfer ☐

File organisation:

Storage medium: Mag. tape ☐ Disc ☐ Single ☐ Multiple ☐

Retention period	Number of generations	Number of copies

Recovery procedure:

Keys:

Labels:

Level	Record name/ref.	Size	Unit	Format	Occurrence

Block/batch size
- Actual, for fixed length
- Maximum, for variable length

Unit of storage: Records ☐ Words ☐ Bytes ☐ Characters ☐ Cards ☐

Number of blocks: Average / Maximum

File size: Average / Maximum

Growth rate: ____ % per ____ or determining factor

MAG. TAPE ONLY
- Tracks: 7 ☐ 9 ☐
- Recording density
- Speed
- Length

DIRECT ACCESS ONLY
- Addressing/accessing method
- Packing density ____ %
- Frequency/condition of re-organisation
- Level | Type of overflow | Size of overflow areas

Notes:

S42

Author | **Issue Date**

© 1969. The National Computing Centre Limited

File specification (S42), published by NCC

Record specification (S44), published by NCC

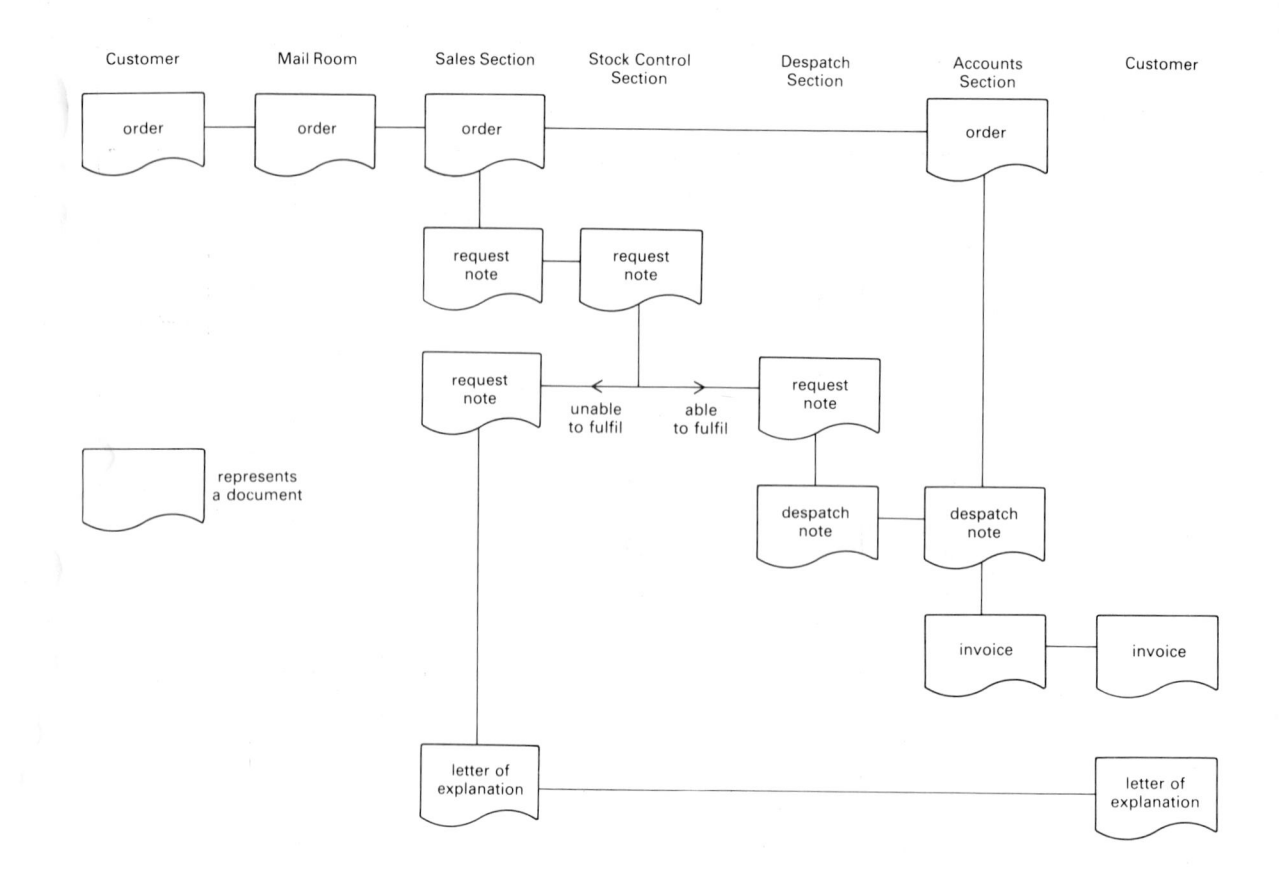

A document flowchart for a mail order company (Note: this diagram only shows documents and does not specify processes. The flow of information is shown only—not the flow of goods).

6.6. DRAWING UP A STATEMENT OF REQUIREMENTS

includes the sending of copies of all or part of the original data into other parts of the company. It is usual to divide a document flowchart into columns representing different parts of an organisation, and to show the flow of information within the organisation from left to right across the page.

Systems flowcharts

A **systems flowchart** is a diagram showing not only the documents as they flow within a company, but also the procedures and processing steps involved. Thus a systems flowchart can be used to understand how the data within the documents can be interpreted and used. Again, columns are often used to distinguish the parts of the organisation.

Having investigated the current system and drawn up a design for a computerised system, these requirements must be presented to potential suppliers. This can enable them to say how and when they can provide what is wanted and what it will cost. Such a statement of requirements is sometimes known as a **call for proposals** or a **tender document**.

It is important that the requirements are stated clearly, so that those suppliers who put in a bid are clear what the customer's expectations are. The less room there is left for interpretation, the less likely it is that there will be a breakdown of communication and the more likely it is that the supplier can be held to a clear agreement.

A tender document is prepared for the potential supplier to complete. Some questions will only require a yes or no answer (can specific

A systems flowchart for a mail order company

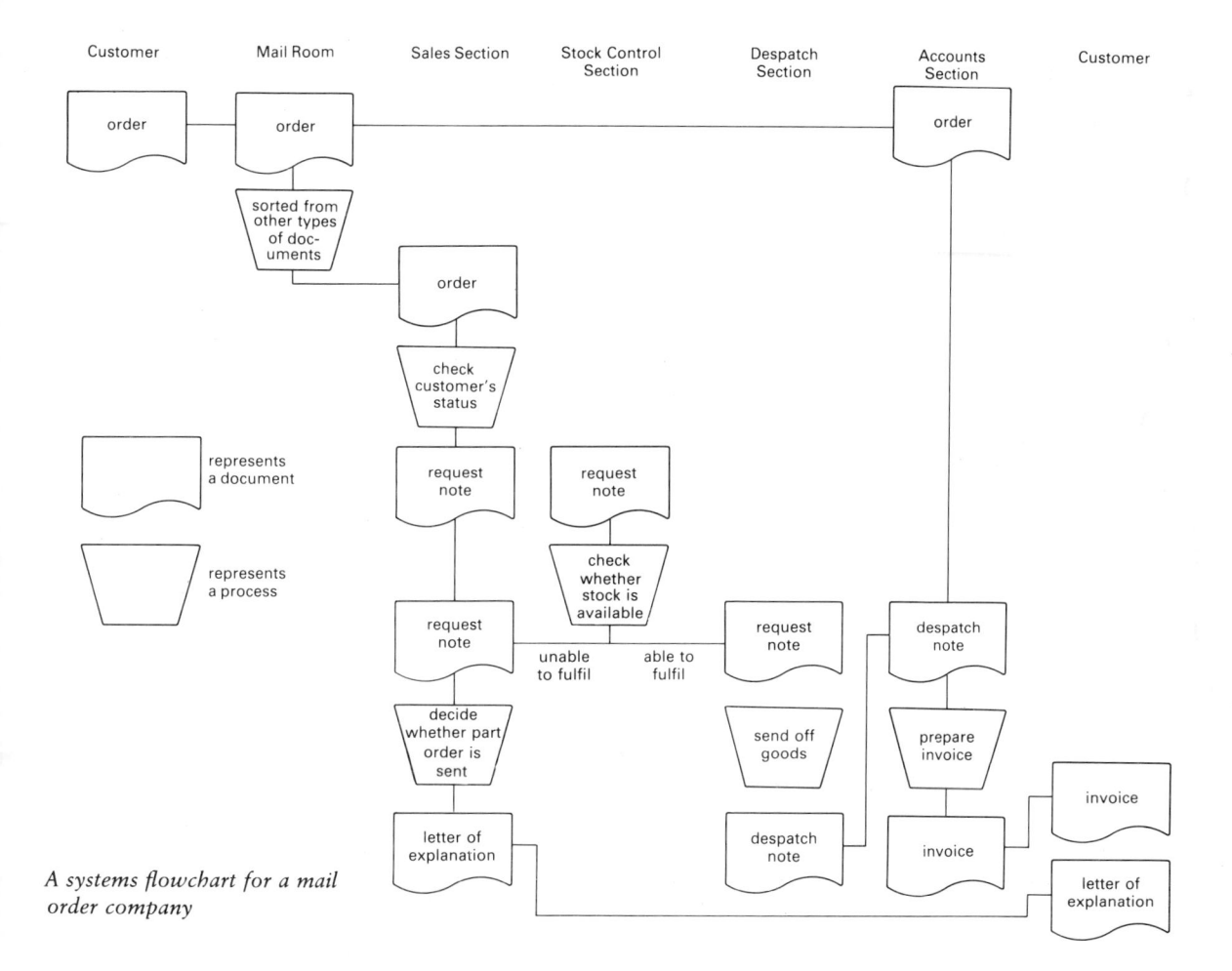

performance targets be reached?); in other cases, respondents will need to answer questions with a detailed description. Technical calculations, such as the size of the computer memory and disc capacity are best left to the supplier. Thus, the tender document is written in terms of business rather than technical requirements.

Points to include in a tender document:

- a description of the business;
- details of the business functions which are to be computerised;
- the objectives of a possible computer system;
- expected workload in terms of input, output, storage and processing (including figures for frequency, volume, average and peak);
- the number of users to be serviced at one time;
- target figures for the system (such as the response time for answering queries);

- operational requirements (such as targets for the proportion of time that the system is fully available);
- a development plan for possible future expansion of the system;
- requirements for maintenance and servicing.

TASK

Outline the advantages and disadvantages of reading magazine articles and reviews of software before drawing up invitations to tender.

It may be that the tender document will consist of two parts. The first section may outline essential features without which the organisation does not think it can effectively computerise. The other section would include desirable features which it is accepted that some suppliers may or may not be able to provide. Decisions about desirable features are often made on the basis of which can be combined together, and their cost is reviewed in the light of the charge for the overall system.

The design and style of the tender document is a crucial part of the process. It forms a basis on which potential suppliers are going to be compared. It is of great importance that all the major areas in which possible systems will differ are identified. The presentation of the call for proposals will determine how vigorously the potential suppliers will compete for the business. Often, suppliers will welcome a detailed call for proposals, as it is often in the companies where the aims of computerisation were unclear in the beginning that dissatisfaction with the final result is most common.

Items which a reply from a potential supplier should include:

▶ details of the business record of the supplier (specific details in this area may need to be asked for, such as number of systems supplied so far, length of experience in the field, links with particular manufacturers and so on);

▶ details of what will be supplied, which will include hardware, software, after-sales support, maintenance, training and documentation;

▶ a detailed breakdown of each element of the costing;

▶ details of adaptations needed to accommodation, staffing levels and other effects on the business, financial or organisational;

▶ arrangements which would have to be made for clerical procedures (such as batch checking and recording);

▶ arrangements which could be made for file security, password control, and back-up hardware, with appropriate costs.

6.7. WHO TO SEND IT TO

At this stage, no firm decisions are being made between different possible suppliers. Thus, in a sense, the more firms which are invited to tender, the better. All the replies which are received have to be analysed, however, and so if several firms have been recommended from various sources, about five invitations may be sent out. If firms are simply drawn from a general list of names, a few more letters might be sent.

Though no firm decisions are being made at this stage, one aspect is clear. If a firm is not invited to tender, it cannot get selected at the end of the process! Thus the process of selecting a list of firms to invite to tender is important; it should ensure that 'good' suppliers are not left out. Thus in drawing up a list, it is important to consider a range of different types of suppliers, such as specialist retailers, national computer chain stores and system or software houses. A list of names can be drawn up using the telephone directory, business directories, advertising material in specialised or local press, and advice from friends or consultants.

TASK

Imagine that you have been asked to help in the computerisation of a common business task, such as stock control or accounts. Suggest ways you would go about drawing up a list of potential suppliers to whom you would send invitations to tender.

6.8. STUDY QUESTIONS

1 How might the improvements to the computer system suggested by the clerical staff differ from those of the management?
2 Why is it best to leave the detailed sizing of a computer system to the supplier?
3 Suggest three sources of the names of possible suppliers other than those mentioned in the text.

6.9. ASSIGNMENTS

Note By far the best way to develop the skills of system analysis is to attempt to do it for real. The ideal way to learn the trade is to try to draw up a specification for a small company with which you have contact. A company might find it of benefit for you to do this sort of preliminary work for them, but you will often find that they are hard pressed for time and are therefore not able to give you that experience. This sort of arrangement is best arrived at by way of personal contacts.
1 The stock control system within a wholesale company uses a centralised system of stock record cards, which are held at a central location. When goods are sold, a form, called a stock requisition form is completed. The data

from this is used to update the stock record card, and if the goods are available, a stock despatch form is completed so that the goods are sent.

The office will also issue order forms when the level of stock has fallen below a specified amount called the re-order level (which may differ between different times). Similarly, a form is required so that the stores can inform the office when goods arrive.

Design the four forms needed and the stock record card.

2 Design the format for a stock status report within a stock control system, which will show, in an appropriate order, for all stock items, the current stock level, the description of the item, the number on order and other data which you consider appropriate. Suggest a way in which items which are out of stock can be highlighted. How could a stock valuation (to work out the value of the current stock held) be incorporated into your system?

3 Bectown is a medium-sized industrial city in the Midlands famous for its manufacture of pharmaceuticals and bicycles.

Bectown Central Library is well stocked with both fiction and non-fiction, with a local studies section. The loans system has been computerised for some time.

A new system is now proposed, which will involve a system of about eight terminals. These will be sited at various points within the building. They are to be used to hold detailed indexes on a number of specialised reference areas.

What is to be established is an on-line reference system so that members of the public can find books or articles about areas of interest. The software may need to be specially written, in a user-friendly way, in order to use the latest technology for user input.

Each member of the library staff will be invited to take on, as part of his or her duties, a specialist interest and to be responsible for deciding on additions to be made as new items are added to the stock. There has been particular interest shown by the local studies section in doing this, and so this will be one of the first areas to be developed.

Behind the scenes, library staff will be required to enter and update information. Much of this will eventually be done on-line by the general library staff, but in the initial stages, a number of them will be reluctant to use their time in this way.

Prepare a report to be sent out as an invitation to tender giving your (estimated) figures for the size of system needed, including performance requirements, and servicing conditions.

Draw up a list of six companies which might be invited to tender for the job.

7 EVALUATING PROPOSALS

No one system will provide the best solution to match all the needs of an organisation. The process of making the final decision therefore involves compromise. It is important that the various factors in the choice are examined formally, so that clear reasons can be given for the final decision. This helps everybody to know what to expect from the new system.

The choice of a particular system is in two stages: firstly we have to ask whether the systems provide the features considered essential and secondly, we have to pick the best of these.

7.1. HOW DIFFERENT PROPOSALS COMPARE

The ways in which systems differ can be divided into two broad areas. The first area of comparison is based on those points which are measurable values, such as operating speed, maximum size of files, and costs. These values are matters of fact and are either readily available, or can be obtained by conducting trial runs. These points of comparison which can be measured are known as **objective criteria**.

Other points of comparison between systems are matters of opinion, such as value for money, the experience of the supplier and the relative merits of different schemes for maintenance. Such areas of comparison, which are open to individual interpretation, are known as **subjective criteria**.

TASK

Draw up a list of the ways in which computer systems can differ from each other. Divide the list into objective and subjective criteria.

7.2. NARROWING THE FIELD

Each proposal returned from a supplier should be evaluated. (Clearly, those suppliers who do not respond to a call for proposals eliminate themselves.) It would be normal to give a final date for tenders to be returned, so that the selection process can start. In order to reduce the numbers of tenders which are examined in great depth, it is usual to draw up a shortlist, probably consisting of two or three suppliers, from the details which they return.

Often the suppliers which can be eliminated are those whose proposal does not match a list of what are considered essential requirements. Such a list is best drawn up before the proposals are returned and should contain features without which the system simply cannot be accepted. This could include minimum guaranteed performance targets and maximum allowed costs, as well as a list of features considered essential. Such essential features might include provision of an audit trail, acceptable VAT features and adequate after-sales service.

It is probably useful at this stage to draw up a check-list in the form of a table, to enable all of the proposals to be checked against each essential requirement. This is desirable so that the process is carried out thoroughly: it is also useful as a permanent record of the decision. This record might be useful for a number of reasons: it could help when choosing a supplier for a future system or in advising other organisations who ask for help. It is a quick reminder of the basis for the rejection of a particular supplier at this stage. Such a straightforward summary can also help explain the decision to others, such as a manager, or a committee.

7.3. THE DETAILED CHOICE

Having narrowed down the field to a shortlist, each of the suppliers on the list must be thoroughly evaluated. As many as possible of the claims made in the proposal by the supplier should be verified. (There is usually no problem the other way round. Potential suppliers are very unlikely to be eliminated on the basis of understating the capabilities of their system!)

Use actual data

It is important for a purchaser to test out the claims of a potential supplier, rather than simply taking a proposal on trust. Good suppliers will welcome the opportunity to show off the attributes of a system which they are advocating. Thus, there should be no hesitation in asking for a demonstration of a system which is being seriously considered. It is important, at this demonstration, for the potential customer not simply to watch the standard presentations, but to ask questions and to run the system using actual data. This will give an impression of the processing speed that will be achieved and will point out any difficulties which the system may have with unusual aspects of the day-to-day data. It is better to discover such problems at this stage.

If typical data is to be tried out, this will clearly have to be prepared in advance. It will also be useful to have decided on the criteria of comparison of different systems before any demonstrations are given. It is most unfortunate when customers think of questions which should have been asked of all the suppliers after several demonstrations have taken place.

TASK

Give examples of problems with a computer system which might only be revealed when it is run with the customer's own data.

Setting standard tests

It might also be helpful to use a set of standard tests of performance on each system, so that systems can be compared with figures drawn up on the same basis. It might be a useful comparison, for example, to see how long a system takes to sort a hundred entries in a database or to print a hundred invoices or to make a back-up copy of a particular file from one disc to another. The process of comparing systems against standard tests is known as **benchmarking**.

Several books and magazines have sections which provide benchmark tests. A number of standard tests have been devised and these are often used in magazine reviews as an objective means of comparison. The earliest benchmarks were generally for the assessment of hardware performance, though standard benchmarks are now being suggested for software performance as well. It might be possible for a company to devise its own standard tests, typical of its daily work. If it will only rarely need to sort a thousand numbers, for example, then there is little point in having figures comparing the time each system takes to do this.

Formal comparison: the weighted ranking system

In order to bring together all the potential pros and cons of a system, it is usual to use a formal evaluation method, such as the **weighted ranking method**. In this method, a list of criteria for comparing systems is written. The importance of each of these criteria is discussed (perhaps in advance of the submission of proposals) and each criterion is given a numerical value reflecting its importance. Thus, if response time to a call-out for repairs is considered important, it might be given a value of 10, whereas a less important factor, such as the time before the system can become fully operational might be given a value of, say, 2. These values, reflecting the relative importance of criteria, are known as **weightings**.

The second part of the process is to take the criteria, one at a time, and to put the different proposals in order under each heading, showing how the systems compare according to each factor. This ordering of the performance of each system according to the criteria is known as the **ranking**.

For a formal comparison, each system is given a score based on its ability to match a criterion. The highest ranking system gets the highest score. Thus, if four systems are being compared, then the top under each heading is given 4 points, the next is given 3, the next 2 and the last 1. This process is carried out for each of the criteria. The rankings are then multiplied by the weighting of the criterion and the results for each system are added up. The system with the highest total will then be the most suitable for the stated purpose. The weighting of the rankings give relatively more importance to systems scoring well on those areas.

A worked example of comparison of systems by the weighted ranking method

Suppose that four systems, A, B, C, and D are being compared, and that the factors to be taken into account are:

1. Speed of response to input
2. Ease of use of hardware
3. Cost of initial purchase
4. Running costs.

It might be that money is limited, and that response times are vital, perhaps in providing a good customer service. These criteria would therefore be given a higher weighting than the others. Thus factor 1 might be weighted 8, factor 2 might be given 2, factor 3 might rate 10, and number 4 might be weighted 3.

The rankings might look like this:

Speed of response (weight 8)	Ease of use (weight 2)	Initial cost (weight 10)	Running cost (weight 3)
A	B	C	B
D	C	D	D
C	D	A	A
B	A	B	C

The weighted ranking is then:

A	B	C	D
8 × 4 = 32	8 × 1 = 8	8 × 2 = 16	8 × 3 = 24
2 × 1 = 2	2 × 4 = 8	2 × 3 = 6	2 × 2 = 4
10 × 2 = 20	10 × 1 = 10	10 × 4 = 40	10 × 3 = 30
3 × 2 = 6	3 × 4 = 12	3 × 1 = 3	3 × 3 = 9
Total = 60	Total = 38	Total = 65	Total = 67

This shows that, although B comes top of two of the four lists, it comes a poor last in the weighted ranking system. The system which scores the highest, D, is not, in fact, top of any list, but its overall rating is highest.

It is a matter of management skill to determine which factors to consider in a weighted ranking system, what weight to give the various factors, and how to rank systems within each particular area. Such choices should be carefully presented, and discussed. Much of this can be done in advance of the return of proposals, and, best of all, should be done before invitations to tender are sent, so that relevant questions are asked.

The weighted ranking system naturally lends itself to implementation with a spreadsheet package. Such tools should not be neglected in making management decisions.

TASK

Design a spreadsheet worksheet for use in comparing systems by the weighted ranking method.

7.4. MAKING THE CHOICE

Look carefully at the supplier: choose a survivor

Many people with experience in business computing will be ready to offer advice about choosing a supplier. Most advice, unfortunately, will be about firms to avoid or problems which might occur after running the system for a few months. Fewer people are prepared to stick their necks out to recommend particular suppliers.

In choosing a supplier, as with many other choices, better service costs money. Those suppliers offering large discounts can often afford to do so because they offer less support to users after the sale. Other suppliers might reduce prices to build up sales in order to establish new products or to get their own name more widely known.

Some purchasers may wish to 'play it safe' and use well-known suppliers, such as well-established firms. This was how several high street chain stores established themselves in the computer market, on the basis that they were much more likely to be around for many years to come than some of the smaller computer specialist shops. The higher discounts are often available at smaller shops. A potential purchaser has to balance the risk of a supplier ceasing to trade against the discount offered. The popularity of the hardware and software being considered is an important factor here, as support for popular purchases might be available from a wide number of places if necessary. The purchase of little-known hardware or software from the sole agent in an area can lead to problems.

In choosing a supplier, it is also important to avoid being a 'guinea pig'. With any product, there must be a first sale by each supplier, but most firms would want to avoid being that first customer. In computing particularly, it might be beneficial to wait until a product is reasonably well established and the supplier reasonably familiar with it, before buying. This should ensure that most minor flaws in the system are ironed out and that the supplier is fairly familiar with common faults. As hardware and software prices continue to drop, established products begin to look a little more expensive. One of the features which a purchaser gets for the extra money is the pool of expertise that is available about the product. The value of this has to be decided by the purchaser.

Suppliers differ in the amount of support they give to smooth the transition into the new computerised system. This can involve provision of some training and of general 'hand-holding' in the first few weeks or months. The price that customers are prepared to pay depends both on their need for and the quality of this initial support. In evaluating this, new customers often contact previous customers of the supplier.

What to look for when comparing the quality of support from suppliers of different systems of hardware and software:

▶ support for hardware breakdown: on-site repair service, warranty period, temporary replacement of equipment while equipment is away for repair;

▶ support over software problems: replacement software on disc, a 'hot line' for enquiries, provision of upgrades following revision of packages, cover for loss of data caused by problems;

▶ speed of response and cost of calling engineers out.

Look carefully at the contract: avoid the pitfalls

Before signing a contract for the supply of hardware, software, training or support, or any combination of these, customers should check what they are getting, and what they are *not* getting!

The contract should include details of the equipment to be supplied and the price of that equipment (possibly including discount). It should also have details of delivery and testing of equipment. The responsibilities of the supplier and of the customer should be clearly specified. There will normally be conditions laid down with guarantees, covering such eventualities as attempted repairs by the customer which invalidate the warranty. Most suppliers use a standard form of contract and are unlikely to deviate from their standard terms. In order to be quite clear what the contract says, it is good practice to consult a solicitor.

Quality assurance

Customers might also require performance guarantees as laid down in the call for proposals. They should seek to ensure that it is clear on both sides how it might be demonstrated in the future that these performance targets cannot be met within the terms of the proposals. This covers the possibility of a dispute about the quality of the goods. It should also be clear what redress there is should this be proved. Again, legal advice should be sought.

Look carefully at the finance: plan the expense

In deciding whether a computerisation project is worthwhile in financial terms, a whole set of costings must be drawn up. As part of the feasibility study, one of the suggested benefits might have been the saving of money, and rough costings would have been done then. Only when the tenders have been received, though, can the precise financial benefits be analysed.

Costs and benefits

A table can be drawn up, showing the costs and the benefits of a computerisation scheme. Some costs and some benefits might not produce a clear financial gain, but may be very important in other respects. It is a matter of judgement what weighting should be given to such considerations. If the overall benefit to the company is to be assessed, then it may be worthwhile to estimate the financial equivalent of such non-financial benefits. (In that sense, how much is a potential benefit 'worth'?) Such benefits are often called **intangible benefits**.

In order to put a figure on some of the financial benefits, it might be necessary to make a few estimates. Producing invoices at the time when an order is processed rather than waiting for clerical work to be completed might mean that customers are asked for money up to a week earlier. This should bring money in earlier and will mean less capital is tied up, allowing its investment elsewhere (or the borrowing of less). The cost of this finance is then saved. Similarly, allowing fewer bad debts will produce savings.

In order to make a realistic assessment of the financial effect a system will have, it is usual to draw up a table of costs and savings. It normally happens with computerisation that a short-term initial cost is outweighed by long-term savings.

Possible costs and benefits of a computer system

Some suggested headings for costs are:

- purchase of equipment;
- cost of installation (adaptation of rooms, relocation etc);
- initial costs (consultancy fees, file conversion, training, initial supplies);
- staffing costs (computer personnel: recruitment, salaries, benefits);
- running costs (supplies, maintenance, overheads, insurance)

Some suggested headings for savings/benefits are:

- staffing costs (the number of non-computer personnel might be reduced);
- other running costs;
- better credit control;
- better control of cash flow;
- reduction in stock held;
- tax benefits (these change according to legislation)

The headings for non-financial or intangible benefits should be gathered from the feasibility study, but might include:

- less paperwork oin astra;
- more business because of a better company image or service;
- increased job satisfaction of staff;
- ability to respond more quickly to market trends

Long-term financial planning.

It is reasonable to evaluate a computer system assuming that it will be used over a five year lifespan. This gives reasonable time for the system to be used to full capacity, but after five years equipment is likely to be well worn and outdated.

If it is considered appropriate, the system can be evaluated in terms more closely related to those which accountants would use. The **net present value** system is based on the experience that money available now can be used productively in the meantime, whereas future money cannot. So, money available now is worth more than money available in the future, as what currently costs £100 may cost £115 next year. Thus future money is discounted by an approximate figure based on the investment potential of current money. Thus, for each successive year, a discount factor is either obtained from tables or calculated.

The total of the discounted cash flows is called the **net present value**. This figure normally gives a realistic saving, because the benefits are generally all in the future and so are worth relatively less.

A spreadsheet can be used to calculate the discounted cash flow. Some spreadsheets have inbuilt functions to help with this, and with the calculation of a figure known as the **internal rate of return**. Such figures are often used to compare all potential projects within an organisation and the detailed basis of the comparison is generally best left to the financial staff.

TASK

Design a spreadsheet worksheet for use in calculating a discounted cash flow for the analysis of the costs and benefits of various systems.

Cash flow analysis

	Year 1	Year 2	Year 3	Year 4	Year 5
Costs					
Purchase of equipment	20 000				
Cost of installation	2 000				
Initial costs	3 000				
Staffing costs	10 000	10 000	10 000	10 000	10 000
Running costs	5 000	5 000	5 000	5 000	5 000
Total costs	40 000	15 000	15 000	15 000	15 000
Savings					
Staffing costs	5 000	15 000	15 000	15 000	15 000
Other running costs	3 000	3 500	3 500	3 500	3 500
Credit control	1 500	1 500	1 500	1 500	1 500
Control of cash flow	1 000	1 000	1 000	1 000	1 000
Reduction in stock held	500	1 500	1 500	1 500	1 500
Tax benefits	1 000				
Intangible benefits	1 000	3 000	3 000	3 000	3 000
Total savings	13 000	25 500	25 500	25 500	25 500
Net cash flow (savings-cost)	−27 000	10 500	10 500	10 500	10 500
Cumulative savings	−27 000	−16 500	−6 000	4 500	15 000

From this table, it can be seeen that the total cost of the system will be £100 000. The total savings are £115 000. From the cumulative figures, the £15 000 saving can be seen more clearly. The initial extra cost is offset by savings in later years.

Figures which reflect the relative value of money in different years can be calculated, in this example using a discount factor of 15%.:

	Year 1	Year 2	Year 3	Year 4	Year 5
Net cash flow (savings-cost)	−27 000	10 500	10 500	10 500	10 500
Discount factor at 15%	1.00	0.87	0.76	0.66	0.57
Discounted cash flow	−27 000	9 135	7 980	6 930	5 985

Totalling the discounted cash flows for the five years gives a net present value of £3 030. The figure is less than the cumulative savings above, because money in the future is worth relatively less than money in the present.

Look carefully at the system: acceptance testing

Before a new system is fully accepted (the contract may define this), and before the final payment is made for the purchase, it is important that the system is put through its paces *on site*. Ideally, a clause to this effect should be included in the tender document, but it is still tempting to take short cuts at this late stage rather than insist on thorough testing in actual conditions. At the acceptance testing stage, it is clearly important to ensure that the system performs to any standard specified in a tender document.

An acceptance test might show up teething troubles such as problems with the power supply or compatibility of particular models with particular software or the features of a printer. It is much easier to get a supplier to undertake to rectify faults when one of the staff is present and when only part of the money has been paid than it is to ring somebody up after all the bills have been paid.

TASK

Imagine that you are responsible for arranging an acceptance test of equipment that your organisation is buying. Write a list of the people who you would wish to be present and the things that they should be looking for.

7.5. STUDY QUESTIONS

1 What arguments might be given in favour of purchasing a new product which has just come on to the market?

2 What would you imagine are typical figures for the running costs of a business system? If possible, draw up a list of running costs for a system with which you are familiar.

7.6. ASSIGNMENTS

1 Devise a series of benchmark tests which could be used to compare the performance of different systems with which you are familiar. Ideally, attempt the exercise of comparing different pieces of software performing similar tasks. If this is not practicable, then compare the speeds of different computers (possibly with standard Basic programs).

   (a) Try to devise generalised tests including features which all the systems have.
   (b) Design tests which use features emphasised in sales literature for the particular products. Is there a greater contrast between the systems on this basis? What does this suggest about who should devise benchmark tests?

2 Imagine you are about to purchase a piece of popular software of your own choice. By using catalogues, magazine articles and other sources (possibly including telephone calls and letters), draw up a list of differing prices. Alongside this list, contrast the ways in which what you get for your money differs between the different sources.

8 GOING LIVE

8.1. PLAN THE CHANGES

The first months of using a new computer system are critical. Attitudes of staff and the style of their work with the system are set during this period. This is equally true whether an organisation is being computerised for the first time or a new computer system is replacing an old one.

The way in which the changeover is handled is crucial in determining attitudes at this demanding time, when everybody is under pressure. Bringing a new system into full use will require the active participation and cooperation of staff, though this must start much earlier in the system's life cycle; attempts to begin consultation at this late stage are very unlikely to succeed.

TASK
Write down a list of the stages of computerisation. Against each stage write down as many suggestions as you can for participation of the workforce.

Timing is crucial in the transfer between systems and so the process must be well planned. There are many tasks that will have to be carried out at almost the same time. Physical installation work may be required, the system must be tested, staff need training or retraining, records require transferring, and the business has to be kept going at the same time!

Clearly, an appropriate time of the year must be chosen, when the major upheaval of the changeover will have the least damaging effect. Thus, it is advisable to avoid busy times, such as the Christmas rush, or periods of staff shortage, such as summer holidays. The end of a financial year is also a busy time, though there would also be advantages in automating the records for a new year on a new machine.

It might be advisable to use a normal holiday period, when the business is usually closed, to perform the transition, with staff being paid generously for this. Such a strategy has to be arranged for some period in advance, probably in consultation with the staff and their trade union. (Staff might then take other holidays staggered through the year.) Such major arrangements are clearly very dependent on previous stages of the systems development being completed on time.

The various activities involved in computer system implementation must be carefully planned, particularly as some activities cannot start until others have been completed. For example, staff responsibilities must be determined and job descriptions drawn up before people can be appointed or redeployed in the posts. Similarly, the system must become fully operational once the files have been transferred, otherwise they will quickly become out of date.

Projects can be planned using wallcharts, with the days or weeks across the top, dividing the chart into columns, and the activities listed down the side, forming the rows. The estimated time for each activity is represented by a horizontal bar, which is placed at the appropriate stage of the timetable. Such a plan is known as a **Gantt chart** (see over).

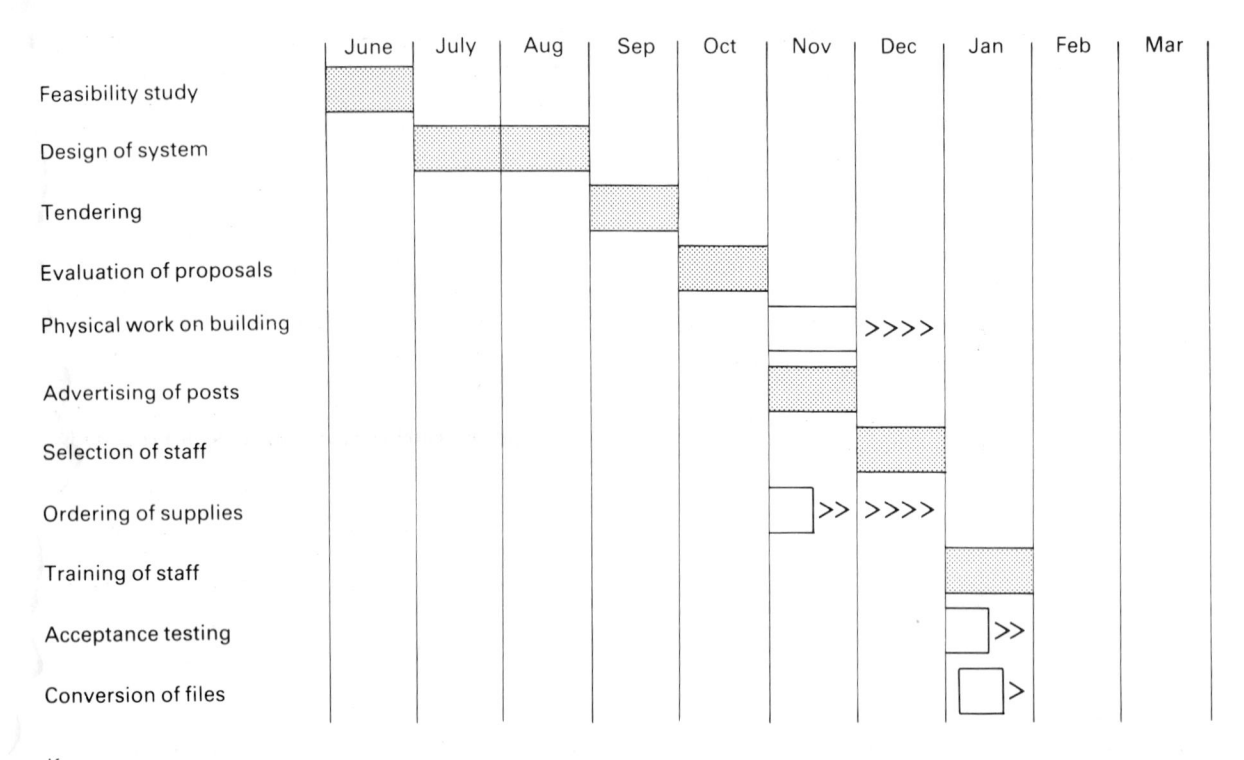

	June	July	Aug	Sep	Oct	Nov	Dec	Jan	Feb	Mar
Feasibility study	▓▓									
Design of system		▓▓	▓▓							
Tendering				▓▓						
Evaluation of proposals					▓▓					
Physical work on building						□	>>>>			
Advertising of posts						▓▓				
Selection of staff							▓▓			
Ordering of supplies						□	>> >>>>			
Training of staff								▓▓		
Acceptance testing								□ >>		
Conversion of files								□ >		

Key

▓▓ Critical tasks — a delay in these will have a knock-on effect and will delay the whole project

□ Non-critical tasks — a delay can be absorbed without delaying the project

>> Float time — a period into which a task could move if a delay occurs

A Gantt chart showing the different stages in the introduction of a new computer system

The use of commercially available boards which can allow writing to be wiped off, or the use of removable stickers will make it easier to adapt the timetable in the light of changing circumstances. Different colours are sometimes used to indicate the priority of tasks. In particular, some tasks are **critical** because other tasks cannot start until they are completed, thus a delay in a critical task will have a knock-on effect and so will delay the final implementation.

TASK

Find out what types of planning board are available. Carry out a brief survey of their features and their cost.

8.2. FINALISE CLERICAL PROCEDURES

The work of the staff who will be operating the computerised system should be designed carefully. Procedures should be evolved so that all transactions are processed, none is left out, and all work is carefully logged, for checking and audit purposes. Double checking on work, particularly that involving money, not only ensures smooth operation, but also provides a safeguard for staff.

In order to keep errors to a minimum, clerical procedures should be designed with as few stages as possible. Errors are particularly likely to happen with tedious clerical tasks, such as copying information from one source to another, for example completing forms, whether by hand or by typing. Such transcription errors can be reduced by reducing the need for such tasks. If a person's address is already within a computer system for example, it should not have to be entered again. Clearly, this would save time and therefore money. What it will also do, though, is reduce the chances of having conflicting data, or storing and handling two slightly different versions of the same thing. For example, one address might include 'Avenue' in full; if another version is entered it might have the abbreviation 'Ave'. Spotting similarities of this form would be no problem to the Post Office, but it is difficult to automate a large number of such checks within a computer system.

At this stage, it is possible to ensure that the input forms, screen layout and printouts are all acceptable to the actual staff who will be using them. They should be clear, easy to use and unambiguous. Care should have been taken in the earlier stages of design to overcome such problems. It is better, however, that problems are pointed out, even at this late stage, before the system goes live, than it is to discover them after the system has been operating (badly!) for several weeks or months.

The clerical procedures to be used will include instructions on the way that transactions are to be handled.

Batch processing

Transactions may be **batched**, so that a number of transactions accumulate and are processed together from time to time. Thus, for example, all orders might be placed in a tray during the day, and then be entered at the end of the afternoon. The frequency with which batches are processed will depend on the application. Wages information, for example, might be processed weekly, or monthly.

The advantages of batch processing include:

(a) monitoring to ensure that all work is processed can be done more easily; work can be logged in registers, the transactions in a batch can be totalled to make sure that they are all entered;
(b) recovery from error is easy, as files can be reconstructed from previous versions of a file and the batches which have been processed since the version was produced;
(c) work can be scheduled and timetabled more easily and the fluctuations in work load between different types of task can be monitored more readily and can therefore be allowed for in future planning.

Examples of batch, on-line and real-time systems

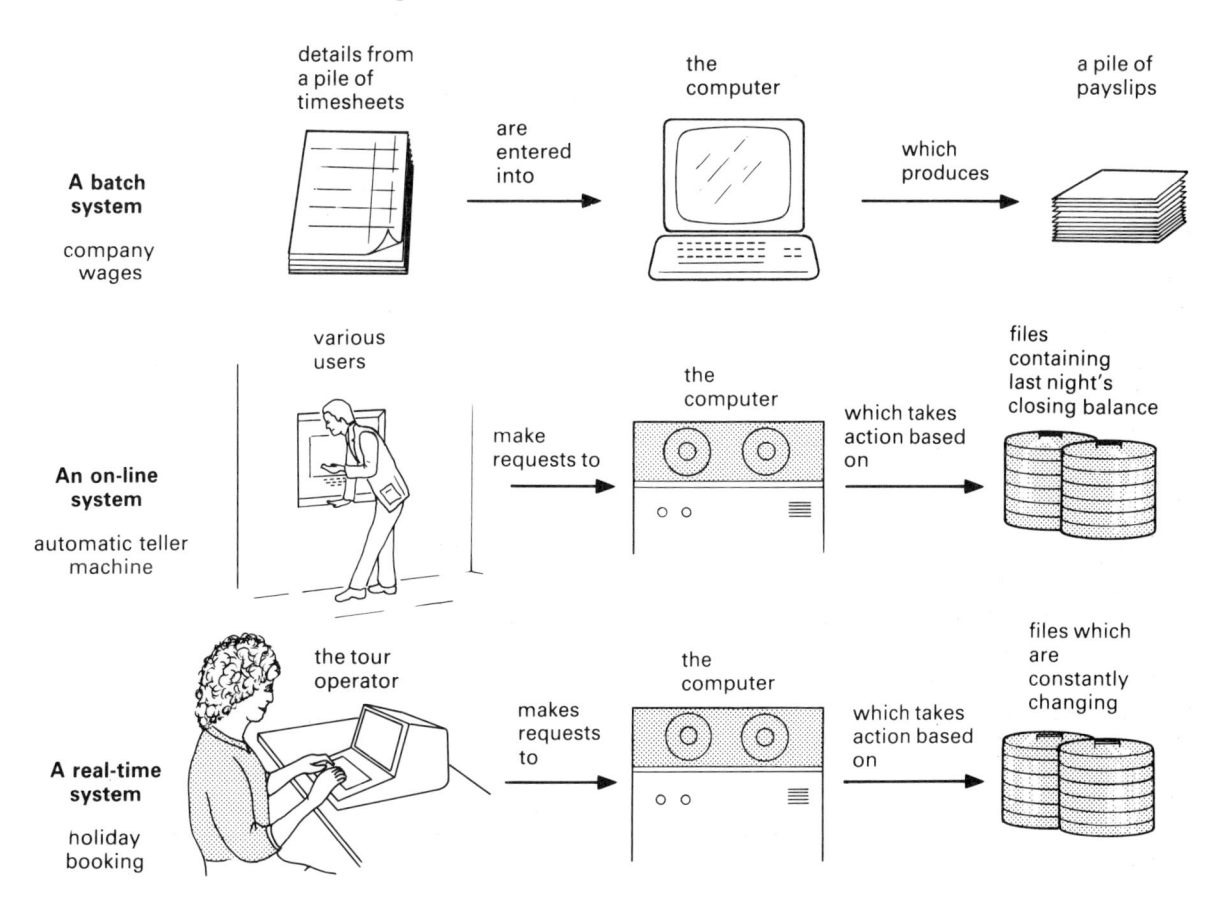

On-line systems

The alternative to batch processing is the **on-line system**. Here, data for transactions is entered directly into the computer system for each individual transaction. For this reason, such systems are also known as **transaction driven**. In some on-line systems, transactions are held and stored for later processing, sometimes in batch mode. If the transactions are processed immediately, however, this is known as **real-time** processing. Clearly, real-time processing is essential for systems such as airline bookings or control of a chemical plant.

The advantages of on-line systems include:

(a) the person originating the data can enter it into the computer. This reduces the chances of incorrect data being entered (as might occur with transcription from a form) and it increases the likelihood that something can be done straight away about errors that do occur;
(b) delays in the entry of data are reduced; transactions do not have to wait until the next batch is processed;
(c) if processing is real time, so that the file is updated immediately, any further transactions, initiated possibly by other members of staff, will be carried out in the light of the updated information.

8.3. ORGANISE THE STAFF

Introducing a new computerised system may require the reorganisation of staff and the reallocation of responsibilities within an organisation. Computerisation might also provide a welcome excuse for a reorganisation which has been long overdue. It is also, however, the point over which some staff will be most sensitive. It can be very threatening for a member of staff to have duties significantly altered after a long time. Some staff might also feel that their livelihood is threatened. These are situations where skills in personnel management are particularly called for.

Discussions of job descriptions will have to take place in the light of estimates of the time required for each task. Responsibilities can then be allocated.

Some staff time will be needed for data entry, some for supervision, batch checking, logging and so on. Other responsibilities include cleaning, maintenance and administration of the system. Some changes in the hierarchy of posts will probably be needed. Careful judgement will be necessary in deciding which staff can be retrained and which staff will not be able to work within the new system. Tact will also be needed in assessing whether posts are advertised to bring new expertise into the organisation.

Clearly staff training can only begin when staff duties have been allocated and the selection of staff has been made.

TASK

Suggest a number of reasons why staff are reluctant to see change in their work.

8.4. INSTALL EQUIPMENT

There may be a period of considerable disruption when new equipment starts to arrive. Building work might be necessary, though this will often only occur in larger organisations. Rooms might also have to be adapted in a number of ways. Staff may need to be moved between rooms or partitions might be required. This work is best done before the equipment arrives.

Similarly, electrical wiring work will have to be carried out, to make the appropriate number of sockets available. This supply may well be a special one to reduce the problems caused by a fluctuating voltage. The introduction of terminals or networks will also involve the use of cabling for signals. If this is well planned, the power supply and cabling can be installed together, using the same style of ducts to carry the wires. This gives both a pleasant and a safe working environment. There are many problems in carrying out installation work after the equipment has been delivered. There is the dust created by drilling, or the need to carry equipment elsewhere for storage (if space is available) and the loss of use of the computers while the work is done.

In order that the equipment can be used properly, furniture must be ordered. Again, this has to be timed properly. Appropriate typing chairs will be needed; desks and stands for monitors will have to be obtained; lighting must be ready and so on. This will all occupy valuable space if delivered too early, yet it must not be too late either.

Some principles of good workstation design

8.5. TRAIN THE STAFF

Realistic estimates must be made of the period necessary for staff training and this must be allowed for in the schedule. The development of staff skills might include general computer appreciation and an understanding of how the new system fits into the organisation as a whole.

Staff will also have to be taught about the particular parts of the system which they are going to be using regularly. There should also be a broadening of the skills so that there are several people capable of carrying out each task. This ensures that the organisation can continue to function when some staff are ill or on leave.

The timing of training can be a difficult decision. It will clearly have to come after staff recruitment and is ideally carried out in the real working environment on the actual equipment to be used. With all the other activities surrounding the implementation of a computer system, this might prove difficult. Training in the use of the system must include an introduction both to the particular hardware and to the particular software.

TASK

Describe the advantages and disadvantages of bringing in somebody from outside a company to carry out training on a new system.

8.6. TEST THE SYSTEM

Before a system is accepted as being fully operational, it must be thoroughly tested. Though, in principle, *all* hardware and software will be tested before paying for it in full, greater care is normally taken with larger systems, as there is much more money at stake. It is common with large systems that payment throughout the project is made in instalments. Upon completion of the project, the customer is asked to sign to confirm that the goods and services have been provided satisfactorily. It is before signing this that full and rigorous acceptance testing should be carried out.

Check the hardware

It is normal to test the equipment when it has been installed, in case damage is done in transit. If the equipment is delivered and/or fitted by the staff of the company selling the equipment, then tests can be carried out in the presence of these staff. With microcomputers, terminals and printers, however, it is common for them to be delivered by a commercial delivery firm. This makes it important to test out equipment on arrival. The supplier should be notified immediately of any problems.

Great care must be taken with unpacking equipment and installing it. Machinery must be handled delicately, connections must be made properly and equipment must only be switched on when such things have been checked. It is normally in everybody's interest for this work to be carried out by more than one person. Particular care must be taken if the case of the computer has to be removed, for example for the fitting of a chip. The first rule for carrying out work on the inside of a computer is 'DON'T'; it is far better to get the supplier to carry out such jobs, and therefore to take responsibility.

Equipment should be tested to see that each part is working. Some equipment has self-testing features and some devices even provide fault diagnosis. After systematically checking all the elements such as the disc drives, monitor and printer, it is useful to run some simple software to see that the parts are all acting in unison.

Check the software

If special software has been commissioned as part of the system, the individual programs will have to be tested to confirm that they achieve what they are meant to. When programmers are testing their programs, they concentrate on ensuring that all individual errors and combinations of errors are trapped and acted upon. They sometimes forget to check thoroughly that the program does what it is supposed to do for valid data! Programs should be tried out with real data.

The system as a whole must be tested to ensure that the various programs in the suite relate together properly. It is also appropriate at this stage to verify that any systems performance criteria specified previously are met when using actual data. If, for example, the invitation to tender includes figures about response times for particular file sizes, checks should be made to ensure that these have been met.

In acceptance testing of commercial packages, it is advisable to try out each feature provided, as a check that the copy which has been sent has not arrived in a corrupted form. Examples for trying out are often suggested by the manual.

It is sometimes difficult with unfamiliar software to know whether an apparent problem with its use is caused by an error in the software, in the manual or in the user's understanding of what the software is supposed to do. It might be useful to get a second opinion to diagnose the problem.

Before software is used, a back-up copy should be made. The original should be kept as an insurance against corruption of the working copy and as proof of purchase. In some cases, software is protected against copying and some alternative arrangement will have to be made for recovery from disaster.

8.7. CONVERT THE FILES

Before a computer system can become operational, there is a major job in transferring files from the previous system to the new one. This will involve a considerable amount of work, whether the transfer be from a manual system or a previous computer system.

If some data is currently held in a computer readable form, it may be possible to transfer files by electronic means. Devices and software for file transfer between popular file formats and disc types are commercially available. These can either be purchased or file transfer can be commissioned, perhaps by mail order, with the converted files coming back by return of post. (Appropriate back-up copies should, of course, be made before sending the discs.)

If the current system is manual, or a partly computerised system is to be expanded, then data will probably have to be transferred from written records into a computer-readable form using a keyboard. The work involved may well take a lot of time, and will have to be carried out extremely accurately. A company may bring in additional temporary staff to do the work or may pay existing staff overtime to do it. Additional staffing hours will be needed for this crucial period, as this work is not productive in itself – the firm must carry on as normal; very little other work can stop to enable the changeover to take place.

There may be many problems in coordinating the initial data entry for the files. The data may come from a number of sources, such as different departments or branches and may currently be held in a number of different ways. (This might be part of the reason why the system is to be computerised and thus standardised.) The data might be incomplete. For example, the name of the previous employer of some staff might not be recorded in a manual personnel system. This will mean either that some records are entered in an incomplete form (the data being desirable but not essential) or that considerable chasing up has to be done.

The data might not fit the new style of record; for instance some addresses might have five lines and only four are allowed by the computer. The fields of a record might be in a different order on a manual system than they are to be entered into the computer. Neither of these problems is insurmountable, but each calls for judgements which can perhaps only be made by a limited number of the company's staff.

Data might also be entered from printouts and other reports, which might be difficult to follow, or some specialist knowledge might be needed for their interpretation. If new codes, for example, are to be introduced, perhaps for a stock recording system, then codes have to be allocated to all existing stock. It may also prove necessary to ask staff to complete special forms onto which they copy the contents of current files which they are using.

TASK

Explain why it is difficult to use a computer to compare addresses to see whether they are the same, for example to ensure that somebody does not appear twice on a mailing list. Suggest ways of overcoming the problem.

In some cases, it may be considered worthwhile to have a special file conversion program written in order to overcome a combination of these problems. Such a program would have to be particularly reliable.

In some circumstances, it might prove difficult to transfer the contents of files which are in constant use during working hours, and data entry during holiday times or weekends may be the only option.

TASK

As the union representative in your company, you have been consulted about the method of file conversion which might be used. Describe how you would go about finding out the views of your members on the issue. Outline some possible schemes which you might suggest and ones that the management might suggest.

8.8. CHANGEOVER

There are several ways in which the change to a new computerised system can be made.

Direct changeover

When an old system is disposed of and a new system immediately takes its place, this is known as **direct changeover**. This involves closing down the old system as the end of one working day and the new one becoming fully operational at the start of the next. If this is done over a weekend or public holiday, this can provide time for file conversion. The method is vulnerable, particularly if teething troubles are experienced with a new system. If problems develop after a few days, there are only out-of-date records from the previous system to fall back on.

The direct changeover may be possible for a limited system. It might be the *only* option for a real-time system, such as a theatre booking system or controlling a steel plant.

Parallel running

It might be possible to run a new system alongside the old system, and so run the two in **parallel**. This will then mean that the results of the two systems can be compared to ensure that they are the same. A direct comparison of *all* results might not be possible, however, as a new system might have additional features not present in the old one.

Parallel running is expensive, as it involves doing all the work twice during this period. It also might not be physically possible to process each transaction in two different ways, particularly if the new system involves a change of departmental responsibilities or even geographical locations.

Gradual changeover

In some circumstances, it might be possible to introduce the new system a little at a time. Thus a payroll system, for example, can be introduced for just one department. When this has operated successfully for a while, and a number of the problems have been ironed out, another department can be put on the system, and so the scheme is gradually introduced to all parts of the company.

This method had the advantage that any initial problems will only affect a limited number of employees (or customers, or stock items, depending on the application). An added advantage is that a 'typical' part of the new scheme could be computerised first. This will mean that expertise and experience with the new system can be built up before those parts having unusual features are added, so that the difficult part can be postponed. This method also allows more time for file conversion; it only has to be done little by little.

Another way of introducing a new system is to use old data from the previous week or month on the new system. Results from the new system can be compared with actual results already produced. This involves extra work in a similar way to parallel running, but as it is a period behind and results are not actually to be used, delays and problems are less crucial.

Once processing is running properly one step behind the old system, an extra processing run is carried out to bring the new system up to date, from when it can be used 'for real'.

There are many systems, however, where a gradual changeover is not possible because of the interrelations of departments or functions or data. The introduction of a new traffic lights system at a junction, for example, could not be done gradually!

Choosing a changeover method

The choice of changeover method will depend on the particular systems, old and new, and on other constraints on the organisation. Important considerations include the costs involved, the attitude and availability of staff and the risks which it is acceptable to take. In addition, some methods might simply not be possible because of the nature of the application.

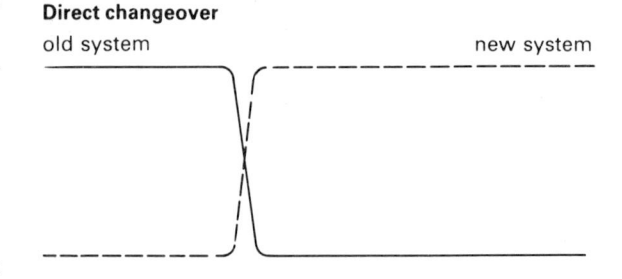

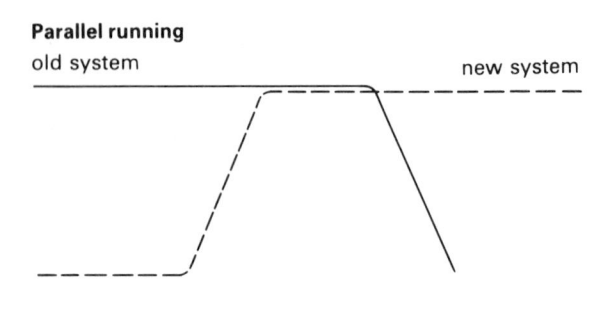

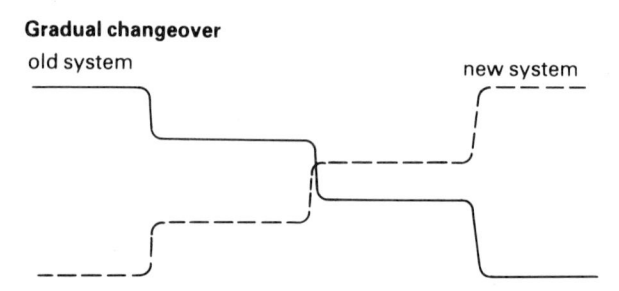

Direct changeover
old system — new system

Parallel running
old system — new system

Gradual changeover
old system — new system

Three ways of introducing a new system: direct changeover, parallel running and gradual changeover

8.9. SYSTEMS REVIEW

Once a system has been implemented and is fully operational, there is a temptation to breathe a sigh of relief, thinking that all the work is over. Surely, the system can now be left to function properly. On the contrary, the system should be subject to regular review.

Reviewing the process of computerisation is clearly important for the organisation, as there will be lessons to learn for the future. It is likely that in the future, a number of other business functions will be computerised; it is important not to make the same mistakes again. A new system which has been introduced will itself begin to look rather dated after a few years. It may be necessary or desirable to replace a system because of developments in hardware, or software, or the business itself. A typical system might be expected to last five years before a replacement is considered, in order that it can be economically viable.

Similarly, a computerised system should be reviewed in the light of changing circumstances in which the organisation finds itself. Room for expansion and development on a reasonable scale should be built into the original specification, but a lot can happen in five years.

There may be major or minor ways in which the company or its operation changes. Changes to the computer system may be needed to fit in with these. Similarly, adaptations to the system might be required because of external circumstances, such as changes in law, tax provision, safety requirements and so on. For these reasons, regular reviews, possibly annually, should be carried out.

A system can be reviewed by asking questions such as:

▶ Is the system bringing the benefits which were expected? If they are not, what can be done about it?

▶ Are the costs within the bounds expected? If not, what can be done about them?

▶ Does the response time match the specification?

▶ Does the storage capacity meet the needs?

▶ Does the system sustain the throughput of actual work?

▶ Are there any amendments needed to cope with changes in law, company organisation and so on?

8.10. STUDY QUESTIONS

1 What are the disadvantages, respectively, of batch processing and real-time processing?

2 What stages of testing would you carry out on a suite of programs to ensure that they are working according to a specification? (Note that to do this, you do not need a detailed knowledge of programming; indeed, you do not even need to know what language the programs are written in.)

3 Which of the following operations can be carried out using a batch-processing system and which must be on-line or real-time systems? Give reasons for your answers:

(a) stock control in a shoe warehouse,
(b) the entry of new hire purchase agreements for customers,
(c) the payment of gas bills,
(d) the retrieval of instructions on how to get to a particular address for use by the fire brigade.

4 For the four applications listed in study question 3, what would you consider to be an appropriate form of changeover when the new system is introduced?

8.11. ASSIGNMENTS

1 Imagine that you are one of two people who currently work in the wages department of a firm employing a hundred people. The system is to be computerised and the post of computer wages supervisor is being advertised both within the company and in the press. Write two letters, one applying for the post, the other to your union expressing whatever fears you might have about the new system.

2 A public library in a small town is about to computerise its lending service for books (both fiction and non-fiction) and records. Write a report giving the advantages and disadvantages of each possible method of changeover. Include a particular recommendation.

9 RUNNING COMPUTER SYSTEMS

It goes without saying that a computer system is only as good as the people who operate it. This idea led to the slogan 'Garbage In, Garbage Out', often abbreviated to GIGO. A system is also only as good as its *worst* operator. Thus any computer installation, be it large or small, should have a defined set of operating standards and procedures which are an insurance against possible failures.

9.1. THE BASICS OF USING A COMPUTER

At all levels within a modern organisation, people will be called upon to use a computer. In the forseeable future, this will mean using a keyboard for at least part of the time. A rudimentary knowledge of how to get the best out of a keyboard is therefore required.

Infrequent users of computers do not have to be able to touch type. The old 'hunt and peck' method will suffice for occasional use. All users need to be aware of the basic keyboard layout of the particular model being used.

Alphabetic characters are always laid out with the traditional QWERTY arrangement, devised for the early typewriters.

Numeric keys are normally either directly above the alphabetic keys forming an additional row, or they form a separate area on the keyboard, sometimes called a numeric key-pad.

A user will need to be familiar with the SHIFT and SHIFT LOCK keys and the RETURN key (sometimes called ENTER). Other keys with special purposes include DELETE, ESCAPE and BREAK. The CTRL key is normally used in combination with other keys, and many keyboards include function keys, which can be allocated a specialised use by each program when it is run. Uses of all these keys vary considerably between machines. New users are best advised to consult manuals and user's guides to their machines.

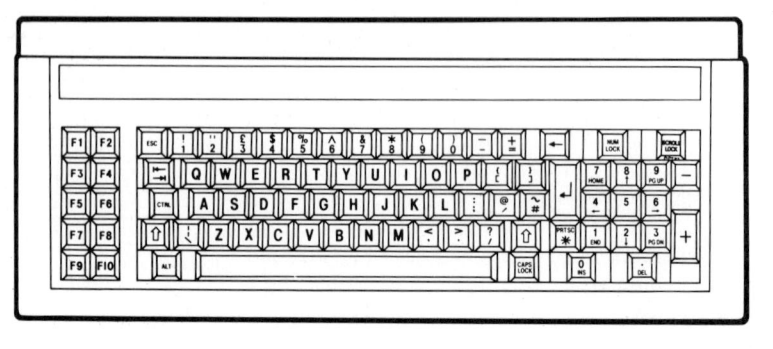

A typical microcomputer keyboard layout (Research Machines Nimbus)

TASK
Suggest reasons why the QWERTY keyboard layout remains so popular.

TASK
Describe the advantages and disadvantages of a keyboard layout which you know.

9.2. SWITCHING ON AND OFF

Before a computer can be switched on and used, the various parts must be linked together. Connections are marked with varying degrees of clarity on computer equipment. Leads should normally connect each part of the system to the central computer. These leads should be obtained when the hardware is purchased. Often the points at which to connect devices are marked and there is an appropriate socket in the device itself. Most connections are now designed so that leads can only be inserted one way. Normally, the most convenient way to connect a piece of equipment is the correct one. In any case, there should be no need to exert great force to make connections. Most good manuals will explain how connections are made.

The number of power sockets required can vary greatly. On the first BBC microcomputer systems, for example, users needed a socket each for the computer, the monitor, the disc drive and the printer. On other systems such as the RM Nimbus, the computer, screen and disc drives come as one unit, and only one socket is needed (with an additional one for the printer, where appropriate). Most wall sockets for electrical power supply now include a switch. Only when all the leads have been connected should the power be switched on. Under no circumstances is it advisable to connect or disconnect leads when the system is switched on, as stray signals can cause damage.

When switching on equipment, the power socket should be switched on first and then the equipment. If this rule is not followed, a power surge when switching on the socket can damage the equipment. Additionally, if there is a master switch for the complete power supply (which is a sensible precaution), this should be switched on first, before the sockets and the equipment itself. It is also advisable to switch the main computer on before the peripherals, as this reduces the chances of stray signals affecting the rest of the equipment when the computer is switched on.

The powering-down sequence of a computer system should be entirely the reverse of the powering-up sequence. Thus the peripherals should be switched off first, then the main computer, then the sockets, then the main supply (if appropriate).

9.3. THE FACILITIES OF A PRINTER

Loading paper into a printer can be a cumbersome and tedious job. Paper should be lined up precisely so that it passes through in a straight line. It is usually preferable for paper to be fed up from the floor so that it has ample opportunity to unfold before reaching the printer on the table. Different

Connections available to a microcomputer (Research Machines Nimbus)

paper feeding mechanisms are sometimes difficult to get used to. A good printer manual will explain this in some detail, but most users will not need to load continuous stationery frequently.

TASK

Suggest reasons why a typical computer user in a small business might not need to change the paper on the printer frequently.

When they are first switched on, using the POWER ON switch, most printers perform some simple test to check that everything is working. This might include tests of the circuits, ensuring that some paper is present and so on. In addition to this, if necessary, most printers have a self-test procedure, whereby a thorough check of all the facilities is carried out. This usually involves the printer repeatedly producing its complete set of characters. Such self-test features are explained in printer manuals and are completely self contained, in that they can be used without having the computer switched on (or even connected to the printer).

There are two modes in which a printer can be used. One is called ON LINE. This state is usually set up by pressing a button on the printer marked in this way. Once a printer is on line, it is under the control of the computer for printing and moving the paper. In this state, many of the features on the printer for which there are buttons and switches are not operational, as control has been passed to the computer. The other mode is OFF LINE, when the printer can be controlled from the various buttons on the printer. These allow such facilities as LINE FEED, which moves the paper up one line, and FORM FEED, which moves the paper to the top of the next page. The printer works out where the top of a page is by counting the number of lines used since the printer was switched on.

The discipline of printer usage

People who use printers should consider both their own convenience and that of the person who will use the equipment next.

When the printer is first switched on, the paper should be in a position so that the first line printed will be at the top of a new sheet (usually about three lines down). A considerate previous user will have left it in this state, because when a printer is switched on, it takes the current position as the top of the page. *After this, the wheel for moving paper up is no longer required for normal operation.* If all paper movement is now done under the control of the computer or by using the control buttons on the printer, then the printer will keep proper track of the paper position. At the appropriate time, the paper will be thrown to the top of the next page in order to skip over the perforations between pages. Any movement of the wheel will upset this arrangement.

When a portion of printing has been completed, this may have finished in the middle of a page. (A good program would seek to avoid this, by incorporating a 'page throw' command when it finishes.) To throw the paper to the top of the next page, the user should switch the printer off line and then press the FORM FEED button on the printer. The printer should be put back on line if further output is required. A little patience in waiting for the next document to be started before tearing off the page can save a lot of sheets of paper in the long run. This is particularly important when using expensive pre-printed stationery.

Computer printouts should be disposed of properly, particularly waste paper. Some printouts can be used in the future as scrap paper and there

A range of computer stationery

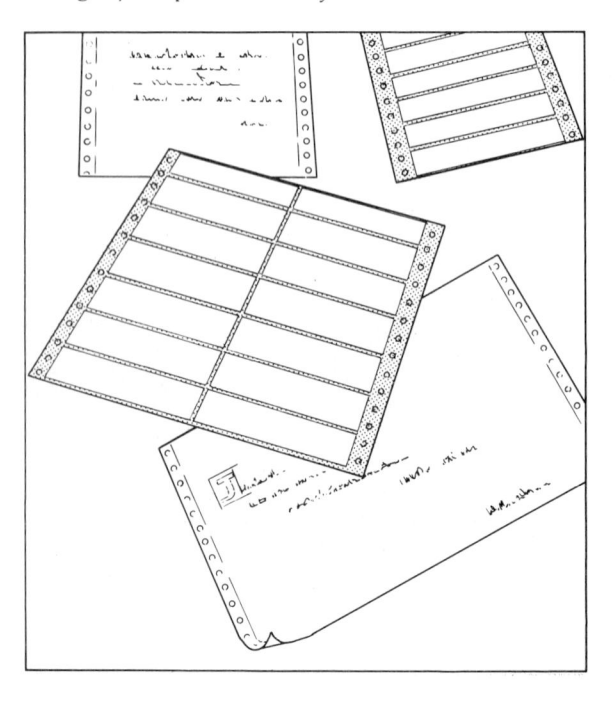

could be a box kept for this purpose. In some cases, however, printouts must be destroyed for security reasons. Even the tightest security procedures can be thwarted by careless disposal of printouts.

9.4. LOGGING FAULTS

It is also important to report and log problems with equipment, particularly printers. When something goes wrong in printing, it is most frequently not the user's fault; often it is because the paper or the ribbon has run out. Some printers signal these conditions with loud bleeps, others with flashing lights. When these or other conditions occur, then something should be done immediately, so that a printer is left in a working state if possible. Replacement of the paper or ribbon can take place immediately and if supplies have run out, then these can be ordered straight away.

More serious problems can also occur when using a printer. Most printers have mechanisms which detect blockages to the movement of printer heads so that the printer will cut out properly before doing any more damage or burning out the motor. Problems can be simple, such as jammed paper or a frayed ribbon, or more serious, such as mechanical failures. In all cases, it is best for the fault to be reported promptly to the person responsible for dealing with such difficulties.

Errors might be recorded in a faults log book which can help in tracing the history of a fault with equipment for its repair. In serious cases, this might form a document recording the unsatisfactory nature of the goods sent by a supplier.

9.5. THE FACILITIES OF A DISC SYSTEM

Floppy discs, like any magnetic medium, are sensitive and so have to be treated with considerable care. As the disc head moves over the surface of a disc, various forms of dirt on the disc can cause the loss of data on the disc and could also cause damage to the disc drive's head.

Discs should be handled carefully. They should only be taken out of their wallets so that they can be put into the disc drive. They should preferably be held by the label and never by the exposed part of the recording surface. They should be stored in a

The distance between the head and a disc compared with some possible hazards

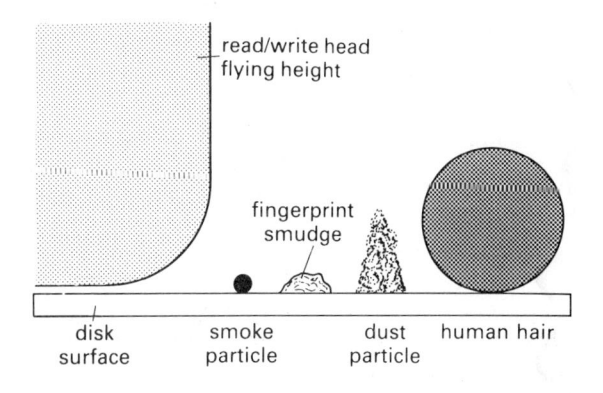

closed box, preferably upright. There is only one correct way to load a disc; the disc drive and the disc could be damaged if it is put in the wrong way. The disc should never be forced into the drive or bent in any way. It is best only to write on labels before they are stuck to the disc, and once they are stuck on, writing should only be done using the special felt tip pens designed for the purpose. Discs should not be exposed to magnets or to extremes of temperature. The smaller 3 inch and $3\frac{1}{2}$ inch discs have rigid plastic cases, which make them somewhat robust than the floppy variety.

Though there are differences from machine to machine, a user should become familiar with the methods of obtaining a directory of the files held on a disc. It is also important to know how to lock and unlock files if this facility is provided by the software. A user should also be able to copy files from one disc to another, and know how to 'back up' a disc by copying it in its entirety. Learning how to erase a file is also useful.

Write protection

Discs usually have some way of physically preventing data being lost by having it recorded over by mistake. On floppy discs, this works by placing a write-protect sticker over a notch near the top right hand side of the disc. On 3 inch and $3\frac{1}{2}$ inch discs, a write-protect tab is used, which can be placed in one of two positions, on or off. These methods ensure that the disc drive will detect that the disc is not to be written on. Physical protection must be removed when the file is to be changed. This hardware protection works independently of any file-locking mechanisms provided by the software.

Using only certain makes of discs

It is common practice within a computer installation to use a limited number of makes of discs. This can often avoid difficulties when damage is caused to disc drives, when the drive's manufacturers might blame the use of poor quality discs. The use of better quality discs also reduces the chances that the disc drive will break down in the first place. Disagreement with the disc drive manufacturer can further be reduced if an installation uses a make of discs recommended by the drive's manufacturer. The use of a limited range of discs also helps to ensure that all users of the system are registered through the centralised issuing of discs. Questions can then be asked of anybody using a non-standard disc.

Installations should also encourage users to keep their discs in a suitable environment; they should not be carried around, unless this is unavoidable. A standard issuing procedure also helps with organising supplies, with the formatting of discs and with the issuing of standard software to users, and of later versions of software when this arrives.

Warnings about care for discs (Elephant Memory Systems)

TASK

For as wide a range as possible of sites where small business computers are used, discover what make or makes of disc are used and the reason for restrictions on brands (or the reasons for having no restrictions).

The discipline of disc usage

Users of a computer system need to be trained in good disciplined use of discs. Firstly, there is a need for regular copying both of data and programs in use. Depending on the regularity with which files are updated, it might be necessary to copy them daily or weekly. Copies should then be kept in a fireproof safe away from the original. Most software suppliers allow users to make a single copy of programs for back-up purposes, so that the copy can be used on a day-to-day basis. The original should be locked away safely as a safeguard against the corruption or loss of the working copy. The original discs sent from software suppliers must be looked after and catalogued, as these are normally used as proof of

Standard symbols from the back of a disc envelope

NEVER FORGET.

Even though we guarantee your Elephant Flexible Disks to meet or beat all industry standards, we can't promise they'll forever retain their memory — unless you promise you'll forever do (or don't do) the following things:

1. DON'T TOUCH THE SHINY PARTS. (The exposed "plastic" slits or dots that show through the black paper liner.) And don't touch them with *anything*. They're vulnerable to fingerprints, dust, coffee spills, cigarette ashes, sneezes, and maybe even dirty looks. The best way to keep things from touching them is to keep the disks inside their protective sleeves whenever you're not actually using them.

2. DON'T JAM THEM INTO THEIR SLOTS. Ease them gently into their drives, so they don't bend, scratch, or otherwise become offended.

3. BEWARE OF MAGNETISM. The disk's "memory" comes from a critical arrangement of the tiny magnetic particles on the disk's surface. Therefore, exposing the disk to close contact with any kind of magnetic field (which you'll find in and around television sets, electric motors that run fans, typewriters, air conditioners, etc., as well as the coils in most loudspeakers) can muck up the arrangement of particles — and your disk will end up either with amnesia or madness.

4. HANDLE LIKE GLASS. Which means don't bend them, sit on them, drop things on them, use them to prop up table legs, etc. If you do so, they will spite you.

5. KEEP THEM COMFORTABLE. Meaning between 50°F to 125° Fahrenheit (10° to 52° Celsius). Intense heat or cold can cause lost memory or weakened sensitivity. As an egregious generality, though, if the room's comfortable enough for you, it's more than comfortable enough for your disks.

6. IF IT'S IMPORTANT, COPY IT. Let's face it: the information on the disk is usually worth a whole lot more than the price of the disk. (Just in man-hours alone to recreate the stored information, let alone in what it could cost you if something like your entire accounts receivable file should all of a sudden "forget.") So by all means, if the data is valuable, make a copy of the disk and store it someplace safe — like a deposit box or fireproof vault.
Made in U.S.A
© Dennison Computer Supplies, Inc.
Waltham, MA 02254

DISKETTE CARE AND HANDLING INFORMATION

	Protect Protéger 保護	Protéger Schützen
	No Non 注意	No Falsch
	Insert Carefully Inserer avec soin 挿入注意	Insertar Sorgfältig Einsetzen
	Never Jamais 絶対禁止	Nunca Nie
	10°C - 52°C 50°F - 125°F	
	Never Jamais 絶対禁止	Nunca Nie

purchase when there are problems, or when an upgrade is issued.

As a further safeguard, regular printouts should be taken of important files, so that if all magnetic recordings of the data are lost, then, if all else fails, all the data can be typed in again!

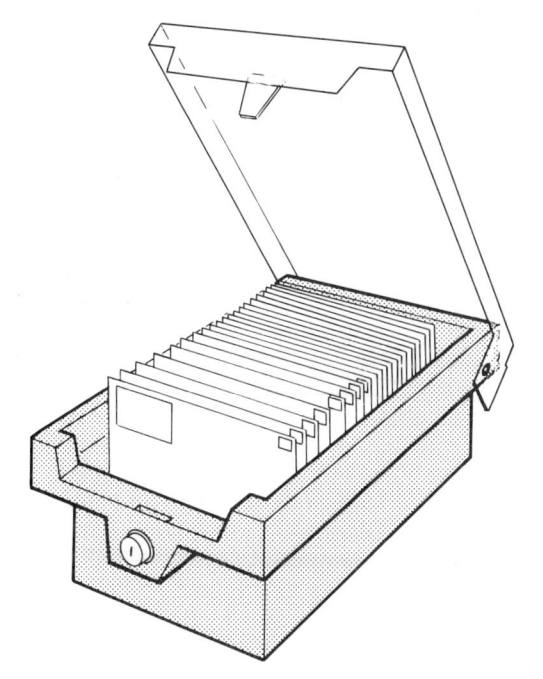

Discs can be locked away as protection against accidental or deliberate damage

9.6. OTHER HAZARDS

Computers are common in most offices nowadays and they should be treated as part of the normal office environment. Like other office equipment, computers have to be looked after as delicate and valuable assets. With computers, it is worth taking sensible precautions to protect the environment in the office, as the results of some possible office accidents can be particularly far reaching and costly.

Fire

One possible serious hazard to be avoided is that of fire. Clearly, everything must be done to prevent fire and everything must be done to minimise its effect if it does happen.

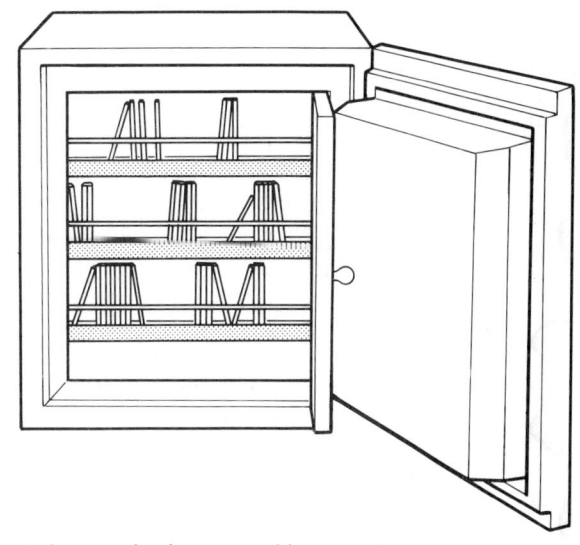

A fire-proof safe is a sensible precaution

One of the most obvious ways in which fire can be prevented is to ban smoking in and around computer rooms. This has the added benefit of reducing the chances of damage to discs by smoke. Secondly, bulk paper supplies should be kept well away from computer rooms and any scrap paper left in a computer room should be organised in a disciplined manner. This also adds to the appearance of the room, which can in itself encourage other good computer practices. Fire risks can also be reduced by seeking expert advice about the power supply for equipment, so that power lines do not get overloaded and other electrical hazards do not occur.

Power problems

Steps can also be taken to prevent surges of power passing through the computer by fitting surge prevention units, which smooth out any peaks in the supply. Similarly, voltage drops, while they are unlikely to damage the equipment, can cause mistakes in a program's execution, loss of data or errors in the operation of a disc drive. In the worst case, where there is a complete power failure, the work currently in memory can be lost and files being accessed at the time could be corrupted. Some computers will continue to operate for a sufficient time after a power failure for the memory contents to be written to disc. Large installations also protect against power failure by the use of battery back up.

FLUCTUATIONS of voltage, caused by abnormal loads

SPIKES caused by lightning or switching other equipment on or off

NOISE from other electric motors in office equipment

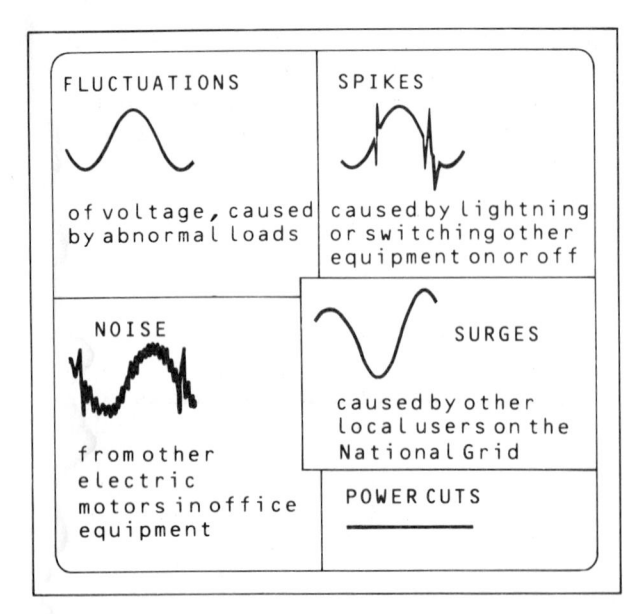

SURGES caused by other local users on the National Grid

POWER CUTS

Electrical hazards for computer systems

Flood

Adequate measures should also be taken to protect computing equipment from the effect of possible flooding. The measures necessary will depend on the particular location. For example, it would be foolish to place a computer room directly below a toilet if this is easy to avoid. Equipment must be kept within reasonable limits of temperature and humidity at all times. This includes periods when the building is not occupied. Damage might be done to computers if there is a particularly heavy frost overnight causing low temperatures indoors. When the building is occupied, the equipment will function effectively in conditions which are comfortable for office workers.

Theft

Equipment should also be protected against theft. Computers are valuable and fairly easy to transport. The value to a company of the data on discs is far greater than the replacement value of the actual disc. As a simple precaution, one organisation took down all the signs to the computer room. All the staff knew where it was already and so all the signs were doing was to make life easy for potential thieves!

Recovery from failure

The planning for recovery from failure has to involve all operations, so that the ability to recover from failure is always there. Indeed, planning for failure involves thinking the unthinkable.

In the most sophisticated software, facilities are built in so that as data is entered and processing is taking place, it is also being logged so that recovery could take place. In addition to this, copies of the main files are dumped onto other discs for filing elsewhere in case error recovery is needed. (This technique is known as dumping and logging.)

In the more typical small business situation, the user will have to perform all the dumping and logging. Thus procedures should be established to copy files regularly and to keep a record of all transactions which have been entered since the last dumping took place. This might, for example, entail a recording of all batch numbers for the batches entered. From such detail, the current situation at the time of failure can be reconstructed when necessary. Such a system must clearly be operated by all users, otherwise this guarantee will not hold.

TASK
Design a set of operating standards for a computer system with which you are familiar. Pay particular attention to the order in which the items are set out, both in terms of their relative importance and their relation to each other.

9.7. WORK SCHEDULING

During the systems analysis stage, a detailed study of the tasks to be performed will have been made. Once the system is operational, the work to be done will have to be scheduled so that jobs are given an appropriate priority.

This scheduling involves an analysis of the activity cycles – the frequency with which each task is needed. The planning of some tasks depends on a deadline for completion. The most obvious example of this is the payroll, where there is an agreement to have all the work completed by a particular time. All the deadlines for data collection, entry, processing and so on are worked out with reference to this completion date.

In other cases, work is scheduled forward from a known time before which the data will not be available. An example of this is the return of details of goods sold from branches in order to update stock records.

Other processing will be on demand and an allowance of an estimated time to be spent on this activity must be made. On-demand activities can be of two types. There are those, such as customer enquiries, which will be processed immediately, and there are the routine tasks, such as the entry of new hire-purchase agreements into a system, which can be fitted in at any appropriate point during the day.

It is also important when scheduling work to note which processes are within the control of an organisation and which are dependent on external factors. External factors can disrupt the regular work substantially.

It is also useful to consider which tasks it would be useful to put on a shorter activity cycle. One such example is the increase in frequency of preparing invoices, which will improve cash flow.

When an overall analysis of work scheduling has taken place, a clear set of guidelines should be laid down to ensure that the various people who complete tasks know what the next process is to be so that this can be initiated. One such method would be the issuing of decision tables which define the next step for all possible situations.

9.8. EQUIPMENT CLEANING

All computer equipment has to be cleaned from time to time. Cleaning reduces the dangers from dust in the disc drives. A clean screen eases the user's task. A clean printer produces a better product. Cleaning must be performed carefully, otherwise the dirt and dust that is already present will simply be disturbed and redistributed. If done incorrectly, cleaning can simply transfer contamination from one disc drive to all the others.

Keyboards

Keyboards should be kept clean, primarily by using a dust cover whenever the equipment is not in use. The dust that does settle on and around the keys can be removed with a small brush, or with a wooden-stemmed cotton bud. These are used either dry or with a cleaning solvent. In some instances, the case of the computer might have to be removed so that keys can be fully cleaned. This is usually only necessary, however, when a liquid has been spilt over the keyboard, or keys are beginning to jam for some other reason.

Screens

Screens tend to attract dust, which clings to the glass because of static electricity. Screens should be wiped regularly with a lint-free cloth, and an anti-static spray can prevent some future build up of dust. Such sprays must only be used sparingly so that a very thin layer of anti-static is built up. If anti-static spray is used too liberally, a considerable film will eventually build up, which will be sticky and will retain dust. Anti-static screen wipes are also available, which come in sealed sachets to keep them damp. These must be applied sparingly to avoid leaving a sticky film. Aerosol cleaners are available for screens to give an occasional thorough clean. There are special sprays and materials for the anti-glare screens which are becoming more common. Other materials will harm these anti-glare screens.

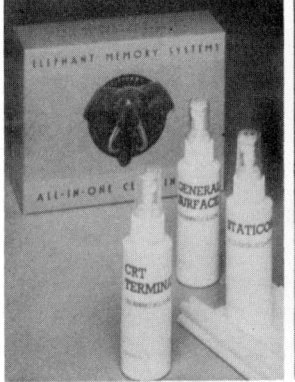

Computer cleaning materials (Elephant Memory Systems)

Disc drives

Disc drive heads should be cleaned occasionally, depending on their frequency of use. Cleaning kits for these consist of lint-free, non-abrasive circular cloths which fit in to a traditional disc jacket for placement in a disc drive. These kits are either wet or dry, the wet ones using a fluid provided to clean the head surfaces. By operating the heads for reading, the head surface will be cleaned. This process takes less than a minute. The cloths are designed for once only use, as once they have removed dirt from one head, it is not really appropriate to introduce that dirt to another drive.

For areas of equipment which are difficult to reach, compressed air sprays can be purchased, which release air under pressure.

Printers

Printers tend to accumulate a surprising amount of paper dust, which can be removed with a brush. The roller of a daisywheel printer gets inky through accidental printing onto it when no paper is present. This can be removed using either a dry cloth or a damp anti-static cloth. Printing on the roller will clearly have done damage to it. Special devices are available to clean removable daisywheels. The daisywheel is placed inside a tube, the lid of which has plastic bristles, and alcohol is poured in as a cleaning agent. Moving the top around brings away a lot of the dirt. Some people also find that a proprietary product like Blu-Tack is an effective way of lifting dirt.

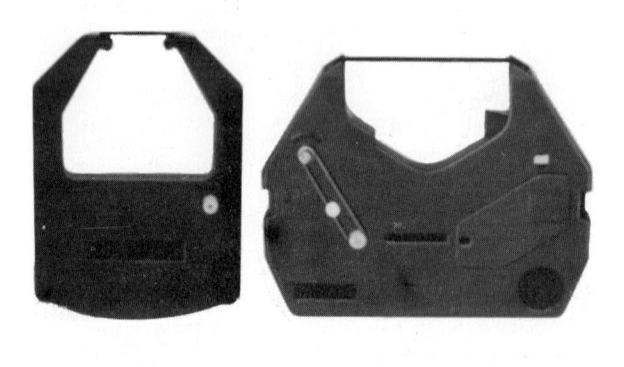

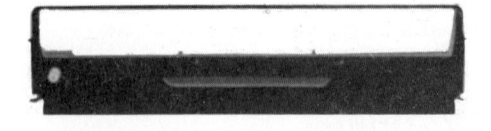

A range of printer ribbons (Elephant Memory Systems)

Casing

The casing of all computer equipment will begin to show the dirt after a while, particularly if it is a light colour. There are special foam aerosol cleaners for this purpose. Ordinary office cleaning materials should not be used. If a keyboard is polished with ordinary varnish, it can take six months before the keys stop feeling sticky to the touch.

TASK
For a computer installation of your choice, find out the arrangements and responsbilities for cleaning.

9.9. IF SOMETHING GOES WRONG

Warranties

All computing equipment which is sold will carry some form of warranty from the manufacturer. In the computer business, however, it is common for this warranty to last only ninety days. In some cases, a card is provided which is completed in order to register the sale. This card is normally date stamped by the dealer. The use of equipment for three months is likely, however, to show up only minor faults in manufacture, many of which would be covered already by the purchaser's statutory rights. It is unlikely that difficulties caused by poor design will show up in this first period.

It is important to be clear precisely what is covered in a warranty before making a purchase. Does the warranty cover both the cost of labour and the cost of the parts? It is unlikely that a warranty will include the provision of replacement equipment while the original is being repaired. This could be a major problem once an organisation becomes dependent on equipment.

Maintenance contracts

For the longer term, it is possible to take out a maintenance contract at the time of purchase. Such an arrangement must be part of the initial budget estimate.

A maintenance agreement might cover hardware, software or both. Software has to be maintained in a useable state just as much as hardware. Thus, when the tax regulations change, most proprietary payroll packages will have to be slightly amended. Are these covered in the purchasing arrangement? If they are, will the software by maintained indefinitely?

What is more likely, in the cases of both hardware and software, is that the initial agreement will cover a fixed period. To cover the period after this, a maintenance agreement should be considered.

An annual maintenance agreement will usually cost between 10% and 15% of the price of the hardware or software covered. A maintenance agreement will ensure that, within a specified time, stated in the contract, an engineer will come out in response to a telephone call, to solve the problem.

Conditions vary considerably, and so it is worth finding out whether a contract:

(a) covers the cost of parts as well as labour,
(b) includes a charge for a call out,
(c) provides advice over the telephone about simple problems,
(d) provides repairs on site or only back at a workshop,
(e) incorporates an arrangement for the provision of temporary replacement equipment (particularly when equipment has to be taken away for repair).

Maintenance charges generally run on a yearly basis, but it is important at the outset to determine what charge will be made in future years, as older equipment is clearly likely to break down more often.

There are three main sources of maintenance agreements.

Contracts with the manufacturer

The manufacturer of the equipment may be prepared to offer a maintenance contract. Clearly the manufacturer is in the best position to know how to repair the equipment and would be expected to have the best stocks of supplies. This does not always follow, however, if parts have to be ordered from abroad.

Contracts with the supplier

A supplier might provide a centralised maintenance contract for all the equipment. This reduces the chances that one installation has to deal wih several sources for repairs, as equipment purchases are often made separately. Printers, for example might be a different make from the main computer. A single contract might prove particularly useful when it is not clear in which part of a system a fault lies. If the same organisation is responsible for all the maintenance, it cannot evade its duties.

Contracts with a specialist maintenance company

Specialist maintenance companies also provide maintenance contracts. They will quote an annual charge for the maintenance of a complete system. This also has the advantage of covering all the equipment in the same way.

It is sometimes difficult to know whether a problem is caused by hardware or software. This will always be a point of contention if the supplier of the hardware is different from the supplier of the software. Difficulties are compounded in that the development of a hardware problem can cause the corruption of software. Thus, what begins as one problem ends up as two. The worst effects of such disasters can be overcome by a rigorous approach to backing up software and data.

It is also possible to have a regular service contract where all the equipment is overhauled. This, in a similar manner to a medical check up, is designed to detect problems early and to prevent serious problems developing, prevention being better than cure.

As an alternative to a contract, some maintenance companies will perform repairs and charge on a call-out basis. In rough terms a one-year maintenance contract will cost something between the charge for two and three average calls out. Thus, such an arrangement is a gamble.

Insurance

It is clearly foolhardy not to insure computer equipment against fire and theft. This could either be appended to an existing contents insurance policy or could be covered separately. The consequences, financial or otherwise, of the loss of the services of a computer for whatever reason, can, however, be much greater:

(a) valuable records might be lost, which in the case of invoice details could be very expensive;
(b) when an organisation depends on the computer, the work done on it might be impossible to do by hand or might be very costly if extra staff had to be hired;
(c) if data has to be reconstructed for future use, this might take considerable time for both computer and employees.

Contents insurance policies often only cover fire, theft and accident. Thus, the spilling of coffee on to a terminal would be covered for the cost of replacement. On the other hand, damage or loss attributable to normal wear and tear would not be covered. Thus the cost of the repair has to be borne by the organisation. There might be consequent loss of data caused by a head crash and there may be a loss of service while repairs are carried out.

A computer insurance policy could be taken out to cover both hardware and software. Such special computer policies often provide for the replacement of the damaged property *as new*. In some instances, computer equipment can be insured on and off the premises. This should be a particularly important consideration where portable computers are being used.

Some policies also cover what is termed **consequential loss**, which would be those financial losses suffered as a result of the computer breakdown and would include such things as temporary staffing cover. In cases where data would be costly to replace when recovering from a problem, this cost can also be covered by insurance, with an appropriate premium.

As with all insurance policies, it is important to read the *small print*, to check precisely what exceptions are stated. These can include normal wear and tear, war risks, radioactivity, sonic bangs and so on. Most policies also include an **excess**, so that the insured might pay, for example, the first £50 of any claim.

Some companies now also offer a complete cover, combining what would normally be provided by both a maintenance agreement and an insurance policy. This has the clear advantage of removing the grey area when there is a doubt whether a repair is covered by insurance or not. This **complete cover** insurance allows the insured to get any repairs done by an engineer and to present the bill to the insurers. This final option is an attempt to leave absolutely nothing to chance.

9.10. AUDITING AND OTHER REQUIREMENTS

Within any computer system, as in any accounting system, provision must be made to allow for auditing of transactions. The need for this sort of monitoring must be borne in mind throughout the year.

There are two forms of auditing. **External auditing** is required by law. In an external audit, an independent analysis of the financial statements of an organisation is carried out by accountants to ensure that they give a true picture. It is not the function of external auditors to carry out checks on the internal workings of the organisation. Such checks would be carried out by **internal auditors**, who keep a regular check for errors within a system, whether accidental or fraudulent.

An **audit trail** is used within most computerised systems, from which the history of an individual transaction can be traced through the whole of its processing. In large-scale applications, this has often been through the recording onto a tape of details of each transaction. This tape is then treated with great security. The knowledge that transactions are permanently recorded is often enough to prevent attempts to commit fraud. Such audit trails have also proved useful in correcting major errors in computer systems.

In batch processed systems, many of the controls on processing which provide trails for auditors are techniques such as batch totalling and numbering systems. With the advent of more complex computer systems, the computer is involved at many more stages of the processing and there are consequently fewer written records to trace the processes through. Indeed, the benefits of a computerised system include the reduction of such paperwork.

Some internal checks which were previously performed by hand will now have become part of the computer system. Thus, when a batch of data goes missing, this will be reported by the computer, rather than be spotted by a clerk.

The principle should be carried over from manual to computer systems that no one person has sole responsibility for a particular function. For example, the storekeeper is not given primary responsibility for updating the stock records. Similarly, the person responsible for receiving cash payments does not also have responsibility for manipulating customers' records. thus, fraud can only occur when two people conspire to achieve it. Additionally, the chances of similar mistakes being made twice are greatly reduced if two people are responsible for them.

Security measures should also exist to prevent unauthorised access to operational programs, so that undocumented amendments, for whatever reason, do not take place. When rigorous procedures are established, it is also more apparent when people have taken deliberate steps to get round them.

Many of the controls which are suggested might be considered inappropriate to a small business, and where only a few employees are involved, the clear separation of duties might be difficult or impossible. It is likely, however, that in a small business, a greater degree of trust exists and a manager will have a clearer picture of the day-to-day situation, which helps internal control.

TASK

Imagine that a set of public examination entries, including your own, are to be prepared by computer. Write down a list of the possible errors which could creep into the process and draw up a table showing the means of avoiding such errors.

9.11. STUDY QUESTIONS

1   List arguments in favour of using a log book for the recording of faults with computer systems.
2   What sort of cleaning schedule would you devise for a computer installation in a small business?

9.12. ASSIGNMENTS

1   Using a supplier's catalogue, describe what materials you would acquire for regular cleaning in a small business computer environment with a number of different makes of computers and printers. Show what could be purchased in a cleaning kit costing about £100.
2   Write a letter to an insurance company to determine their scales of charges for insurance of computer hardware and software and precisely what is and what is not included in the cover.
3   Write a report, for an installation of your choice (either real or imaginary), on the relative merits of taking out an insurance policy and of having a maintenance contract.

SECTION C

SOFTWARE NEEDS

10 THE GOOD SOFTWARE GUIDE

10.1. SOFTWARE: THE TOOLS FOR THE JOB

The usefulness of computer equipment will be entirely dependent on the software used on it. The choice of the applications software is vital in order that the equipment can be made to do the job for which it has been acquired.

There are broadly seven types of software available.

Operating systems

An **operating system** is a set of routines provided to organise the computer's internal functioning, the running of programs and the handling of peripherals (discs, printers, screen and so on). Such routines are used frequently to perform each part of a program. Thus instructions are needed to ensure that data is recorded in the correct place on a disc and that the disc is rotating at the correct speed when data is recorded. The operating system also controls printing, ensuring that the printer has received the character sent to it and is ready for the next one before it is sent. The operating system also also allocates internal memory for programs and parts of programs and organises the passing of control between them. These and numerous other functions of an operating system are essential for running all programs, but are 'back room' in nature. The internal workings of such programs are not the concern of the average user. The choice of operating system is important, however, as all software is written to run under the control of a particular operating system. Thus the choice of operating system limits the choice of software to perform general business functions.

Language compilers

A **language compiler** is another form of 'back room' software used when programming in languages such as Cobol and Pascal. These are essentially a means to an end, as they help in producing working application programs.

Utility programs

Utility programs are similarly used for background work within computer systems for functions such as copying files, printing the contents of files and so on. Such facilities may or may not be provided as part of an operating system.

Pre-written application packages

These form the bulk of an organisation's software purchases. Such programs provide generalised solutions to typical business problems and can be adapted to fulfil the needs of an organisation. Such a process will inevitably involve a compromise between the theoretical ideal system for the particular application and the best that can be achieved by use of a standardised approach.

Vertical market software

This consists of programs which have been specifically written for a particular trade or industry. Thus there are specialised packages for use by estate agents and others for use by garages, pharmacists, publicans and so on. These are generally advertised in the specialist press and are normally written by specialists within the field. Advice about such packages is available through trade associations or professional bodies. Such packages will have to meet strict professional standards and, because of their limited market, they are generally much more expensive than generalised packages. In contrast to the term vertical market, generalised packages are sometimes called horizontal packages, because their use is spread across a whole range of companies. Many vertical packages include aspects of specialised accounting and an accountant should be consulted at an early stage in the introduction of such a package. Judgements about the quality of vertical software are best left to experts in the particular fields.

Program generators

These are tools by which a user can define the processes involved in a business system in a form of English, often in response to a question-and-answer dialogue. From the responses, the program generator software will produce code for a program to perform the tasks specified. Thus a program is being used to generate another program. The generated program will normally be less efficient than a hand-written program, but the time saving in its production may well compensate for this drawback.

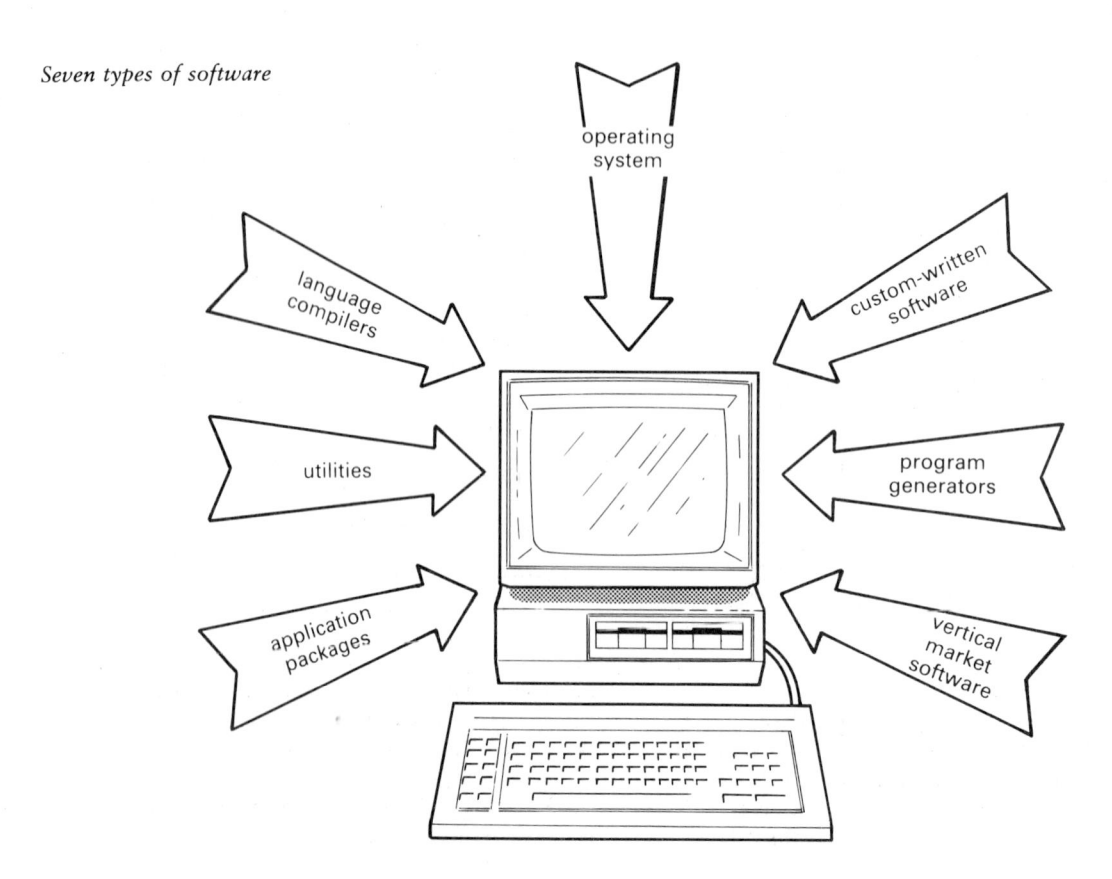

Seven types of software

Custom-written software

This is specifically written software for one particular situation. In many cases, this option is only considered when all the other options have been exhausted. The development costs of such a project are enormous and the delay before the product can be used might be considerable. In some cases, the needs of an organisation might be so specific that this is the only practicable solution.

TASK

Take a software supplier's catalogue, and try to put the various software packages it describes into one of the above categories. Analyse how closely the headings in the catalogue reflect the seven software categories above.

Applications and systems software

Applications packages, vertical market software, program generators and custom-written software are together referred to as **applications software** in contrast to operating systems which are termed **systems software**. Applications software is provided in order to carry out the tasks for which the computer has been acquired. Systems software on the other hand, is the necessary evil needed to 'breathe life' into the computer. In some cases, the operating system is provided on a chip. This means it does not have to be loaded every time the computer is to be used. It has the disadvantage that upgrading is made more difficult, because the operating system is fixed on a chip and is harder and more expensive to replace than a disc.

10.2. CHOOSING THE TOOLS

From a huge range of programs which are on the market, a choice has to be made. Firstly, the needs of the organisation must be assessed. Then the potential computer user must become aware of the range of software provision on the market. This calls for the detailed exploration of the capabilities of the available software. A computer practitioner must be competent at comparing analytically a range of programs in the same software area.

Until a detailed study is made of them, most commercially available packages would appear, from the sales literature and documentation, to be broadly similar. One package would appear to provide a facility which another does not, but then might omit some other features. The question which should be addressed is therefore: 'What makes a good program from the user's point of view?'

A package should be well documented

A program will normally be supplied with appropriate documentation both to set up and to use it within a company. The program will be a generalised one, which serves the needs of the 'typical' company. The program and documentation together form the **software package** and it frequently does a disservice to the product to use the term 'package' to refer to the program only.

Packages are available to perform many of the tasks which are carried out in any business. These cover such diverse business functions as invoicing, word processing and stock control. Because packages provide more generalised facilities, however, they may run somewhat more slowly than specially written software.

The user of a package will often not have and will not need detailed knowledge of the internal working of a sytem. A user requires only an appreciation of the functions that a program will provide, and needs to be able to operate it effectively.

Tailoring a package to a company's needs

Some packages can be tailored to the requirements of a particular user, by setting values when the system is initialised. For example, the accounting period for a payroll may be set to be a week or a month. Packages differ a lot in the ease with which they can be modified when circumstances change in major or minor ways. Future enhancement is normally easier than with specially written software, as adaptability may be built into the package, or add-on modules might be available providing further features.

TASK

Using examples of packages you know or business tasks with which you are familiar, suggest some reasons why a standard generalised package might have to be tailored to an individual company's needs.

Points to look for

Packages can have their disadvantages as well. They might be some way from meeting the precise requirements of a particular company and it is often difficult to judge how far to amend company practice to fit in with what is available.

Documentation for the user of a package can leave a lot to be desired. There is no easy way for users to improve it for their own purposes, as they can only be aware of the program's capabilities from the information the supplier gives them. No standards exist for quality, reliability and maintainability of packages and the standard of the products available varies enormously. With a constantly developing market, new and better products are always coming on the market. It can be frustrating when a much improved competitor becomes available soon after an organisation has purchased an expensive product. This problem is emphasised when new and better products are also cheaper.

Some packages have been implemented on several different computers. This means that the user encounters exactly the same response from a particular package on a *different machine*. This is arranged despite the fact that the machines have completely different internal workings and so the programs are running in different codes. Such portable packages are popular because there is no need to retrain users when switching between machines.

This portability has accounted for popularity of products such as Wordstar as a word processing package, and VisiCalc as a spreadsheet. Indeed, it is claimed that the success of these packages has been a major factor in the sale of the particular computers on which they will run. Popular packages have also had books written about their use, which can benefit the user.

10.3. SOFTWARE LOOK-ALIKES

Early market leaders have spawned look-alikes. Thus VisiCalc was followed by SuperCalc and CalcStar. There are also families of packages which can be linked together into a total system, for example SpellStar and MailMerge are used with Wordstar. Some packages are constructed from various modules, which can be combined to serve particular situations, such as the Pegasus accounting system. In these cases, users simply buy the modules which they need or can afford.

Purchasers of software packages benefit from immediate availability and so there is no time wasted in waiting for software to be written. A system can be implemented overnight. This might have considerable cost savings. There is also no need to employ specialist staff to develop a system, which avoids the problems of recruitment, training and finding the next job for them. Additionally, the computer time necessary to develop a system will be provided by the supplier, not from the purchaser's own resources. Packages are then developed with the most sophisticated hardware and software aids available.

TASK

Suggest reasons why software for a small microcomputer might be developed on a more powerful machine.

Packages should be well tried and tested both by the manufacturers and users, so there should not be the teething troubles of a new system to contend with. Existing users can be contacted for their comments. Should anything go wrong with the system, the responsibility will lie with the supplier, whereas the authors of a self-written system carry the responsibility and possible costs themselves.

The availability of software packages is having an increasing impact on the choice of hardware which users make. Hardware is effectively limited by the range and quality of the software which is available to run on it.

TASK

Make a list of the advantages and disadvantages of purchasing software packages.

TASK

Draw up a table of software manufactured by a number of major software companies and from the companies' literature, or otherwise, tabulate which operating systems they will run under.

10.4. PACKAGE TYPES

Many successful packages have been produced by new software companies and there have been considerable rewards for those companies who have produced the most popular packages. Establishment as a market leader in a particular software area itself leads to increased sales as people buy popular products, believing in 'strengh in numbers'. Some companies who are market leaders in one application area have then attempted to launch other products in different fields, sometimes with limited success.

This has led to **families** of software which have been produced by the same company. Thus Wordstar has been followed by SpellStar, CalcStar and InfoStar. Similarly, there are PerfectWriter, PerfectCalc and PerfectFiler. Such families are designed to run under one operating system, but are portable in that they are available on several machines.

In such a family of software, each part performs the tasks of a major software application, such as a spreadsheet or a database. The purchase of a number of these pieces of software has several advantages. These include:

(a) some transfer of data from one program of the suite to another,
(b) the standardisation of presentation of documentation,
(c) the similarity of commands such as the use of particular key combinations for similar operations in different programs (such as 'scroll a screenfull of information').

10.5. DOCUMENTATION

While the primary consideration in evaluating the quality of a package is to consider the quality of the program, the features provided can only best be exploited if they are fully explained and illustrated in documentation.

The documentation which a potential user would need would have to include a description of the program's facilities and how to use them. The documentation provided with a package may consist of five basic elements. There might be a guide to the installation of the package, a tutorial guide, a reference manual, a command summary and an on-line help file.

Installation guides

An **installation guide** will give details of how a package can be adapted to a particular situation. This process will normally be a one-off operation and will include setting codes to using a particular printer, adapting the program to a particular keyboard, establishing discs for files and so on. The complexity of this 'customising' will depend greatly on the sophistication and generality of the package. The process could also involve the definition of the shape and size of files. The installation of a package

A typical family of software

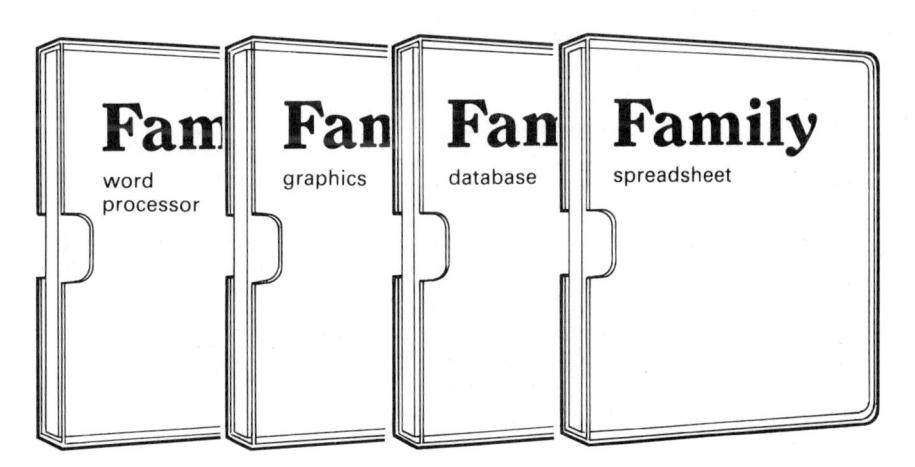

can be a difficult process, but it is not one which the regular user will need to comprehend or perform. Unfortunately, however, the installation must be successfully completed before any use of the package is made. Help in carrying out these instructions may be available through the supplier.

Tutorial guides

A **tutorial guide** will take the user step by step through the facilities provided by the package. The commands available are explained in detail and illustrated with examples and exercises. The order in which ideas are introduced will have been chosen to aid the learning process. A good tutorial guide will also teach some theory about the general concepts behind the package. Thus a word processing tutorial will inevitably include concepts common to most word processing packages. This would normally include descriptions of ways in which a user can benefit from word processing. These benefits are often not specific to the particular package.

Reference manuals

A **reference manual** for a program will provide a formal definition of each of the commands or facilities provided. Normally a comprehensive description of the power of a command and the details of all the different command formats would be extremely off-putting to the first-time reader. Thus the entries in a reference manual, being comprehensive and formalised, differ from those in a tutorial guide. They also differ in the order of presentation. A reference guide might be in sections, with each section covering an aspect of using the program. If it is not sectionalised, the guide might be in alphabetical order of commands. Reference material is for use by experienced users who know what they want to do, but need to look up how it is done. A reference manual is for looking things up, so its organisation should reflect this with a good contents page and a comprehensive index. A reference manual should be available at all times when the package is to be used.

Command summaries

A **command summary** or quick reference guide will be a short document, probably of two or four pages, which gives, in outline, the complete set of commands and their meanings. Such a guide does not need explanations and illustrations and is provided for the regular user who wishes to recap on particular functions. (For example, a user might want to look up whether it is CTRL-R or CTRL-D to move right.) Such a guide would not be very useful in the early stages of using a package, but is made short enough so that all users can be given their own copy.

On-line help facilities

An **on-line help facility** is provided with many major packages. This allows the user of a program to ask for details of the use of a command to be displayed on the screen while the program is being used. The explanations are normally held on disc, so that they have only to be read in when they are requested.

Documentation and discs provided with Wordstar 2000 from MicroPro International

Documentation for dBase III Plus from Ashton-Tate

10.6. DOCUMENTATION

The quality of documentation should be an important factor in comparing packages. There can be major differences between the documentation of otherwise fairly similar packages. With programs which have been on the market for a considerable time, improvement of the documentation often goes hand in hand with the production of later versions of the software.

The company which develops the program will also keep technical documentation about the program, but this will not be for public consumption. The programs themselves will be supplied in machine code form, with the source program, written in a high-level language, not being for sale. This makes it considerably harder to discover how the program works, which few users, but most competitors, would be interested in.

10.7. EVALUATING SOFTWARE

Many of the criteria which would be used to evaluate a supplier of hardware or training would also be applied to suppliers of software, in terms of their quality of service and support. When choosing software, there are also many features of the actual product which should also be considered.

General quality considerations

Any software must be **reliable**. Therefore, the purchaser should look for clear evidence that it has been thoroughly tested by the writers, that it has been widely used in realistic situations and that it will work with the particular data on the particular equipment. Only if a software tool passes all these basic quality checks is it worthy of becoming a tool on which an organisation relies. Suppliers of quality software should be pleased to provide the names of firms who have successfully used a package, so that potential customers can hear of the practical benefits to be gained. A reluctance to supply such information could indicate that there are practical problems with the use of the software or that it is a very new product.

Good software will also be **robust**, handling incorrect input and mistakes in an acceptable manner. In particular, it must not crash. Error messages produced should be unambiguous and either diagnose the error or, at second best, point to a reference book which will explain the error.

Output from programs should be clear and at an appropriate level of detail, neither over complex nor over brief. The provision of documentation and other support materials must be adequate. Any modifications to the system to cope with future changes must be simple to understand and carry out. It is advisable to find out before purchase whether upgrades of software will be supplied free or at a nominal charge, as expensive upgrades can add considerably to costs.

TASK
Construct a list of at least ten pitfalls and things to avoid when purchasing a package.

Presentation considerations

When evaluating a package, it is important to contemplate the background knowledge assumed of a user. Are screen messages at a level of English which the typical user will understand or are they full of jargon? The level of detail of messages will depend on whether the programs are normally to be used by trained staff or by general users. In the design of dialogues, there has to be a trade-off between the ease of use, the amount of memory space available and the time taken to display and read messages. With some packages, such problems are reduced by storing detailed messages on disc files, only reading them in when necessary.

When moving from a manual to a computer system, it is helpful if the computerised system works in the same style and order as the manual system it replaces. Programs differ in the ways in which progress through the various facilities is marked and explained. Thus a good program will tell the user at all stages what it is possible to do next and what has just been done. The presentation of different programs, particularly from the same manufacturer, can be similar in their style. This can be helpful in learning standard approaches, but if programs have some similarities and some differences, this can be confusing.

It is also worth ensuring that it is easy to correct typing errors by use of keys such as DELETE. In all but the most simple cases, the depression of an incorrect key should not lead to the wrong facility being chosen, the wrong file being deleted, or some other undesirable event occurring. Before carrying out such operations, a good program will ask for confirmation that this is what is required. Some programs also incorporate a feature which allows the user to 'undo' the last command, which aids recovery from mistakes.

It is also useful if the individual user can determine the pace at which text is displayed for reading, as people read at very different rates. This reduces the pressure on the user.

User friendliness

Overall, a program should be **user friendly**. This could be described as the program telling users at all times where they are, what they should be doing and what sort of input is next expected. Users should also be told at all points what the computer is doing and, if a mistake has been made, it should be clear what the mistake is and how it can be rectified. Most programs will fall down against such stringent criteria, but the better programs will fulfil most of them.

10.8. DIALOGUE DESIGN

Types of user

The needs of different users should be catered for in the design of computer dialogues. If the use of a program forms a major part of a person's job, then it will be important to use simple and abbreviated codes so that facilities can be used as speedily as possible. When a program is only being used as a minor activity, then the emphasis should be on simplicity of use.

A regular user will be able to remember a wider range of options, whereas it will be necessary to give a member of the general public some guidance in a program's use. An example of this is the extremely simple dialogue used with a bank's automatic telling machine. Such a style of dialogue would be extremely tedious for a program which a person was using hundreds of times a day.

An **active** user is one who gives commands to the system to perform the appropriate tasks, knowing what actions are to be taken at each step. A **passive** user is one who needs to be guided through the program by being prompted with appropriate choices. In this case, the computer controls the dialogue and the messages tend to be more detailed.

Command-driven programs

A typical active dialogue is that which a programmer in dBase II would use. dBase II is **command driven**, and when in use, a full stop appears on the screen. This is called a prompt, and the user must then type in a command, such as 'use stockfile' or 'display all itemcodes for cost > 100 and onhand > 2'.

Menu-driven programs

A typical passive dialogue is provided by Beebug's Masterfile, in which a list of options is provided on the screen with letters A to P. To select an option, one of these commands must be chosen. In this program, the steps in setting the selection criteria and requesting the display of values of a field are done one step at a time, so that they can be confirmed and checked by the user.

A **menu** is used to present to the user a series of options from which a choice can be made, usually with a single letter. Some programs are completely menu driven, giving a uniformity of approach. The use of menus can be frustrating, however, for a regular user, as there may be some delay before the next menu is displayed. The best menu-driven programs allow sub menus to be bypassed by keying the choice before the menu appears. Menus can also be used effectively with light pens, mice or touch-sensitive screens, where the user points to the option required.

Keeping the user informed

Messages to the user are also important in evaluating the dialogue. A message can be used to confirm to a user that something is happening and the system has not simply hung up. A quarter of a

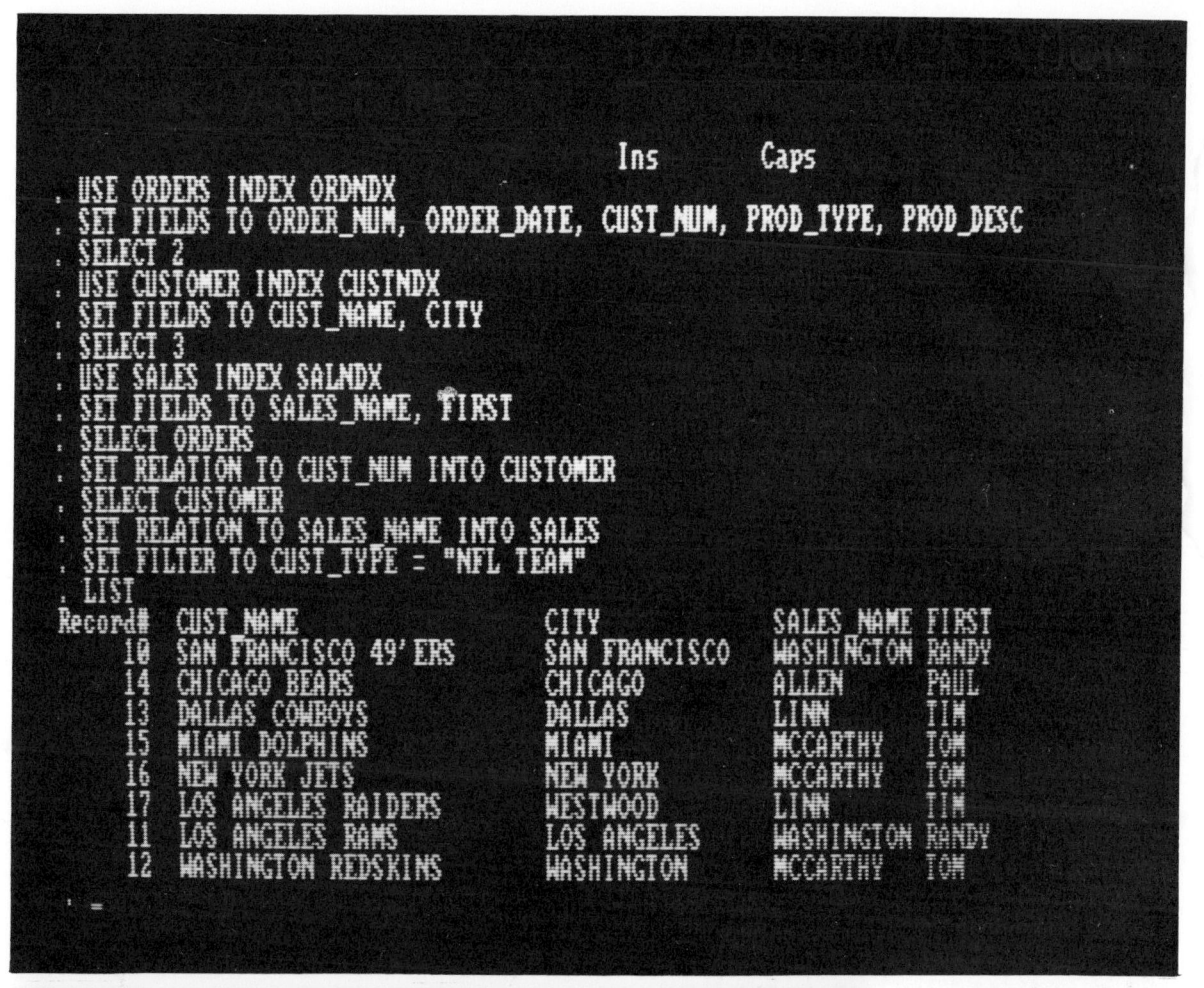

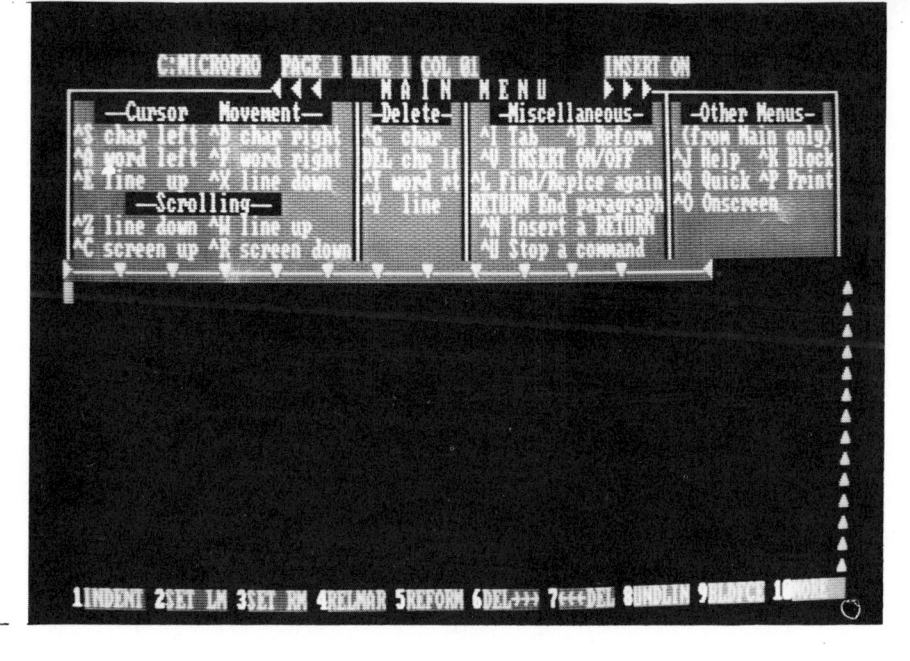

```
                              Ins     Caps
. USE ORDERS INDEX ORDNDX
. SET FIELDS TO ORDER_NUM, ORDER_DATE, CUST_NUM, PROD_TYPE, PROD_DESC
. SELECT 2
. USE CUSTOMER INDEX CUSTNDX
. SET FIELDS TO CUST_NAME, CITY
. SELECT 3
. USE SALES INDEX SALNDX
. SET FIELDS TO SALES_NAME, FIRST
. SELECT ORDERS
. SET RELATION TO CUST_NUM INTO CUSTOMER
. SELECT CUSTOMER
. SET RELATION TO SALES_NAME INTO SALES
. SET FILTER TO CUST_TYPE = "NFL TEAM"
. LIST
Record#  CUST_NAME              CITY            SALES_NAME  FIRST
     10  SAN FRANCISCO 49'ERS   SAN FRANCISCO   WASHINGTON  RANDY
     14  CHICAGO BEARS          CHICAGO         ALLEN       PAUL
     13  DALLAS COWBOYS         DALLAS          LINN        TIM
     15  MIAMI DOLPHINS         MIAMI           MCCARTHY    TOM
     16  NEW YORK JETS          NEW YORK        MCCARTHY    TOM
     17  LOS ANGELES RAIDERS    WESTWOOD        LINN        TIM
     11  LOS ANGELES RAMS       LOS ANGELES     WASHINGTON  RANDY
     12  WASHINGTON REDSKINS    WASHINGTON      MCCARTHY    TOM
```

A dialogue in dBase III Plus, using commands typed in response to the 'dot' prompt

The main menu of Wordstar Professional, showing the key combinations used for each command shown

minute with nothing happening on the screen can seem a long time to a user, who may panic. One of the simplest forms of confirmation that something is happening is for a series of dots to disappear gradually while a lengthy process is taking place, such as a file being read in. Alternatively, a message could be displayed or a pause can be indicated with a picture of an egg-timer. Messages are also useful to remind a user to make a back-up copy of files at appropriate points or to give warnings, such as 'are you sure?' when mistakes are likely to have particularly serious consequences.

Useful techniques: colour, sound and help

The use of colour can considerably improve a program's user friendliness. Standard screen layouts can be displayed in a fairly neutral colour. Thus a heading and a series of questions or a menu could be in white. Data entered by the user could appear in yellow, so that it stands out. Error messages and warnings could appear in red. Flashing colour can also be used to draw attention to messages or values. Another method is to display data in one colour as it is entered. When it is accepted as valid, the colour is changed. It is then simple to see which item is currently being entered. If software is to be used with a monochrome monitor, then the screen layout in this form should be evaluated. Some programs with screens carefully designed for colour monitors can be very hard to use in monochrome.

Sound can also be used, either to confirm the entry of correct data, or to denote the entry of false data. A low, descending note is useful to signify an error. Sound is not popular in offices where it might be a distraction to other people who are working, so it is used sparingly.

Many programs incorporate a 'help' facility, which can be considered as part of the documentation, so that a user can obtain explanations of commands. In the best programs, the help facility provided is context-dependent. In other words, the messages and help provided will depend on the point of the program which the user has reached.

Reflecting the user's needs

Dialogue design should also reflect the **tolerance** of a user. When an error occurs, a program may make 'sensible' assumptions about what the user wanted or may ask for the command to be given again. For instance, a command might have to be typed in upper case and have a complicated structure. Some users will be tempted to give up when their first correction fails to give the correct response, not spotting that there were several errors in the original line. Thus, a program should reflect the likely tolerance level of its users. The likelihood of users giving incorrect commands is reduced by the use of simple command formats, so that a complicated request is built up in smaller stages.

Many programs ask the user to fill in a form on the screen. The purpose of such a screen-based form is to collect information correctly and completely. A form is any surface on which information is to be entered depending on the information already present there and so, in this sense, a screen can display a form. Such a form is most suited to data entry where the expected input is to be in a fixed format. A major advantage of a screen-based form is that the user can be moved from one part of the form to another under program control. This can reduce or even eliminate the need for instructions as to which parts of the form to fill in. (For example: 'If you answered *yes* to question 3 and *no* to question 4, then you need not answer this question'.)

The simplest form of dialogue is a series of questions to which the answer is yes or no. This would be suitable for the very infrequent, or even one-off user, but such a series of questions would be too long for a sophisticated user.

Some dialogues use pictures rather than words for their menus, so that the choices of facilities available are depicted by representative pictures. Such pictures are called **icons**. This approach is popular with some busy business executives, who do not want to learn a wide range of commands and would prefer a pictorial reminder or prompt of what is available. The screen is then said to resemble a businessman's desk. But have you ever seen a desk with a dustbin and a filing cabinet on it?

TASK

Construct a list of questions which you would ask a dealer at a demonstration of a software package which you were considering buying.

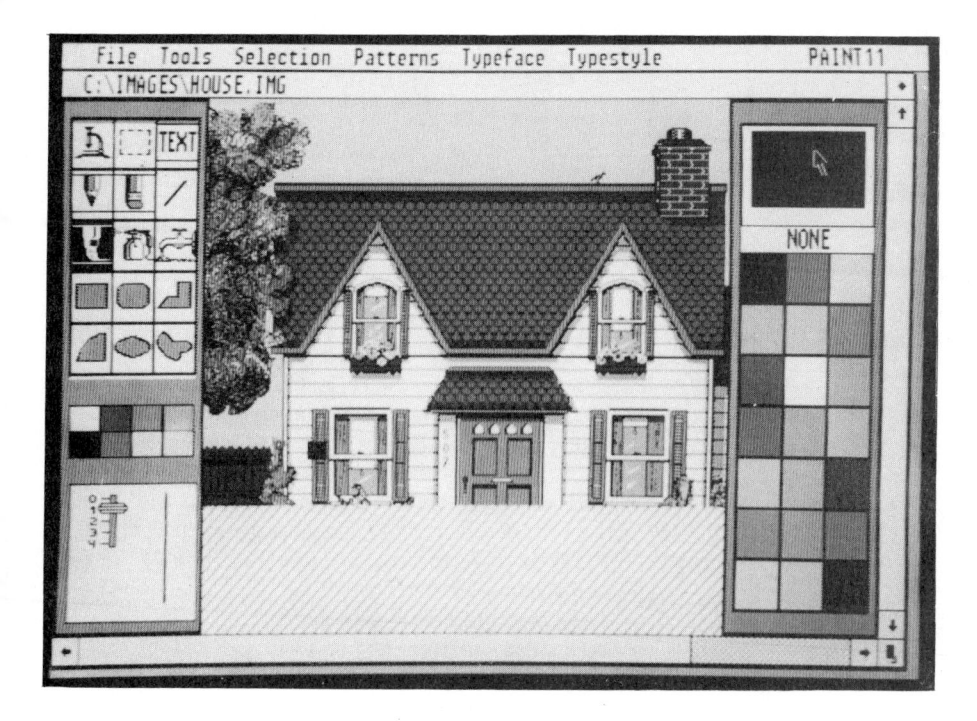

Icons are used in GEM Paint, from Digital Research, each small picture on the left and right of the drawing represents an operation

10.9. STUDY QUESTIONS

1 Write down five questions which you would ask about a package to find out whether you could run the package at all on your system.
2 Write down five checks which you would perform on a package to find out whether it would be a package which feels good to use.
3 What are the advantages and disadvantages of acquiring a number of programs from a family of programs?

10.10. ASSIGNMENTS

1 Write a report on the suitability of one piece of software of your choice for use by:

   (a) a 10 year old,
   (b) a manager who will use it for two hours a week,
   (c) a trainee junior clerk who will use it 30 hours a week,
   (d) yourself.

2 Write a report on a piece of software which you consider to be of average quality and suggest the different ways in which it could be improved for:

   (a) the very infrequent user,
   (b) the daily user.

3 Choose a specialised application area which interests you, such as a garage, a solicitors or a careers office. Find out as much as you can about the vertical market software available in the area of your choice, including prices as well as features. Arrange to visit such a firm if this is possible. Write a market survey and point out how much specialist knowledge is needed to choose between such packages.

4 Recently developed operating systems have used the idea of 'WIMP's, which stands for Window-, icon- and mouse-driven Programs. Windows are used to show more than one part of a document or more than one process on the screen at the same time. Icons are used to give a pictorial description of a facility rather than one in words. Mice are used to reduce the need for the use of a keyboard. Write a report on the significance of the new generation of user-friendly operating systems and software.

11 WORD PROCESSING

11.1. WORDS THAT DANCE

Word processing is the entry, storage, retrieval and manipulation of text in electronic form. Once text has been entered, it can be adapted in various ways. Parts of the text can be overwritten and replaced, whole sections can be deleted. Paragraphs of text can be moved around within the document. Text can be arranged in various formats by altering line lengths and page lengths. All this is achieved on the screen, without having to type or print several drafts. Only when a final document is ready need it be printed out for use.

The use of a word processor allows the exploitation of the various features available on a particular printer. For example, the various character styles or fonts, such as italic and bold characters, can be used. This allows the same text to be presented in a variety of ways. Text can be copied within a word processing package and thus part of one text can be incorporated into another. The facilities of word processing are useful when a document must go through several drafts before it reaches its final state.

Word processing programs are currently available for most makes of computer, though these vary in the range of facilities which are available and their ease of use. Many of the computers at the lower end of the price range have a specially written word processing package. At the top of the range there are a number of good packages which have been implemented on several machines. If a package is portable in this way, it enables the user to operate a different machine, yet with a program which works in a familiar way. The programs will not be identical in terms of their instructions (one machine may be 8-bit, the other 16-bit, for example), but they are identical in the way the user sees them.

11.2. THE MARKET

One example of a word processing package which has been implemented on a large number of different business microcomputers is Wordstar. This was one of the earliest popular word processing programs and a few years ago was the industry standard word processing package. In recent years, the increase in memory sizes has meant that word processing is now also available on home microcomputers. Generally, at the lower end of the market, word processors have limited features, but they can still be put to serious use. Sophisticated features exploiting the capabilities of 16-bit microcomputers have been included in powerful packages such as Microsoft Word, MultiMate and Volkswriter.

TASK

Make a list of all the word processing packages which are available for a computer of your choice. Find out the prices and the manufacturers of the packages.

All word processing programs have to strike a balance between the range of facilities provided, the convenience of the use of facilities and the difficulty experienced by the first-time user. Another consideration is the ease with which the facilities available are remembered by regular users. Some programs provide menus and submenus from which the facilities can be selected. Others use the function keys for various commands and a plastic card or a liquid crystal display is used as a reminder of the functions of the keys.

11.3. DOCUMENTATION

The manuals provided with word processing packages vary considerably in quality. A number of different manuals may be provided or several jobs may be carried out by a single document. For the first-time user, there is often an introductory tutorial guide, which begins with a brief introduction to the ideas of word processing and takes the reader through a series of lessons gradually building on previous learning. Additional training may be provided by a disc-based tutorial program, which might also have associated written materials.

There should also be a reference manual giving details of the operation of all the commands. This will include formal definitions and details of all the options. This is normally not the most digestible form in which to learn the commands initially. With the reference manual may come a quick reference guide, which is a summary of basic facilities and is useful for refreshing the memory. Both these guides are of most use, at their differing levels of detail, to those who have used the word processing package or a similar program before.

For a portable package particularly, there will be an installation guide which enables the tailoring of the package to a particular hardware system. This guide can include instructions on how to specify the storage to be used, the character codes for printing and the ways that user-defined keys will operate.

TASK

List the documentation available for three word processing packages which can be used on a computer of your choice. Briefly summarise the types of readership for which each part of the documentation is suitable. You might consider the suitability of the texts for people with no computer background, those who have used other word processing programs before, those who have used this program on another machine and so on.

11.4. WHERE WORD PROCESSING PROGRAMS ARE THE SAME

Text manipulation

The user will want to look at different parts of the text in order to edit it. The current position within the text on the screen is normally indicated by a cursor, showing which part of the text the next operation will refer to. There are usually at least twelve cursor movements which can be made from the keyboard. In some cases, cursor movement is achieved with key combinations, such as pressing the CTRL and D key at the same time. In this case, the letters used are generally in some easy to remember form, such as a set of keys which are all together on the keyboard. The use of special keys, such as cursor up and down, delete forward and backward, can make a program easier to use, but this depends on the design of the computer hardware. A mouse device allowing the user to move to the appropriate part of the text by pointing can also make a program easier to learn and quicker to use.

CURSOR MOVEMENTS

Right a character	Up a screen-full
Right a word	Down a screen-full
Left a character	To the start of the line
Left a word	To the end of the line
Up a line	To the top of the text
Down a line	To the bottom of the text

Typical cursor movements available in a word processing program

As text is displayed onto the screen, any word which will not fit on the end of the current line will be automatically placed on the next line, thus enabling the user to avoid typing RETURN (or ENTER) characters. This is called **word wrapping**. As text fills the screen, the text at the top of the screen will be **scrolled** off to make room for new text. Text can be changed either by typing over existing text on the screen (**overstrike**), or by **inserting** extra text at the cursor and moving existing text to the right. Switching between these alternatives is usually easy. Commands are usually provided for deletion of an individual character, a word, a group of characters or a line, either forwards or backwards from the cursor position.

TASK

Make a list of all the commands for movement within the text for a word processing package which you are able to use. If possible, compare this with the features in other packages.

Text can also be amended in most word processing programs by a powerful find and replace command. This allows the user to search for a particular combination of characters (called a string) within a text and to replace it when found. Such a replacement can be **global**, which will replace all occurrences of the phrase named, or **attended**, when the user is asked whether each replacement is to be made. With an attended replacement, the user is shown each occurrence of the string in turn and can indicate whether the change is needed in each case. This avoids the problem of unforeseen occurrences of the string being changed when this is not required.

In some cases, matches are only found with the complete word indicated. In other cases, all occurrences of the set of letters are found, including cases where they occur as only part of a word. In the most versatile programs, the user can choose which of these types of search to carry out.

The replacement command can be used to enter a frequently occurring phrase in an abbreviated form for later replacement. For example, whenever the

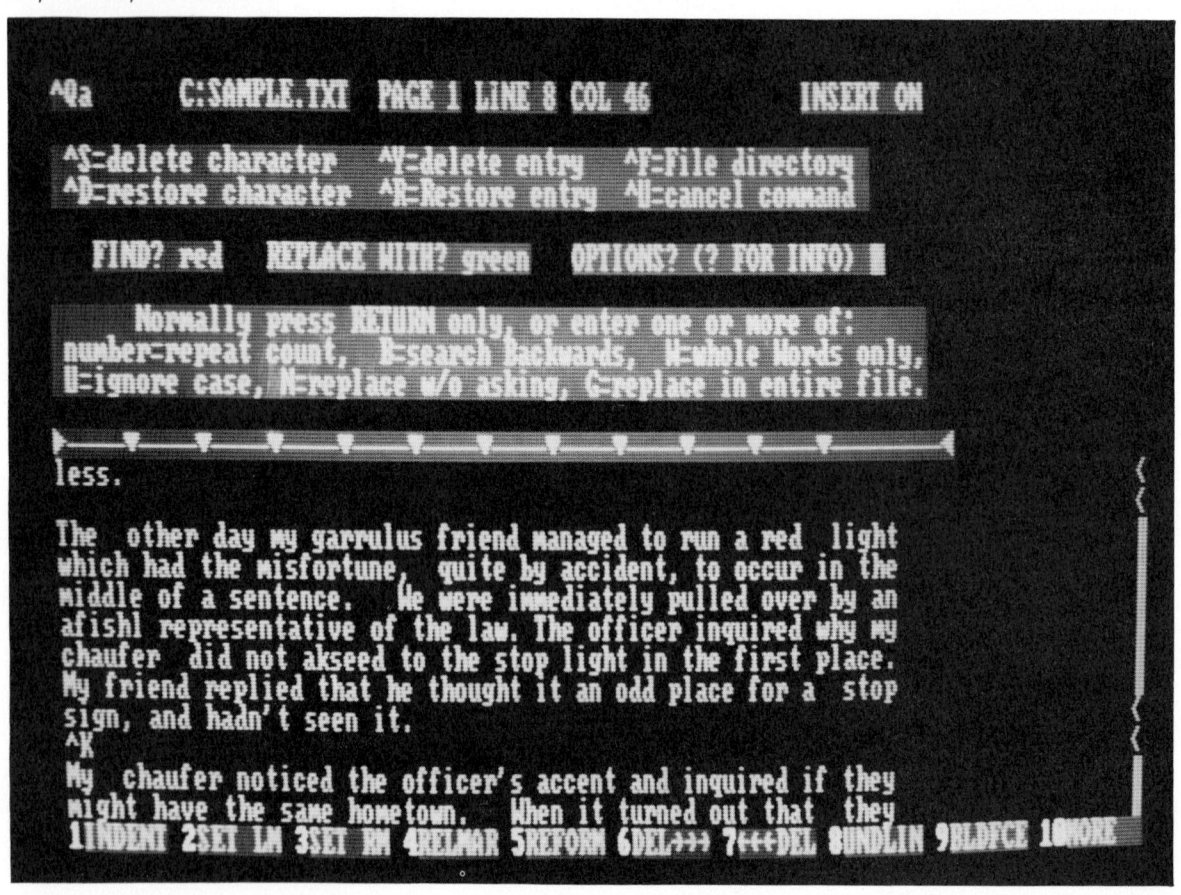

The Find and Replace command in Wordstar Professional from MicroPro

phrase 'word processing' was to be entered in this text, it was typed as 'WP' and then replaced globally. The same principle could be used to enter names in abbreviated form. Replacement is also useful for correcting consistent spelling mistakes and for checking whether a word has been used too frequently in a text.

Text formatting

The layout of text within a page can be controlled by setting values, such as the page length and the length of lines. Different line lengths can be used for various parts of the text, to emphasise paragraphs, to leave space for illustrations and so on. A margin can be set at the left of a text, so that all text is indented, to allow for holes to be punched there for filing.

Paragraphs of text can have one of two main formats. The first of these is **right justification**, where extra spaces are inserted within each line by the computer, so that all text finishes with the last character in the same column. This paragraph has been justified in this way. Extra spaces which are inserted to pad out the text are called **soft spaces**, as they may be removed automatically when, after changes to the text, the paragraph is reformatted.

The alternative format for a paragraph is called **ragged right**, which is the normal style produced by a manual typewriter, where all the spaces between words are the same size. This paragraph is formatted in this way.

Another feature is the centring of a line
within the text.
Text then appears in the style of a hotel's menu.
Titles can be done like this.
Very useful!

The user can define a standard heading to be placed on every page of the text when printed. This is known as a **header** and can be included for all or part of a text. Headers can be useful for chapter headings, or to identify a particular document. A similar feature, known as a **footer**, allows the inclusion of a standard feature at the bottom of every page. Many word processing programs also provide a feature which will number pages as part of the header or footer.

Text presentation

Different printer features can be exploited by word processing programs, but this is clearly limited by the printer's features as well as the program's. Thus, on more versatile printers, text can be produced containing **bold** text, underlined text, subscripts and superscripts, as well as different print fonts, such as *italic* lettering.

In a similar manner to a manual typewriter, column values can be set for tabulation of text. Markers known as **TABs** can be set, so that a single keystroke will move the cursor to the next defined column. This is particularly useful for the preparation of indented text and for preparing financial reports or other tables of figures. The alteration of a single TAB mark can allow the user to move a whole column of figures within the screen layout.

When documents are being printed, various features might be provided. It might be possible for a printout to be aborted, or paused and later resumed. The user may be allowed to start printing from a particular page within the text or to print a selected page number or to print multiple copies, simply by setting values before printing commences. Features might also be provided to produce output using only every other printing line (**double spacing**) or every third line (**triple spacing**). Similarly, the horizontal spacing of

Use of headers and footers within a word processed document, including page numbering

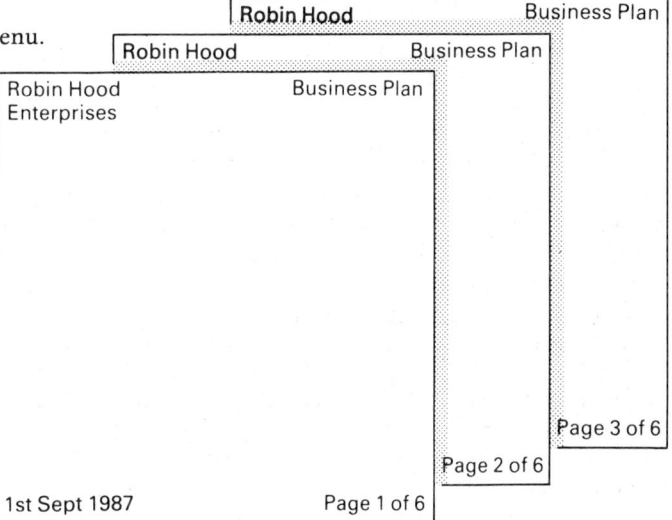

characters might be under the user's control. In some cases, a user might be able to preview the text to see how it will look when printed, by getting simulated output on the screen.

11.5. WHERE WORD PROCESSING PROGRAMS ARE DIFFERENT

What you see and what you get

The basic difference

Word processing programs fall into two main types. The term 'what you see is what you get' (sometimes abbreviated to the initials WYSIWYG, pronounced 'wizzy-wig') has been coined to describe programs where the display on the screen will reflect what will be printed. Thus text is formatted on the screen and the user can decide to reformat paragraphs and immediately see the effect.

In the other main type of word processing program, formatting is achieved by the use of commands within the text which describe how the text is to be laid out. These instructions are not part of the text which is printed, but are commands which are obeyed when printer output or simulated printer output is requested. In this way, different parts of a text can be formatted in different ways. As they are shown at the point in the text where they take their effect, these commands are called **embedded commands**. This style of using embedded commands is sometimes known as **Emacs** format.

In an Emacs style of package, the screen display is designed to make the entry and manipulation of text on the screen easier, the screen text being an appropriate width for the screen, and the printer output for the printer. This can mean that the user is frequently switching between an edit mode, where text is changed, and simulated output mode, where the effects can be seen. The 'what you see is what you get' packages may not be able to display the whole width of printer output on the screen and so sideways scrolling has to be used, showing on the screen only some columns of the text at any one time.

Two contrasting approaches

Wordstar is an example of a WYSIWYG approach. Text appears on the screen with each line of each paragraph set to the width at which it will be printed. As text is entered, it will be laid out in the format specified. When changes are made to the text, the new paragraph layouts can be seen on the screen. Dotted lines are displayed by the program to indicate where one page ends and another page starts. A menu at the top of the page indicates the current options available. An indication of the width and format to which paragraphs are being set is displayed as well.

Wordwise, on the other hand, has a screen where formatting commands are highlighted in a different colour from the main text. All text is displayed to the same width and commands to alter the paragraph format and text layout will only be interpreted on output.

TASK

How WYSIWYG is your program? Make a list of all the features of word processing which might be available in a package, using this chapter as a starting point. For three word processing packages of your choice, preferably ones which you can run, draw up a table showing which facilities are provided by the use of embedded commands within the text and which are not.

Grey areas between the two styles

There are a number of grey areas, in that some word processing programs which take a WYSIWYG approach might have particular aspects which are not presented in this way. One category in which this might happen is in line layout, with such facilities as centring and right justifying. When a command is issued to centre text in Wordstar, the text will be physically moved to the correct place on the screen. In View, however, a command is displayed indicating that the line will be centred at output time. The Wordstar approach has the advantage that the user can see precisely what will

```
........*........*........*........*........*........*........*........*
This is an example of the WYSIWYG approach. Each line of text is
formatted on the screen to look like it will when it is printed out. The
length of lines of text will be set according to a ruler (made up of dots
and asterisks above).
.......*........*........*........*........*........*......*
When lines are to be of a different length, a new
ruler is defined, and text is a differnt length
actually on the screen. This can be a problem if the
printed text is to be wider than the screen.

LL 60
This is an example of text entered in a
word processor using the Emacs style. All
the words in this paragraph are laid out
on the screen at a width of 40 characters.
It is only when the text is actually
printed that the commands (such as LL to
set the line length) are obeyed. In this
case, the text will be reorganised and
printed at 60 characters per line.
BL 2 LL 30
This second paragraph will be printed
after two blank lines, and each line will
then only be 30 characters long.
```

The contrast between WYSIWYG features (top) and Emacs features (bottom)

happen, but has the disadvantage that, if the line length is altered, the centred line must be recentred, which is something that can be overlooked.

A second grey area, where what you see might not be precisely what you get is in the use of different typestyles, such as italic, bold and underlined characters. These styles are displayed on screen as they will be printed by some packages. In many cases, however, they can not be displayed as italic, bold or underlined characters because of the limitations of the hardware. What is normally displayed in this case is a code indicating, for example, where bold printing will commence and where it will finish. These codes are known as **control codes**. The display of such characters within a line will affect its appearance, as the control characters occupy a character position on the screen, but are not printed as separate characters. In some packages where they are used, the control codes can be displayed or hidden on request.

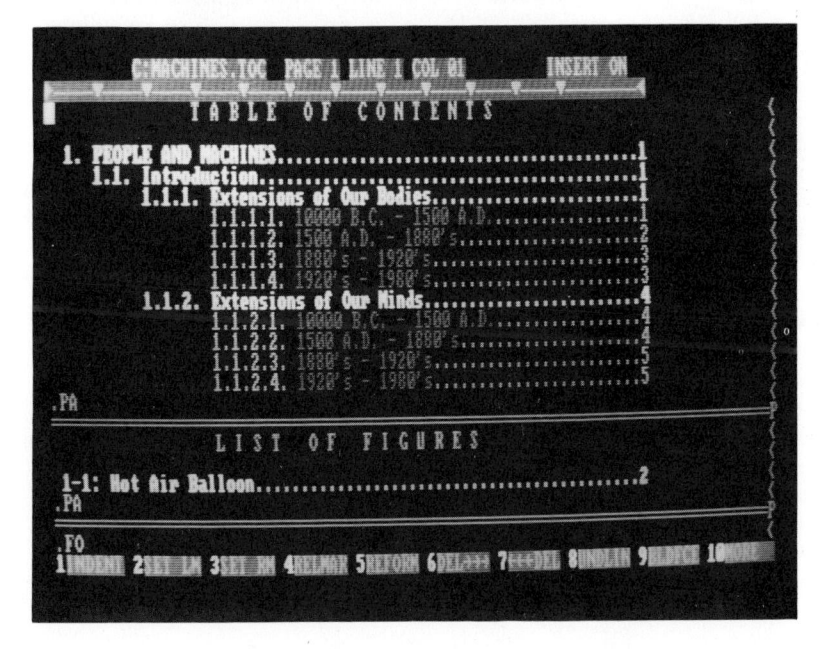

Approaching true WYSIWYG – bold characters appearing as they will be printed and a page break being displayed in Wordstar Professional

Double and triple spacing of lines leaves blank lines between each line of text. A literal application of the principle of WYSIWYG in this case can mean that very few actual lines of text are displayed, particularly when part of the screen space is used by a menu. In this case, it is useful to allow a style which only displays non-blank lines.

Choosing from a menu

Irrespective of which of these two fundamental types a word processing program falls into, it may or may not be menu-driven. The advantage of a menu is that all available facilities are displayed, which is a helpful prompt to the user. There are frustrations with menus, because of the screen space that they use and the time taken to work through several menus. A first-time user might be put off by a large range of features in a complicated menu.

Default values

When the program is first loaded, various values such as the page length and line length are set. Assumptions will also be made, such as whether paragraphs will be justified and whether new characters will be inserted or typed over existing text in what is called overstrike mode. If the values automatically set (the **default** values) are not what is required, then it is normally simple to alter them. When a document is saved to disc, some word processing packages remember such values; others reset them each time the package is used or when each new document is loaded.

Windows

Some word processing packages provide **windows**, whereby parts of more than one document or more than one part of the same document can be displayed on the screen simultaneously. A command is provided to switch between the different windows. Thus, if two parts of the same document, such as financial figures, are to be related, they can be displayed together, which helps in editing. A block can be copied from one document to another.

The use of windowing in word processing (Microsoft Word on a Research Machines Nimbus)

Of mice and menus

Although word processing involves considerable text input, which is normally performed by means of a keyboard, a mouse can be used for all input apart from the actual text. Thus, the cursor can be moved around the screen by rolling a mouse around the table, and editing can be achieved by pressing one of the buttons on the mouse over the appropriate entry in a menu of options. This enables editing to be performed without reference to the keyboard. For features such as moving through the text, marking and moving blocks and moving between windows, a skilled mouse user can save considerable time, compared with searching for keys on the keyboard.

Mice can also be used for choosing from a menu of options. Some programs include **pop-up menus** or **pull-down menus**, which will temporarily appear on part of the screen when requested, but when menus are not needed, the maximum space is allowed for text. Thus only one line is used permanently for the main menu.

Block commands

A number of operations are provided by many word processors which operate on a block of text. A part of a text can be marked, usually with a special character at the beginning and the end of the text, to be treated as a block. Block operations will then allow the block of text to be moved to another part of the text, copied to another part or deleted.

Commands are sometimes provided to allow the saving of a block of text only. This can be useful for combining one piece of text within another. In some packages, a block can also be defined to be an area within certain columns. This can be particularly useful when manipulating tables of figures.

Boilerplating

In some word processing applications, such as the preparation of legal documents, there is a requirement to include standard phrases or paragraphs with some regularity. An example of this is in writing a contract, where similar paragraphs are included in various documents in different combinations. The idea of **boilerplating**, supplied with some word processors, is that standard phrases or paragraphs can be identified by particular key combinations. Typically, ten or twenty such phrases would be accessible at one time.

A standard phrase can then be included either by copying it into the new text, or by incorporating a code (sometimes called a **macro**) within the text, enabling the calling of the phrase from file when it is to be printed. This latter approach has the advantage that duplicate copies of text do not have to be kept. It also allows for the change of standard paragraphs (for instance, to reflect changes in legislation), which will then appear in amended form whenever a new document is requested. Some packages allow part of a text to be saved into a buffer which is given a name by the user, so that it can be recalled easily at appropriate points in the text.

Page layout

An enhancement of the word-wrap facility is sometimes available which points out to the user when a word might be usefully split between two lines to improve the appearance of the text. The user can then decide whether to split the word with a hyphen, and where. Such a hyphen is incorporated as a **soft hyphen** and will not appear in printed form if the text is subsequently reformatted and the hyphen is no longer on the end of a line.

When changes are made to the text within a paragraph, the lengths of lines will alter, making some shorter and some longer than the width set. In most packages the user will have to issue a command to reformat the paragraph to correct this. In some word processing packages, however, the paragraphs are automatically reformatted as the text is altered.

The layout of text as it will be printed, in View from Acornsoft

Printer features

Some packages allow customising of the program for use with a particular printer, with code allowing the use of special hardware features. It is particularly useful when the printer routine can be switched so that the same text can be sent to several different printers.

Some printers also support a feature known as microspacing, whereby the spaces between words can be made the same size (or the same size to within a 1/120 of an inch). This means that right justified text does not have greatly varying spacing between words. Some word processing packages contain within them the programming instructions to use this facility.

Differences in performance

In actual operation, word processing programs can differ considerably in their speed. The rate of moving between pages (scrolling), for example, can differ considerably between packages. Potential users must judge for themselves how important a factor this is. Similarly, there is a marked difference between those programs which will allow a user to begin editing a second document while a previous one is being printed, and those which will not.

Users can also be limited by design features which force them to save documents before printing them. With other programs, documents have to be loaded before they are printed. These features can be particularly frustrating if several similar documents are to be prepared.

Some of these limitations on the order of carrying out operations are provided as a safety net for users so that, for example, they do not forget to save a document they have printed. Such a 'safety first' approach might be spurned by a competent and confident user.

Print layout

It is poor printing style for a sentence or paragraph to be split between the bottom of one page and the top of the next. The term 'widows and orphans' is used to describe this type of effect. Some packages have features which ensure that if a paragraph cannot be completed within the current page, it will not start until the next page. In other packages, the user can issue a special command to indicate any paragraphs which must not be split in this way. It is normally important to ensure that a table of results, for example, is not split between pages.

Some packages allow text to be printed with several columns on each page, as in a newspaper, while still having standard page headers and footers. Often text will not be displayed on the screen in such a format, but in one long thin strip, as wide as one column of the printing.

Layout standards

Some organisations have a number of standard formats in which text is to be presented. There might be different styles, for example, for internal reports, memos and public reports. It is possible that the same text might be presented in a number of ways, perhaps in one way for proofreading, in another for publication. The feature that some packages have allowing the user to store a document style can be particularly useful for this.

Standard document formats can also be given to staff who are new to the system, so that they do not have to worry about page length, page width, space between paragraphs and so on.

TASK
Choose two different newspapers, two books and two magazines. Compare them with regard to their text layout. Some features which you could consider are: use of headers, column width, text justification, microspacing and character fonts. Add your own comparisons to this list.

Footnotes

In texts where footnotes are to be used, some packages allow the linking of a footnote marker in the main text with the text of the footnote. When the document is printed, the user can request that footnotes are included at the end of the text or at the bottom of the page on which they are referred to. Some packages will calculate how much text will fit on the page when footnotes are taken into account and will number the references appropriately.

Undo

Word processing packages sometimes have a very valuable feature called 'Undo'. This will allow the user to cancel the effect of the last command. This can be particularly useful when a serious mistake has been made, such as the accidental deletion of a large block or an unwise multiple find and exchange.

TASK
By reading through brochures for three commonly available packages, draw up a list of features which a word processing program may have. Draw up a table showing which of these features you would consider to be essential, which are present to make the use of the program easier and which are particularly useful for different users of word processing, giving examples of where they are useful.

11.6. WORD PROCESSOR 'ADD-ONS'

Many word processors have additional features available for them, which sometimes come as standard with a package, but on other occasions have to be purchased as an additional feature.

Mailing list facility

A **mailing** facility is one which allows a user to establish two separate files. One of these files contains a set of records such as a list of names and addresses. The other file contains a text, within which there are entries (called parameters), which must be supplied to complete the text. When the mailing option is initiated, a copy of the text is printed for each of the people in the list, with the values from the list substituted at appropriate points. In this way a standard letter can be personalised, and the necessary number of copies produced. The operation is sometimes known as merging the files, as parts of each file are combined together in the specified way.

Once a file has been established with a list of names and addresses, this list can again be used with a different letter. Also, the same text can be used with a different mailing list. A development of this feature is a conditional merge, where the exact form of the output depends on the values held in the file. Thus, for example, all customers who have spent over £1000 in the last year can be offered a discount in a standard letter, others are not.

TASK

Describe in detail a suggested business application where a mailing facility would be useful. Choose a situation where several different documents have to be sent to different lists of people.

Spelling checkers

A program to **check spellings** may be available for a word processing package. This will read all the separate words within the text and test whether they are known words. Such a program comes complete with a standard dictionary on disc. A word may not be recognised for one of two reasons. It may be incorrectly spelt, in which case the text should be amended, or the word could be correctly spelt, but not in the dictionary, in which case it can be temporarily or permanently added to the dictionary. Specialist or technical words and names of people, places or companies are not present on the standard dictionary and so the user can build a dictionary of such words. Some dictionaries use American rather than English spellings. This should be avoided unless this is what is required.

A spellcheck program will find typing errors as well as genuine spelling mistakes. Some also suggest alternative spellings for a word which they do not

The use of Mailmerge in Wordstar Professional. Note also the various options enabling the user to specify the type of output produced

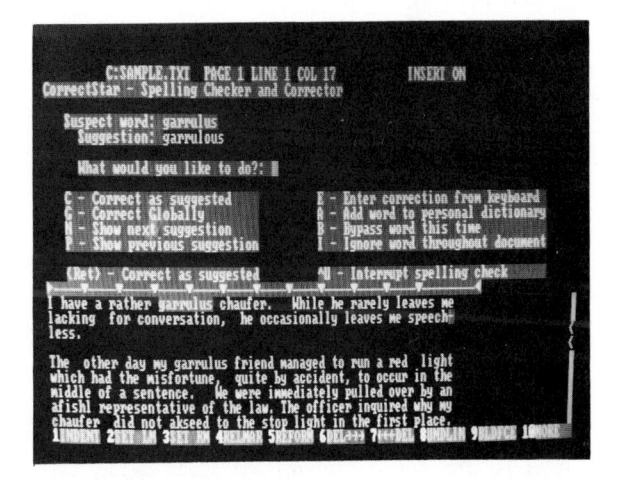

The menu-driven spelling corrector in Wordstar Professional, showing the options available for each word which is not recognised

recognise. This means that the user can choose the correct word from a list, without having to type the whole word again.

Many spellcheck programs operate by reading straight through a complete document and marking all the unknown words. This means that the operator can be getting on with something else while this laborious task is carried out. Later the doubtful words can be presented one at a time to the user, without a delay between words. A few packages, however, check all words as they are entered, and the operator is given a warning as soon as a combination of letters not in the dictionary is used.

Thesaurus

A **thesaurus** feature allows the user to type in a word and have displayed words of a similar meaning, from which an appropriate choice for use in the text can be made. This helps the well-informed user avoid using certain words in certain places with a certain monotony.

Indexing

Another feature sometimes available allows words or phrases to be marked for inclusion in an index or contents page. The index will be constructed in alphabetical order, with the appropriate page numbers being calculated by the computer.

11.7. DEDICATED WORD PROCESSORS

No discussion of word processing would be complete without a mention of dedicated word processors. These are specially designed pieces of equipment which are for use solely as word processors. They are built around the same types of microprocessors, but are adapted and enhanced in ways which mean that they cannot be used for other purposes.

The advantage of this approach is that specialised facilities can be provided, most obviously in the use of a keyboard with extra keys available for all the main word processing commands, such as load, save, format and print. Such word processing stations can also be linked, so that they can share filing systems (such as hard disc) and other peripherals (such as printers). In a medium- to large-scale organisation, where word processing is in wide use throughout the working day, this lack of adaptability to other uses is not too great a price to pay for this extra ease of use.

TASK

Write down a list of desirable features of a word processing program in an order of priority for their use by the staff of a public library.

TASK

Write a report on the need for specialist word processing features, and packages which provide such facilities, such as the inclusion of a wide range of mathematical symbols or the use of foreign alphabets.

11.8. CASE STUDY

Nottingham City Council uses word processing for the preparation of agendas and minutes for Council meetings. Some of the items on the agenda are the same from month to month, such as confirmation of the minutes of the previous meeting and Question Time. Because of this, these items do not have to be retyped.

The papers and reports which are submitted for discussion use standard headings and are often concluded with a formally worded resolution which authorises the spending of money. These motions are in a standard form, which again can be word processed.

When the minutes of the meeting are being prepared for approval at the next meeting, the agenda papers can be used with the supporting detail erased, but the formal motion copied as a record of the business. Again, this is done with no retyping of text.

If a list of all members voting for and against a motion is to be included, this can often be copied and adapted from a previous occasion, as the lists are similar each time, with voting on party lines.

TASK

Outline how a small community newspaper in your neighbourhood could benefit from access to word processing facilities.

11.9. WHERE TO FIND OUT MORE

Manufacturers' literature obviously paints a rosy picture of software available, but it is often as interesting for the things which it omits to say as for the things it includes. By collecting a number of brochures, a fairly detailed list of facilities available can be drawn up.

Both new and old word processing packages are regularly reviewed in the specialist magazines on business computing, but the hobbyist magazines make relatively little mention of the topic. Many magazines aimed at managers in particular industries carry general articles from time to time about application areas such as word processing, but rarely contain detailed reviews.

Manuals can be a useful source of information, even if there is no intention of using a particular package; in this case, though, the tutorial guide is probably the best documentation to look at. There are several books on the market dedicated to particular word processing packages, particularly on Wordstar. These can be worth reading for step-by-step training in using a program.

There is no substitute for the best way to learn about using word processing, however, and that is to use a word processor!

11.10. STUDY QUESTIONS

1   Why is a reference guide needed as well as a tutorial guide?
2   Why is different code needed to get features like bold characters on each of the different printers?
3   What could go wrong with the global replacement of Thomas for Tom in the text 'I think that Tom Brown is a valued customer'?

11.11. ASSIGNMENTS

1   How could authors make use of word processing? By choosing a specific example of an author of a particular type, suggest ways in which he or she would find word processing beneficial. Draw up a list of criteria which an author could use when choosing a word processor.
2   Write a report on the impact of the use of word processing in an office environment, in particular describing the effect of changes in the working lives of secretarial staff.
3   As a computer consultant, you have been asked to write a report on word processing by a group of solicitors. Your report should be presented with a formal structure and should recommend three packages which the solicitors could consider.
4   You have been asked by your manager to go to a conference on 'Computing and the Small Business', at which you are to give a talk entitled 'Progress in Computing in the last 12 months'. Your manager would like to see the complete text in advance. Using a word processing package at each stage, you must therefore produce an outline of your speech, not more than a page, for initial approval. Based on this, you should then produce a full text. This might involve a number of adjustments, including several stages of drafting. Once the text is completed, you are required to summarise the main points of your speech in not more than 750 words for inclusion in papers to be published at the conference.
5   Describe how a teacher or lecturer could make use of a word processor. Include details of how word processing would help improve notes and handouts, both in content and presentation. How could word processing be used in producing an examination paper?

12 FOR THE RECORD

12.1. COMPUTER DATABASES

Database programs are used for the storage, manipulation and retrieval of data. As the size of computer memories has expanded rapidly over the last few years, it has been possible to create very sophisticated data handling programs. While the tasks carried out on the data are simple in concept, it is the ability to handle large amounts of data at speed which proves such a useful tool to the modern organisation.

12.2. THE MAKE-UP OF A FILE

A file will be made up of a set of **records**, each of which is a set of related data items which have meaning by being related together. Each of the items within a record is known as a **field**. Thus, a personnel record might consist of a name, an address, a date of birth, a national insurance number and a telephone number. This record therefore has five fields. In each record, each of the fields has a value and the five values for one particular employee are related together. The contents of the fields are of little or no interest unless related to the values of the other corresponding fields for the employee. The set of all personnel records relating to all the staff is the **file**.

Fields, records and files: *a file is made up of a number of records, each of which is made up of a number of fields*

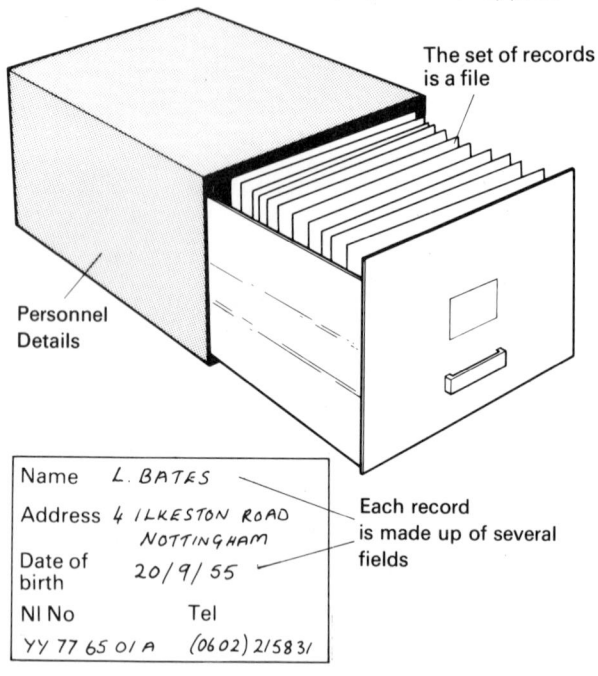

12.3. THE TERM 'DATABASE'

The term **database** was initially used in regard to programs written for mainframe computers, and because of this, the technical term has acquired a number of specific meanings. Thus a number of microcomputer programs sold as 'databases' would not meet the technical requirements of a database. The term has now, though, come to be used to describe all those programs which are concerned with the storage and manipulation of data held in a file as a series of records.

It is rather confusing that people use the term database on some occasions to describe the program and on others to refer to the data itself. Thus, people talk about 'buying a database', clearly meaning a program, and 'accessing a database', meaning the data itself. One means of avoiding the confusion is to refer to the 'database program' or 'database package' when referring to the software and to the 'data' or 'files' when referring to the data.

An understanding of a number of the features which have been found important in the development of mainframe databases can be helpful in thinking about the use of microcomputer databases.

A distinction can be drawn between the way in which the data is actually stored, known as the **physical** file structure, and the way that it is viewed by the user, known as the **logical** file structure. A user need not be concerned about the form in which data is held (are numbers held as binary or in character form?) or the way in which backing storage is used (is all the data on one side of the disc?). All the user has to consider is the make-up of the records as fields, how to add, delete, amend, retrieve and so on. Thus a user specifies to the database package what is required; how this is achieved need not be a concern.

Databases were first developed with the intention of reducing or eliminating the duplication of data. Thus, a user should seek to avoid the situation where a customer's address is held both in the accounts file for orders and payments and in the mailing list file for sending copies of new catalogues. The aim would be to hold the address in a file which both applications can access.

The keeping of a single copy of a data item:

(a) saves storage space, meaning that more useful data can be on-line when required;
(b) reduces inconsistency between applications;
(c) means less data has to be input; one operation changes the data accessed by all applications.

The design of files in order to minimise duplication can be achieved by a process called normalisation. Though a discussion of the techniques of normalisation is beyond the scope of this book, an appreciation of the process can help in efficient file design.

TASK

Draw up a list of as many circumstances as you can think of where a customer's address is needed by a company. Point out some of the problems which would be caused if these different applications had different versions of the address.

An employee's address might be accessed from several different applications

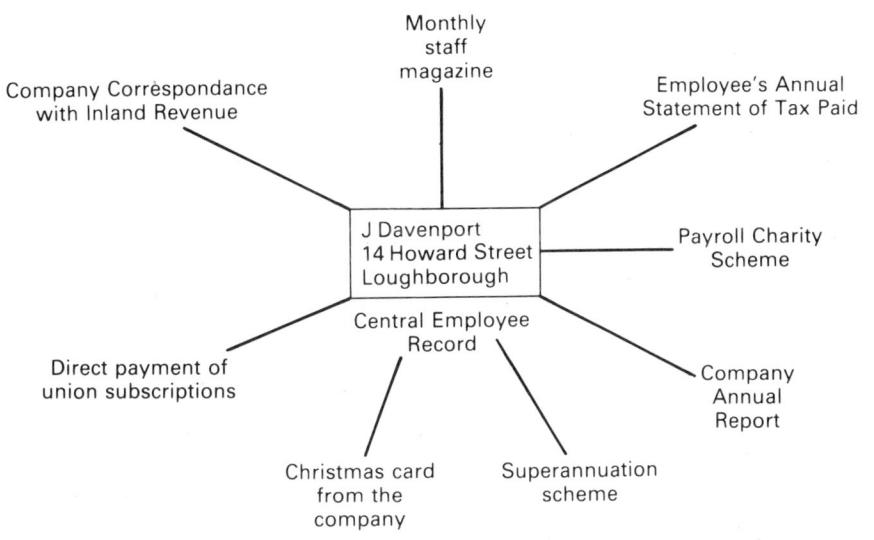

12.4. THE BASIC IDEAS

In formal database terminology, a distinction is made between a **data description language**, which specifies the form of the records to be held, and a **data manipulation language**, by which the user describes the ways that records are to be added, deleted, modified, re-ordered and so on. While the two terms are not always used in describing operations with microcomputer databases, the two distinct areas are present in using a package.

12.5. DESCRIBE THE DATA

Database programs allow for the establishment of a set of **records** of data. In order for this to take place, the format of the record has to be defined. This will usually mean that a user will have to specify the names of the fields, their character types and their lengths.

Each **field** is given a name so that it can be referred to in formulae or commands. Thus a search can be carried out for a particular value in a named field, or records will be sorted according to values held in one or more specified fields.

Field types are used by a system to determine the form of storage to be used and the forms of operations which can be carried out on the fields (such as arithmetic). Field types are also used in any forms of validation which are provided by the package, so that, for instance, alphabetical characters cannot be entered into a numerical field. The number of field types provided and their use differ widely between different packages; the user must choose which are appropriate for a particular application.

Many packages use fixed lengths for fields, so the user must define the maximum number of characters that a field should have. The imposition of a maximum permitted field length aids the producers of packages to limit file size and helps in the arrangement of record display. Thus a typical maximum length of a field may be 80 characters, the width of a screen. Other packages have no limit on field length or have a maximum such as 64 000 characters which covers all practicable applications.

The ability to have longer fields allows the use of records which include full descriptions, perhaps several sentences, such as a brief synopsis of a book for a catalogue. If a maximum field length is set, the data actually recorded might only consist of the characters used in entering the data and not the spaces left at the end of the field. This will not be the user's immediate concern, except that it might affect the size of files which can be fitted onto a single disc.

When establishing the file, the user may have to state the maximum size that the file will reach. This will usually be so that appropriate space can be reserved on the disc. An inappropriate choice of a maximum size might later become a serious constraint in the future development of the use of the data.

FIELD NUMBER	FIELD NAME	TYPE	LENGTH
1	Emp Name	A	30
2	Address	X	80
3	DoB	D	6
4	N Ins No	X	9
5	Telephone	9	10
6			
7			
8			
9			
10			

The records in a file are designed by specifying the fields in them

TASK

Consider a database program with which you are familiar or for which you can obtain literature. Write down the different field types that are available (such as alphabetic, numeric, date and so on). Draw up a list of the ways in which these different data types are handled differently, such as ways in which arithmetic is carried out on them, ways in which they are displayed, ways in which they are stored and so on.

12.6. ENTER THE DATA

Once the shape of the records has been described, the actual values must be entered. A screen is displayed showing the names of the fields, in the order defined earlier, with areas allocated into which the values of the fields for a particular record can be entered. The sizes of the areas displayed will reflect the field lengths. Data is then entered using this 'form filling' technique. Once all the fields have been completed, the user can move on to the next record, thus entering as many data items as are initially required.

A **browse** facility allows the user to look through all the records entered, having them displayed on the screen. This feature is generally linked with facilties to **add, delete** or **amend** records. A good package will allow the user to go back to the first record and view it. It should then be possible to change any or all of the fields of a record using a simple editor. This would allow a user to specify the field to be changed, and either allow its replacement or the insertion or deletion of characters within it. Some more simple packages only allow the complete retyping of an entry, which can prove tedious, time-consuming and error-prone.

As the records are browsed through, they will probably be numbered 'record 1', 'record 2' and so on. As in all database manipulation, this numbering will reflect the logical organisation rather than necessarily being the physical order in which the records are kept. It should be possible in the browsing mode to delete records or to add a new record (logically) between two other records. When this is done, the records are automatically renumbered by many packages. In other cases, records are only marked for deletion, which means that they can be recalled if necessary. Actual deletion only takes place when a request for this is issued, or storage on the disc is tidied up in some way.

```
    Record Number                           72

Emp Name    1       : L Bates              :
Address     2       : 4 Ilkeston Road
                      Nottingham           :
DoB         3       : 20/09/55:
N Ins No    4       : YY776501A:
Telephone   5       : 0602 215831:
```

Records can be browsed through on the screen

Some of the data entry features provided by the more sophisticated packages include inbuilt **validation**, so that the contents of a field can be specified as being within a particular range of values, and any attempt to enter data outside that range will be rejected immediately. Thus, for instance, it might be possible to specify that an employee's age must be between 16 and 70. It might also be possible to limit the values allowed in a particular field, so that 'M' and 'F' are the only entries accepted in the 'Sex' field. 'Y' would be rejected, even though it is an alphabetical character, entered in an alphabetical field.

Special **field types** also exist, so that a field might be a time (in the form hh:mm), or a date (in the form dd:mm:yy), or might be a money field (automatically having two decimal places). More generally, a numeric field might allow the specification of a number of decimal places to be held to which all entries are rounded. (Users need to check whether rounding takes place when the data is stored or only when it is displayed.)

One other feature of data entry to investigate is whether a distinction is made between upper and lower case alphabetic characters. This is important when searching data or sorting or when printing data (such as people's names).

TASK

Examine one particular database package in detail and describe the facilities for data entry. Include in your description:

(a) validation of entries,
(b) features of the editor,
(c) facilities for copying fields from one record to another (such as the name of the town).

12.7. MANIPULATE THE DATA

Once data has been entered, the power of a database package lies in its ability to **sort** and **search** records with varying degrees of sophistication.

Sorting

Sorting of records is achieved in one of two ways. The first method is to rearrange the records physically, that is, to put them in a different order on the disc. The alternative method is to establish an index so that records can be retrieved in a different order from that in which they are stored. The advantage of the use of indexes is that more than one of them can be established, so that data is

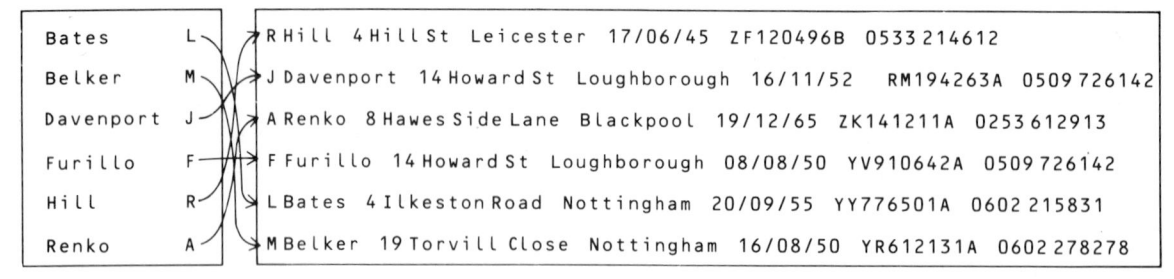

Index File			Data File
Bates	L		R Hill 4 Hill St Leicester 17/06/45 ZF120496B 0533 214612
Belker	M		J Davenport 14 Howard St Loughborough 16/11/52 RM194263A 0509 726142
Davenport	J		A Renko 8 Hawes Side Lane Blackpool 19/12/65 ZK141211A 0253 612913
Furillo	F		F Furillo 14 Howard St Loughborough 08/08/50 YV910642A 0509 726142
Hill	R		L Bates 4 Ilkeston Road Nottingham 20/09/55 YY776501A 0602 215831
Renko	A		M Belker 19 Torvill Close Nottingham 16/08/50 YR612131A 0602 278278

Sorting can be carried out by creating an index, rather than physically moving all the records

The (smaller) index file is maintained in alphabetical order, whilst data is added, amended or deleted in the data file.

accessible in more than one possible order. Thus, a personnel file might have one index in alphabetical order of surname and another index in date order of joining the company. Again, although it need not concern the user how this is implemented, it is an important aspect of the use of a package whether more than one sorting order can be established. Where the physical location of the data is changed rather than an index being used, there can be a considerable delay involved while the program re-sorts the data for each different order of retrieval which is required.

Sorting is usually available in ascending or descending order, either numerically, alphabetically or in date order, if provided. Where values in a field to be sorted prove not to be unique, it is sometimes possible to specify a second or further fields whose values are used to resolve such conflicts. If it is not possible to specify several fields in this way, a complicated procedure of sorting and re-sorting on different fields may be necessary. (Ask anybody who used one of the old punched card mechanical sorting machines to explain how!)

In cases where more than one index is allowed, some packages automatically update all indexes when new data is added. This can be an extremely useful facility when data is frequently changing, as the rebuilding of indexes from scratch will take some time.

TASK

Investigate three database packages. Describe the ways in which they handle sorting and indexes. From this information, describe an 'ideal' package which would have all the features you can think of. By using examples, show how these features would be useful.

Searching

A **search** facility is useful when attempting to locate a particular record. To achieve this a value must be specified for a field or set of fields (such as a name), which will uniquely identify the record which is required. Such a value is called a key. When the matching field value is found, the record is usually displayed in browse mode. In order for efficient searching to be carried out, the file will have to be sorted or have an index based on the relevant field. Where searches are carried out in cases where more than one record has the specified field value, normally the first record encountered with the required value will be displayed, the others being found when the user gives some form of 'continue' command.

Reporting

Users will often wish to produce a report based on the data held within a database file. A typical example might be a request for a list of the names and addresses of all employees over 40. This is achieved by the database program looking at each record in turn and determining whether it matches the conditions set by the user for inclusion in the report. These conditions are known as **criteria**.

Setting up a simple report

When producing a report, there are four major factors to consider:

(a) the order in which the records which are selected are to be printed;
(b) the definition of which records are to be tested to see if they match the criteria;
(c) the setting of the criteria;
(d) the statement of which fields are to be printed for those records which match.

The order of records

The order of the records in the report will be determined by the order in which records have been sorted, either physically or according to an index.

Which records are tested?

There is no need for a test to be carried out on all the records in a file. It must be established within the set of all records which shall be the first record to be tested and which shall be the last.

Setting the criteria

The records specified are taken one at a time and checked against the criteria to determine whether the appropriate fields of the record match. If a record matches, the appropriate printout takes place.

Database programs differ considerably in the number and nature of tests which can be carried out in reporting. Most provide separate tests to determine whether the content of a field is equal to, less than or greater than a specified value. With an alphabetic field 'less than' will mean 'precedes alphabetically' and 'greater than' will mean 'follows alphabetically'.

Conditions can normally be combined using AND and OR, or reversed using NOT, so that a number of tests can be carried out on the same field. For example, to find people who are in their thirties, the field can be tested with the combined condition >29 AND <40. Tests are sometimes extended so that compound conditions can be examined between fields, such as 'Female AND in her thirties OR male AND holding a driving licence', though many programs allow only AND combinations of different fields. The usefulness of such features will vary from one situation to another.

TASK

Some packages allow the user to specify selection criteria which are then used to produce a new file containing only those records from the main file which match the criteria. Suggest some ways in which this might be used.

Stating the field to be printed

Whatever the form of the search, the user should also be able to specify the fields which are to be printed. In many cases it is possible to state the order in which the fields will appear (which need not be the order in which they are stored). Other text printed with the record and the layout of each record might also be under the user's control. The production of standard letters incorporating data from the file and the printing of labels might be additional features in this category.

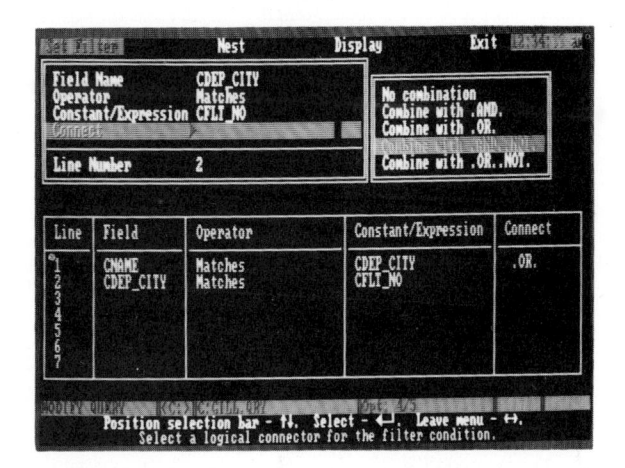

Setting conditions for a search in dBase III Plus from Ashton-Tate

More sophisticated reporting features

One development of search criteria includes the ability to search for a series of characters within a string (all people living in Sussex, whether it be East Sussex or West Sussex). Another is to be able to search with conditional criteria. For example, suppose that we wish to search for those who have been with the company more than five years if they are over 50, or more than ten years if they are under 50. This will require different tests on the 'length of service' field depending on the value in the 'age' field. Another useful feature is to be able to search some or all of the fields for a value. This is useful, for example, in searching for a postcode when different people have it on different lines of their address.

Reports may be produced on the screen, on the printer or both. It is clearly helpful if details of the format of a report can be stored as a file, as this saves having to enter a specification every time. In the more advanced programs, it is possible to specify a header and footer to go on each page and the numbering of pages. Other features might include the rounding of arithmetic and the precise placing of fields within the report according to a coordinate system. It is also useful to be able to include the record number as an output field, so that the record can be referred to later.

A field calculated from a number of existing fields might be incorporated in a report. For example, an item where the stock held is less than the re-order quantity in a stock recording system could be labelled 'RE-ORDER'; where the stock level is zero, it could be labelled 'OUT OF STOCK'. Several mathematical functions are sometimes provided, so that the total, the mean, the maximum, the minimum or the standard deviation can be calculated for fields of all records matching the criteria.

TASK

By examining a database package of your choice, outline the searches which are available and the ways in which they can be combined.

It is also possible for reports to be spooled, which means that they are sent to disc for later printing. This can have a number of uses, such as:

(a) producing more than one copy of the list,
(b) discovering the size of a list without using considerable paper and time,
(c) preparing some text for inclusion in a larger word processed report.

```
        STOCK STATUS REPORT
  Item   Location   Quantity   Value
  S013      17         14        28
            19         10        20
  S162      14          3        30
            19          8        80
            21          6        60
  S195      14          8       164
```

```
              LOW STOCK REPORT
    Stock items with total held
    less than 20
    Item     Location    Quantity
    S195        14           8
    S162        14           3
                21           6
                19           8
```

```
              STOCK HELD REPORT
              For warehouse 17
       Item    Qty      Item    Qty
       S013    14       S276     8
       S196    12       S295    16
       S199   103       S300    32
```

Database packages can be used to produce reports

12.8. UPDATING THE WHOLE FILE

In some circumstances, it may be desirable to perform an operation on the whole of a file. For example, at the turn of the year, all records must have one added to the 'age this year' field. It would be a tedious job to browse through all the records updating them one at a time. A useful feature is therefore to be able to perform the same calculation on all records. This is called a **global field calculation**.

Some fields of a record might be specified as **calculated fields**. Entries in these fields are not entered in the usual way, but are based on other fields of the record. For example, when the 'number of sons' and the 'number of daughters' have been entered, a field containing the 'number of children' may be needed. This can be calculated by adding the two other figures together. Some packages provide automatic updating of calculated fields, so that, in our example, if the number of daughters was changed, then the field for the number of children would be altered without any user intervention. In other packages, the user has to specify when calculated fields should be worked out again. Calculated fields are sometimes known as dependent fields in contrast to fields which have to be entered individually, which are known as independent fields.

In field calculations, mathematical functions, such as SIN, COS and LOG might be available. These can be invaluable features for some specialised applications. The rounding of mathematical calculations to a specified number of decimal places can sometimes also be specified.

12.9. MORE SOPHISTICATED RECORD FEATURES

Some database programs allow additional fields to be added easily to existing records; in others, this is a more difficult process, or, indeed, may not be allowed at all. Fields may have to be added to develop an application beyond what was initially considered. It would clearly be a mammoth task to have to type all existing data in again. In some systems, all the user needs to do is to describe the new field and the new structure will be displayed in order for the values in the field to be entered. In many systems, however, a new record structure must be defined and then all the data from the old system must be copied over to the new format before this process can begin. This is another case where, though storage organisation need not be the subject of detailed study by the user, it can have a serious impact on ways of working. Considerable extra disc space might be needed at the point when both the old and the new copies of the data are held.

Some database packages allow more than one field in a record to have the same name. This can be useful if it is not known how many occurrences of the field there will be. If a record were to hold names of an individual's children for example, a fixed format would suggest providing about five fields, 'Child 1', 'Child 2' and so on. The two main drawbacks of this are that for many people several fields will remain blank, hence wasting file space, and that for some people five would not be enough and special arrangements would have to be made. A more flexible approach is to allow an appropriate number of fields with the same name to be specified. This has the added advantage that all fields with this name can then be searched using a simple matching statement. (Thus all such fields are searched when looking for children called 'Jo'.)

When a group of related fields is repeated within a record, a number of alternative strategies can be adopted. A personnel record might hold details of an individual's previous employment, including the name and address of the employer, date of leaving and number of years service. The number of such entries will vary considerably from person to person, from no occurrences to several. The problems associated with repeated fields occur again, in that providing a fixed number of repetitions could be both wasteful and insufficient. Searches through all previous employers could be time consuming if an inappropriate structure is used. Such a problem is particularly crucial if a lot of such searches have to be made.

One approach to the problem is to use what is termed a **transactional database**. This will allow a variable number of groups of items to be associated with a single file record. Thus a personnel record might consist of nine set fields (name, date of birth, date of joining and so on), with as many or as few grouped items (such as name of employer, date of starting, date of leaving), as is appropriate in each case. Such a group of repeated items is termed a 'transaction'. As a series of transactions are associated with the rest of a record, the structure is viewed as a three-dimensional record. This contrasts with the fixed field record type which is then called a **flat record** system. Purists point out that the transactional database is not a true database according to the formal definitions, because of its lack of symmetry. In the example, it is much easier to determine which employer an individual has worked for than it is to determine which individuals have worked for a particular employer.

A transactional database, showing repeated group items

```
STOCK CODE
ITEM DESCRIPTION
PRICE
PRICING CODE
```

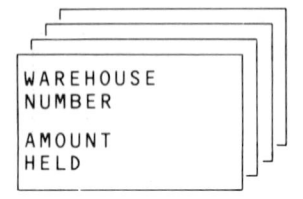

```
WAREHOUSE NUMBER
AMOUNT HELD
```

Each stock item is held at several warehouses.

TASK

Describe how a transactional database could be used to administer some aspects of an organisation's accounts. By using your examples, discuss whether the lack of symmetry is a drawback.

12.10. USER DIALOGUES

The user dialogues of database programs are in some cases menu driven and in others are command driven. The most sophisticated packages provide both.

With a **menu-driven** program, the user is presented with an initial menu, listing the various options available. These allow the defining of a new file, browsing the records of an existing file (allowing amendments), printing a report and so on. Once an option is chosen, further menus are displayed or questions are asked which the user simply responds to in order to carry out the tasks necessary. This is the simplest way in which a new user can establish a new file, or what is more likely initially, use and interrogate an existing file.

A **command-driven** database will simply wait for the user to issue an instruction. Thus, on starting the program, the computer displays a 'prompt' such as a full stop with a flashing cursor, in anticipation of a command from the user. Clearly, the user needs to know the set of instructions available in order to use the package. This is similar to learning a new programming language. Ultimately, however, this is the source of the great flexibility of command-driven databases, as a series of instructions can be saved as a program or procedure. For this reason, command-driven databases are also known as **procedural** databases. Once a set of commands is recorded as a file, it can be recalled and used again, perhaps upon the issuing of a single command. For an established and regular process, an operator can be told how to carry out such commands and so needs relatively little instruction.

The power of procedural databases has been further developed with the provision of structured commands within the procedural language. Such advanced features include the abilities of procedures to call up other procedures and to pass values to them, so that the benefits of a structured programming language can be reaped. In building a dialogue with the user from a procedural database, it is possible to build a menu-driven application program. Some would describe the writing of such instructions as programming in the higher level language of the database. It is therefore possible for a user to have very little contact with running the database program direct, as basic tasks can be programmed. Indeed, a system might be established where pre-written procedures are automatically run when the disc is loaded.

In summary, then, it will be easier for a user to begin using a database program proper when it has

Commands in the structured programming language of a procedural database

```
use stockfil
do while not eof
    if warehouse = 17
    display item qty 1ptr
    endif
    next
enddo
```

a menu-driven approach. With a sophisticated procedural database, on the other hand, the user can be shielded completely from contact with the database program itself as long as application programs are written. The menus provided by a menu-driven database program are general and the same for all applications, whereas those written when using a procedural language can be made to suit the application.

12.11. SETTING UP THE INPUT SCREEN

Many packages allow a user to design an input screen or form to suit the particular application. This is sometimes known as a 'paint a screen' feature. Screen design can be done by specifying how to lay out on the screen a record which has already been defined. Alternatively, the record type can be defined and at the same time the screen layout determined. Thus a user may specify where on an input screen the fields to be requested are placed, irrespective of the order in which fields are stored and used.

It may also be possible to establish a set of questions for the user to answer when data is entered, in preference to displaying only the names of the fields. Thus, a field might be called 'AGE' within the database, for the purpose of sorting, calculating and so on, but when a value is asked for as part of the screen dialogue, the question 'How old is this person?' appears.

Some screen dialogues also **lock** some fields, such as those fields which purely depend on other fields, so that they cannot be corrupted on data entry. When data is being entered, locked fields are simply skipped over by the cursor. Additionally there may be compulsory fields, which must be filled in within a record, and optional fields, which may or may not be completed, such as comment fields, where a blank entry is allowed.

12.12. USING MANY FILES

The uses of a microcomputer database are considerably enhanced by allowing the use of several files at once. When this is possible, a user can, for instance, have a single file of customers' names and addresses, which is referenced whenever a customer's address is required. In some packages, there is a limitation that only two files can be open at the same time. Though this is considerably more flexible than a single file system, there is a limit to what can be achieved with only two files. A more practical provision is made by programs which allow, say, ten files to be available at once.

It is only when a number of files can be handled at once that the full potential of formal database theory can be achieved, such as the removal of duplicated data. The handling of several files is generally more common with procedural databases than with non-procedural ones.

12.13. MANY USERS

Some packages are **multi-user** allowing the sharing of a common database by users in a computer network. This has clear benefits in that all users will have access to data which is entirely up-to-date, from whatever source it has been updated. This could be particularly useful in cases where several operators are performing similar tasks, for example on customers' accounts. It is important that action is not based on out-of-date information to avoid difficulties such as two different people sending a customer a credit note for the same account.

Multi-user databases have posed a number of implementation problems for their writers, not least in resolving conflicts of access. Steps will have to be taken to ensure that only one user at a time has access rights to update files, otherwise a user can find that data being used suddenly changes in the middle of an operation. The design must also ensure that it is not possible for two different users manipulating the same data to update the records partially and thus produce mutually inconsistent data. With multi-user packages, it is generally made very clear in the documentation what is and is not possible and messages normally inform the user when data is not available.

TASK

Imagine that you are a member of a small computing team, which has been asked to give a presentation to careers officers on possible uses for databases in their work. You have been asked to draw up a set of slides to illustrate actual practical and relevant examples. Design a set of drawings, on paper if you do not have access to other equipment.

12.14. LINKS WITH OTHER PACKAGES

In some organisations, it can be of particular benefit that files produced by a database program can be 'exported' for use by other packages and that files produced by other packages can be 'imported' for use within a database environment. Such features have proved particularly popular for linking packages which are market leaders in their own particular application area. Thus, many database programs provide output which can be used as a mailing list for a personalised letter produced by a word processor. Similarly, links might be made to or from a spreadsheet program.

12.15. MAKING THE CHOICE

With such a wide range of features and capabilities, it is clearly important before making a choice to consider which facilities are essential and which are desirable within a particular application. It is vital to consider also which particular machine and operating system the program can run on.

File capacity

Frequently manufacturers' literature and reviews of software provide a list of statistics of the capacities of a database program. This may include:

(a) the maximum number of characters per field,
(b) the maximum number of fields per record,
(c) the maximum number of records per file,
(d) the maximum number of characters per record,
(e) the maximum number of characters per file,
(f) the maximum number in arithmetic,
(g) the minimum number in arithmetic,
(h) the maximum number of digits held accurately,
(i) the maximum number of conditions for a search,
(j) the maximum width of a report.

TASK

For three database packages of your choice, make a table of these 'vital statistics', as listed above.

Operating system

There are clear advantages in choosing a database program which works with an operating system with which the user is familiar. Apart from the saving in purchase costs, the use of a known operating system will help a user get to know the package more easily, will aid in disc maintenance and will open up the potential to pass data from one application to another.

Machine features

Special machine features may be exploited by database programs. For example, function keys may be given particular meanings, colour displays can be used effectively by databases and the full potential of printer features can be exploited. In all these cases, the facilities will have to be written in to the version of the package for the particular machine, and mention will be made of them in manufacturers' literature.

TASK

For three commercial packages which are described by their manufacturers as 'databases', draw up a table of points of comparison. Divide the table into three sections:

(a) values which can be measured, such as fields per record and number of records;
(b) features which may or not be present (simple yes or no);
(c) aspects which are matters of judgement, such as quality of documentation.

Help

Another measure of the user friendliness of a package is the range of 'help' facilities provided and the stages at which help can be obtained. This can be particularly useful in providing reminders about commands available and in giving more details about error messages.

Discs needed

Some packages will only function with either or both the program disc and the data disc being present in the drive during operation. The program disc might have to be left in the machine so that various parts of the program can be swapped in and out of memory when necessary. This arrangement might be made either because the memory of the computer cannot hold the whole program or in order to maximise the amount of space available for data. The data disc may be updated whenever a data item is altered, or the program may only save when a block of data in a file can be written. When a large amount of memory is allocated to hold a copy of part of the data file, it becomes more likely that a command can be carried out without the need for disc access.

When handling data and amending files frequently, there is much potential for error and loss of data. An important part of the discipline of use of databases in business is to ensure that effective security is carried out. Comprehensive file copying routines must be adhered to. In many cases the user will have to initiate this and it should be part of the regular routine. In cases where data is updated on line, there will clearly be some data lost if equipment breaks down, and transactions since the last copy of the file was made may be lost. Careful recording of data entered is therefore essential.

12.16. ADD-ONS

A number of add-on utility programs have been produced, particularly for procedural databases. These programs enhance the features or provide aids in using the database packages; users must already have the appropriate database to make use of the add-ons.

Screen design

Add-ons are frequently written by different companies from the authors of the original software in order to extend the features. For example, an add-on might enable the user to specify and generate data entry screens and to develop a menu-driven enquiry system. This might allow the generation of a program in a procedural database from the user's requirements without the user having to write the coding.

Graphics

A graphics add-on package might allow the production of graphics, perhaps in full colour. This might be used to produce bar charts, line graphs or pie charts from stored data.

Programmers' toolkits

For programmers in a database language, toolkits might be available which aid in the preparation of programs. A feature may allow the saving and merging of files of commands, enabling the building of programs from frequently used procedures, as in other programming languages. Another programmers' aid might be the inclusion of features to help in listing programs, such as the indentation of sections of a program, as this helps program debugging.

Another add-on feature is a compiler for a procedural database, which increases the speed that the program runs, as most database programs run by interpreting a line of code at a time. A file sort routine might be useful if large files are sorted frequently, as the generalised sorts provided in many packages can be slow and specialised sort packages can be much more efficient.

TASK

As a member of the data processing staff in a medium-sized company, you have been asked to represent the team at a meeting about possible computerisation of personnel records. Some members of the personnel department staff are worried about their own technical capabilities. People from other departments are concerned about security and privacy, particularly if incorrect data creeps into the system. Write an imaginary set of minutes of the meeting, reflecting the arguments which you consider might be used on each side for these and any other relevant concerns.

12.17. CASE STUDY

Ashton–Tate produced dBase II, which is a procedural database program. Commands can be entered one at a time for immediate execution, but the full potential of dBase II is only reached when a series of instructions is saved as a procedure to be called up at other times. This allows the setting up of screen menus and document formats, so that the data held can be used and manipulated by operators who need not be familiar with the dBase II commands. Purchasers of dBase II can either write their own applications in the dBase II programming language, or can buy pre-written software in a number of forms.

Realising the potential for the sale of programs written in dBase II's procedural language, Ashton–Tate has also produced a dBase II Run-Time System. This allows programs written in dBase II to be translated to a form such that, with the addition of code provided by Ashton–Tate, the system will run as if it were dBase II with the program. It is not possible, however, using the system either to list the source code in dBase II's procedural language or to enter dBase II proper. This is to protect both the authors of the procedural language program and Ashton–Tate. This scheme makes it possible, therefore, to market database instructions, just like selling any other program.

Ashton–Tate itself produced Friday!, which is sold as a stand-alone system. It does not require dBase II to operate it, and indeed, the full dBase II is considerably more expensive.

12.18. WHERE TO FIND OUT MORE

In choosing a database package, it is particularly vital to establish early in the selection process what precisely is required. It is important to identify the amount of data which is to be handled. The type of user who will make use of the package will also be a crucial factor. If there are to be a lot of occasional users, then the ability to present a user-friendly menu-driven dialogue will be important. This can be achieved either by a menu-driven database package or by judicious programming in a procedural database. The ability to produce your own programs may appear attractive in the advertising, which stresses the flexibility this provides. Purchasers should be aware, however, that writing their own programs requires time for development, debugging, documenting and so on. Indeed, people often buy packages to save this effort. Clearly the choice whether to go down the path of procedural databases depends on the scale and the timescale of the work.

When viewing demonstrations of the power of particular database software, it is important to balance the potential long-windedness of menu-driven software against the difficulty of learning with a command-driven approach. It is also worth asking to see the power of pre-written programs in a procedural package, but it is also worth asking how long it took to produce the demonstration!

A number of books have been written about particular database packages. These books frequently seek to develop the reader's knowledge of commands by introducing a few new commands in each chapter. Examples are included as well as sample programs to try. Reading such a book, even without access to the particular package, can give a picture of what can be achieved in using the package. It is possible to learn what is generally available in such software by reading about the specific features of one package.

12.19. STUDY QUESTIONS

1 In what ways can different methods of logical structure of data allow a more flexible approach to physical structures of data?
2 Why would a field be given a name different from the message which is displayed on the screen for that field?
3 What implementation problems are there when changes are carried out on variable-length records?
4 In some file handling programs, a feature known as file reorganisation is included. Why might the need for this arise?

12.20. ASSIGNMENTS

1 Using a database package with which you are familiar, design a set of files which can be used for a company's stock control. This should allow for the amendment of existing

stock level, the introduction of new stock items, the deletion of discontinued lines, the production of a list of items which are out of stock and any other features which you consider useful. Design a simple guide to the features which a regular user could use for reference.

2   You are required to reply to a memorandum on the use of databases.

You are a senior clerk in the Department of Administrative Affairs. The way your section does its work has changed significantly in the last five years, and has become microcomputer-based, moving away from a mainframe, batch-based system. Many new applications have been computerised in the last few years and many of the senior staff are now competent in using the microcomputers, which are allocated at the rate of roughly one between two workers.

Very little use has so far been made of databases, as the primary concerns have been to computerise accounts and to introduce word processing. The latter has been particularly successful in generating new and edited reports. The time has now come, however, to keep records of suppliers and tenders in a database system and this will have a major impact as each area moves over to a new way of thinking.

You should prepare a detailed (and well-organised) report in response to the memo. You should point out any assumptions you have made about the existing system on which your answer depends.

Memorandum

From: Sir Humphrey, Permanent Secretary, Dept. of Administrative Affairs
Subject: Use of databases

Rt Hon. Jim Hacker (the Minister), has asked me to look into the possibilities of us using databases in our computers.

I'm a bit pushed myself at the moment (fame has its price!). Could you possibly dig out the appropriate gen? And then bang out a report in draft form so that I can juggle it around a bit. (I can cope with most word processors, if you can run to that.) Use all the standard headings in the report – that'll save me time.

As you know, we have rather a mix of Apricots and various breeds of IBM PCs. Is this going to pose a problem of compatibility?

The Minister points out that he has heard of dBase II. Could you find out some detail of this. I myself am worried, because, unbeknown to the Minister, I have heard, through the usual channels, that there is already a dBase III on the market. Do we want to go for an outdated piece of software? I also hear that you can get plug-in software units for dBase II. Is this right? If so, what are they?

Are there alternatives to dBase, though, something more up-to-date, or easier to use? Come to think of it, in what ways do databases differ and how can you choose between them? Could you draw me up a list of criteria? (Let's show the minister we thought about that!) Do I need to know how these different packages differ?

What will I need to know and what will my staff need to know to use one of these things? Somebody once told me that the only databases to consider are programmable, others talk about procedural databases. Is there any difference? Will I need to program? Who else will?

The Minister also wants to know about CardBox and Friday! In order that we can present enough options, I think that you should also say something about either Delta or Superfile. They all sound the same to me, but he has contacts who are insisting that one is better than the other. Are they leading him on? What would be good is two or three examples (related to our admin).

One final point. Can a database be linked to other software, including the sort of things which we already have?

Sorry that this is rushed. No need to rush the reply until the Minister gets back from his fact-finding tour of Clacton, but you know how particular he can be about detail in his reports!!!

13 SPREADSHEETS AND THEIR USES

13.1. THE BASIC IDEA

A spreadsheet program is a business modelling tool commonly used in business and financial planning. The first spreadsheet, released in the late 1970s was 'Visicalc'. This extremely popular piece of software achieved unprecedented sales and is believed to have helped boost considerably the sales of Apple computers, on which it was originally implemented. 'Visicalc' was followed by many similar packages, which were termed by some VisiClones or CalcAlikes. Spreadsheet programs are now available for almost all modern computers.

The basic idea of a spreadsheet is the manipulation of a table of figures. A set of rows and columns of numerical values is established, providing a set of **cells** into which entries can be made. The numerical values in the various cells can be related by using formulae which refer to the contents of other cells. This is done by referring to a cell by specifying its row and column. Alternatively, in order to aid interpretation of a table, text can be included within a cell instead of a number. Clearly a cell containing text should not be used within a formula for calculation. In summary, there are three kinds of cell entries:

(a) a numerical value, entered through the keyboard;
(b) a numerical value, calculated from other cell entries according to a formula;
(c) a text entry, entered via the keyboard.

13.2. WILD DREAMS AND FRIGHTENING NIGHTMARES: ASKING 'WHAT IF?' QUESTIONS

The great power of a spreadsheet is the facility for the user to change one or more of the numerical values, after which the program can recalculate all the cells which have a formula using the values that have changed. This enables a user to consider a number of possible options or scenarios in quick

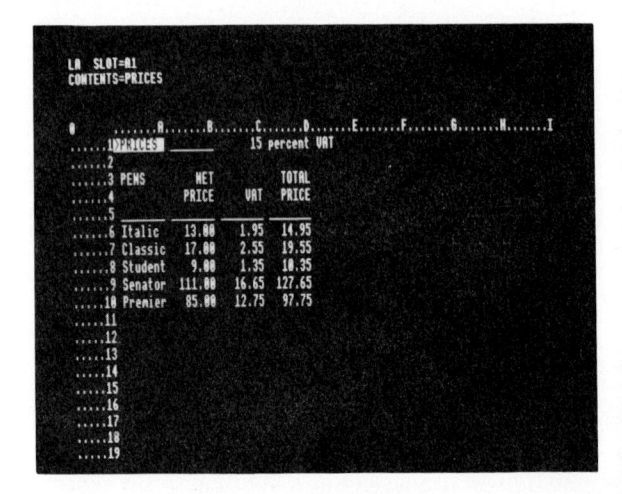

A typical spreadsheet screen: ViewSheet from Acornsoft

succession without the tedious task of performing several calculations each time. Thus a user is able to consider what the effect would be if a wide range of conditions applied. For this reason, spreadsheets are sometimes known as 'what if?' programs.

Spreadsheets can be used to see the effect on an organisation of an individual's wildest dreams, by entering data for the most optimistic forecast. Alternatively, the most pessimistic values can be entered, in order to evaluate the most frightening nightmares. The process of manipulating figures to forecast effects is known as **modelling**, and so the values, text and formulae entered into a spreadsheet are sometimes referred to as a **model**.

13.3. A WINDOW ON THE WORLD

Not all cells can be displayed on the limited screen space simultaneously, so only a small rectangular part is shown at any one time. This is known as a **window** on to part of the worksheet. The user can move around the worksheet by use of the keyboard. The cell currently under consideration is indicated, often by appearing in reverse lettering (for example, black on white), and is referred to as the cursor position. As this cursor is moved about the sheet, the sheet will be redrawn on the screen to enable other cells around it to be displayed.

A spreadsheet screen showing the right-hand edge of a worksheet (Acornsoft ViewSheet)

13.4. WHAT THEY ALL DO

Different kinds of cell entries

The number and the range of facilities provided within a spreadsheet have both grown and continue to develop as each new product is released. A number of features have now come to be expected as standard, though views of which are necessary will vary between users and between applications.

All spreadsheets will allow the three standard forms of entry: numbers, text and formulae. The contents of cells may be displayed in a variety of formats or **cell layouts**. These can include:

(a) left justifying (starting at the left-hand edge of a cell, leaving spaces at the right),
(b) right justifying (ending at the right-hand edge of a cell, leaving spaces at the left),
(c) centring (as far as possible, having an equal number of spaces at each end),
(d) an ability to set the number of decimal places to which values should be calculated and displayed (which includes monetary values, which may or may not be preceded by a currency sign).

Where a cell is specified as a formula, the normal display will show the results of this calculation as a numerical value. The formula which lies behind this value generally only appears as the contents of the cell when the cursor is placed at that particular cell position.

Saving and printing

As in all computer applications, it is essential that data, once entered, can be saved for future use, and a spreadsheet program will allow a model to be saved (including values, text and formulae). This can then be recalled at a later stage. Equally essential is the ability to produce hard copy output and spreadsheets usually provide for all or part of the data to be printed. Thus a set of final figures can be produced. It is also common to want a hard copy of the basis on which these figures are produced in terms of how each cell was calculated;

that is, the user will want to print the model. Thus facilities are provided to print what lies behind each cell, whether it be a value, text or a formula.

Cell references

There are two main ways of referring to the cells. Some spreadsheet programs label all the rows numerically down the side, and all the columns alphabetically with letters running across the top of the screen. Columns after column Z are labelled AA, AB, AC and so on. It is quite common for there to be 63 columns which are labelled A to BK. Thus a cell is referenced by a letter (or two-letter combination) followed by a number. The alternative approach is to number both rows and columns, and to refer to cells by means of expressions such as R3C7, meaning the cell on the third row and in the seventh column. This slightly increases the length of formulae, but various facilities are provided to reduce typing when entering formulae.

Cell sizes

When establishing a blank worksheet on to which the user is to place entries, it is normal for all cells to be given the same display size. This size may or may not be under the user's control. Similarly the cell layouts wll be established with all cells having the same default layout. Most spreadsheet programs will allow a cell to hold a value or text which is longer than the display area provided for a single cell. In this case, only that part of the contents which will fit the cell's size on the screen will be displayed. There are normally simple commands provided for setting the widths of columns or the display formats of some cells. Most spreadsheet programs allow different columns to have different widths, to allow for different types of data, such as text descriptions and financial values. All cells in a given column must have the same width, whether columns vary in width or not.

TASK

Suggest why all the cells in a column of a spreadsheet must have the same width.

Illustrating the 'what if?' approach

The following example is extremely simple and could be implemented using any spreadsheet program. It is designed to show how the basic features can be used to experiment with possible situations.

Suppose I am given a loan of £1000, to be paid off in annual instalments, with an interest rate of 10% per annum. What sum must I pay each year to pay off the loan over 5 years?

Clearly the answer is more than £200 as I have to pay some interest as well. In tackling this problem with a spreadsheet, it is important first of all to build a model. In this example, columns are referred to by letters and rows by numbers.

Step 1: The basic model

Column A will contain explanatory labels. Column B will contain the amount owing at the start of the year. Column C will contain the interest charged for the year. Column D will contain the payment made in the year and column E will contain the money owing at the end of the year.

Row 1 will be reserved for text headings of the columns. Rows 2 to 6 will display amounts for years 1, 2, 3, 4 and 5 respectively. Thus the layout will appear as follows:

	A	B	C	D	E
1	Year	Start	Interest	Payment	End
2	1	1000.00	100.00	250.00	850.00
3	2	850.00	85.00	250.00	685.00
4	3	685.00			
5	4				
6	5				

Fig A *The start of a spreadsheet for the loan repayment problem*

In Fig A, entries have been made for an initial estimate of a repayment of £250.00 per year. The entries so far could be calculated by hand, but later values get more complex to work out.

Step 2: Establishing the formulae

To build the model as a spreadsheet, a number of formulae have to be entered. The contents of cell

C2 should be 10% of B2; as a formula this is 0.10*B2. Similarly, the interest in year 2, held in cell C3, should be 10% of B3, entered as 0.10*B3. The interest charges for further years are worked out in a similar manner.

The values of column E are worked out by taking the debt at the start of the year, adding the interest, and subtracting the payment. Thus E2 should contain the formula B2+C2−D2; E3 should contain B3+C3−D3 and so on.

Payments can either all be entered separately in the D column, or, more efficiently, D3, D4, D5 and D6 can each contain the simple formula D2. This has little initial advantage, but is of benefit when the amount is to be changed, using the 'what if?' approach.

Finally, the amount owing at the start of one year is simply the amount owing at the end of the previous year. Thus B3 will contain the formula E2; B4 will contain E3 and so on.

In summary then, the formulae to be entered are as follows:

Cell	Formula held
B3	E2
B4	E3
B5	E4
B6	E5
C2	0.10*B2
C3	0.10*B3
C4	0.10*B4
C5	0.10*B5
C6	0.10*B6
D3	D2
D4	D2
D5	D2
D6	D2
E2	B2+C2−D2
E3	B3+C3−D3
E4	B4+C4−D4
E5	B5+C5−D5
E6	B6+C6−D6

Fig B *Formulae for loan repayment problem*

The cells which do not contain formulae or text must contain values, and these are cells B2 and D2, which contain the following values:

Cell	Value held	Reason
B2	1000.00	Initial sum
D2	250.00	Amount of payment

Fig C *Initial data for loan repayment problem*

The only other value set by the question is the 10%, which is incorporated within the formulae in column C in this model.

Step 3: A solution to the initial problem

The model, once established, can now be used to evaluate the payment needed. 1000.00 is entered in cell B2, and the initial estimate of the repayment amount is entered in D2. From these two values, all other cells are calculated. The contents of cell E6 show the amount outstanding at the end of five years. If this amount is positive, then the repayments are too small and the amount in cell D2 should be increased. If the amount in cell E6, on the other hand, is negative, then the repayment is too large and should be reduced. By such a process, possible values can be narrowed down, until the nearest value to zero is found. It is very unlikely that the amount in cell E6 will ever be exactly zero, but often a value can be found that will leave E6 with an entry which is only a few pence. This is as accurate as is necessary.

Step 4: Further uses for the model

The use of the model does not end there, however. It is easy to enter a different initial loan and to determine repayments for this amount. It is straightforward to expand the table to include more rows with similar formulae (based on the pattern already established) to work out payments on a loan over 10 years or 14. It is also possible to enter a loan sum and a repayment figure and to see how many years it would take to pay off a loan with a fixed repayment figure.

The user could also alter the interest rate and perform any of the above calculations. It would be straightforward, but rather tedious to alter all the formulae in column C to reflect a different rate. In fact, most spreadsheet packages offer a simpler way to alter a set of similar formulae like this.

Armed with these possibilities, a user can ask: 'How much can I borrow at 10% interest if I can afford at most £200 per year repayment?', 'What if the interest rate was 12%. How much could I borrow?' The ease with which users can investigate such possibilities has given rise to the term 'what if?' analysis.

TASK

Using a spreadsheet package of your choice, build a model for the above problem. Investigate the model with the following 'what if?' analyses:

(a) Find the payment needed per year on a loan of £1000 at 10% interest over 5 years.
(b) Find the payment needed per year on a loan of £2500 at 10% interest over 10 years.
(c) How much can be borrowed with a repayment of £2400 per year over 10 years at 10%?
(d) How is the above answer affected if the interest rate is raised to 11%?
(e) What happens if the payment is less than the interest charged in the first year?

Other facilities

Copying formulae

There is often a demand to copy a formula along a row or column. For example, if a cell was to contain the sum of all the other cells on that row, a formula can be established. The cell immediately below it might also have to be set to hold the total of *its* row. The formulae for the two cells, consisting of row and column specifications, will be identical except that the cells specified in the second formula should be those for one row lower. In order to increase the power of copied formulae, relative formulae may be used. These allow the user to refer to a cell as being 'in the current row', or 'three columns back' and so on. When such a formula is copied to a different cell, it will have a different meaning.

In the example above, the formula in cell E2, which is B2+C2−D2, could have been written as RC(−3)+RC(−2)−RC(−1). The parts of this formula refer to 'current row, three columns back', 'current row, two columns back', 'current row, one column back'. The same formula could be copied into cells E3, E4, E5 and E6. Because the formula is relative to the current cell, the same formula in a different place means a different thing. This makes the copying of formulae an extremely powerful tool.

Recalculation

When the value within a cell is altered, this can affect cells whose formulae contain the changed cell. Additionally, these cells might then have further cells which depend on the value held in them. Thus there can be a cascading effect of a simple change throughout a worksheet. In some cases, recalculation would cause considerable delay and would not be particularly useful. For example, if a whole list of new values must be entered before its total has any meaning, then recalculation will be time consuming. In most spreadsheets, this automatic recalculation can be switched off by the user. Subsequently, when all values have been entered, the automatic recalculation can be switched back on, or a recalculation can be forced.

Adding rows and columns

When a model is being built, it may become necessary to insert a row or column at a point within the table, for example, to add intermediate results or an additional category of income. Most spreadsheet programs will allow the insertion of a row of column and will automatically amend all formulae to reflect the movement of existing cells to different rows or columns.

A user most frequently requires the formulae to be evaluated a row at a time working from the top of the worksheet. Where this is not the case, the recalculation order can be changed so that formulae are evaluated a column at a time.

As an example of the importance of recalculation order, consider the following situation:

Cell	Contents
A3	A2+10
B2	A3*10

	A	B	C
1			
2		*	
3	*		

Fig D *Calculation order matters!*

If the values are evaluated a row at a time (the normal order), then B2 is evaluated before A3, and so the previous value of A3 will be used, as the new value will not have been worked out. If, however, the cells are evaluated a column at a time, then A3 will be evaluated before cell B2 is, and thus B2 will reflect this new value. It is clearly important that the evaluation order is specified and adhered to in order to resolve conflicts which occur when two cells both depend upon each other. Cells could be related in a conflicting way, such as B2 containing 2*A3, and A3 containing 2*B2. The final worksheet cannot have both values being twice the other, one must be evaluated using the previous value of the other cell. The recalculation order determines which way round this is.

13.5. WHAT ONLY SOME DO

Editing formulae

As models are manipulated and adapted, formulae held in cells will have to be changed. The simplest spreadsheets will only allow the complete retyping of a formula. The more sophisticated programs will incorporate a line editor, which will allow a user to 'copy and patch' a formula.

Naming cells and areas

Some spreadsheet programs allow a cell or a group of cells to be given a label or **name**, which can then be used in formulae, rather than using cell references. The use of names will reduce the chances of errors when formulae are entered. It is also possible to choose meaningful names to aid understanding of a model. The formula SALES-COSTS, for example, has a more obvious meaning than K9-G7. When rows and columns are added, formulae using names will be unaffected and will so retain their correct meaning.

Cell entry by pointing

Formula entry is also simplified in some programs by allowing a cell reference to be entered by a pointing technique. Thus, as a formula is being entered at a particular cell, the cursor can be moved to the cell which is to be referenced by the formula. Pressing an appropriate key will then incorporate the reference of that cell within the formula. Not only does this simplify entry, but it also cuts down on mistakes. Some spreadsheets allow the evaluation of a formula as a line is being entered, enabling the spreadsheet to be used as a calculator.

> **TASK**
> Suggest why formula entry by pointing cuts down on mistakes.

Mathematical functions

The mathematical functions provided in different spreadsheets vary considerably, reflecting the requirements of different users. All spreadsheets will provide the standard five mathematical operations (add, subtract, multiply, divide and raise to the power) and most will include facilities to take the integer part, calculate the square root, logarithm, sine, cosine and tangent. Such functions are of obvious use for scientific applications. Some programs provide a random number feature for statistical purposes.

Many spreadsheets have functions to give the total of a list (usually specified by giving the first and last cell reference to be considered), the largest in a list, the smallest in a list, the mean (average) of a list and the standard deviation. A conditional function allows simple decision-making, so that a value might be A3 if A1 is less than 50, or A4 otherwise. Conditions may be combined using AND, OR and NOT, the operations of Boolean algebra.

Typical mathematical functions in a spreadsheet

ABS (x)	absolute value: the positive number with the magnitude of x
ACOS (x)	arc cosine: the angle whose cosine is x
ASIN (x)	arc sine: the angle whose sine is x
ATAN (x)	arc tangent: the angle whose tangent is x
AVE (range)	the average of the values in the range of cells
COS (x)	the cosine of the angle x
COUNT (range)	the number of non-zero values in the range of cells
EXP (x)	the value of e to the power x
FV (values)	the future value of a sum of money at a stated discounted rate
INT (x)	the integer part of x

LN (*x*)	the natural logarithm of *x*
LOG (*x*)	the logarithm to the base 10 of *x*
MAX (range)	the largest value in the range of cells
MIN (range)	the smallest value in the range of cells
PMT (values)	the monthly payment needed when borrowing a stated amount at a given interest rate over a stated period of time
PV (values)	the present value of a sum of money at a stated discounted rate
SIN (*x*)	the sine of the angle *x*
SQRT (*x*)	the square root of *x*
STD (range)	the standard deviation of the values in the range of cells
SUM (range)	the total of the values in the range of cells
TAN (*x*)	the tangent of the angle *x*

Cell overlap

In order to aid the readability of tables, some programs allow text entries to overlap blank cells to the right. This can prove particularly useful for headings.

Accounting functions

For accounting purposes, facilities are provided for net present value, future value, interest rate required, period of payment necessary and so on. It may also be useful to have a facility to multiply all the items in one list by corresponding items in another list and give a total of the products. (This is sometimes called the dot product.) Table look-up features allow a cell to have a value dependent on the range within which a value in another cell falls. This might be useful, for example, for the inclusion of different income tax band rates.

TASK

Give an example where the dot product would be useful.

Date features

Arithmetic can also be provided on dates, so that cells might contain dates in the form of day:month:year, but they can be subtracted to give the number of days between them. It might also be possible to strip off the day, the month or the year

Windowing can be used to show different parts of a spreadsheet which are relevant on the screen simultaneously

Mortgage repayments on a loan of £22 500 at 10% over 30 years

Year	Amount owing at start of year	Interest	Payment	Amount owing at end of year
1	22500.00	2250.00	2400.00	22350.00
2	22350.00	2235.00	2400.00	22185.00
3	22185.00	2218.50	2400.00	22003.50
4	22003.50	2200.35	2400.00	21803.85
5	21803.85	2180.39	2400.00	21584.24
6	21584.24	2158.42	2400.00	21342.66
7	21342.66	2134.27	2400.00	21076.93
8	21076.93	2107.69	2400.00	20784.62
28	4335.01	433.50	2400.00	2368.51
29	2368.51	236.85	2400.00	205.36
30	205.36	20.54	2400.00	−2175.10

A payment of £200 a month (£2400 a year) ensures that the capital is paid off in slightly under 30 years. This spreadsheet is most effective using windowing, so that year 1 and year 30 can be seen on the screen together; the values for intermediate years are of less interest.

part of a date for calculations. Some spreadsheets will even work out the day of the week from a date.

Screen splitting

Many spreadsheets allow the screen to be split in various ways. The simplest form is to allow either the first few rows or the first few columns to be designated as titles. These cells then stay in place when the cursor is moved, however far it goes to the right or downwards. This prevents the user losing track of the row or column in which entries should be made. For example, the first column could contain the months of the year, so that each row refers to a particular month. In normal circumstances, when moving several columns across, the first column would be lost. Using titles prevents this.

A development of titling is to allow several **windows** to be displayed on the screen at one time. Thus different parts of the worksheet which are related, but which are too far apart to be shown on the screen together, can be shown by allowing two or more smaller sections to be established. Thus a chosen part of the worksheet can be held on one part of the screen while other information is sought in another window. Such splitting can be achieved horizontally or vertically and some programs allow several windows to be created, typically eight. The cursor is manipulated in only one window at any one time and windows can be linked or synchronised, so that movement of the details in one window is reflected by an identical movement in another. This is useful when comparing lists of figures.

Capacities

The size of a worksheet can soon become quite large, particularly in cases where it is not rectangular (for example, where some columns have more rows than others). Different spreadsheets take different approaches to the internal storage of the models, the details of which need not bother the user. All but the least-sophisticated spreadsheets store only those cells with values which are not blank. Where storage space will be a crucial consideration for the user is in the backing storage used for the data relating to a particular situation. In normal circumstances, when the worksheet is stored, all the cell entries are saved. Where the same model is being used with different data, it may be more efficient on space to save simply the values entered for a particular situation, rather than having many copies of the same formulae.

TASK

Outline the extent to which you consider that the establishing of a worksheet for calculations on a spreadsheet should be classed as 'programming'. Suggest situations in which the application of spreadsheet models is preferable to the use of purpose-written software.

13.6. ADDITIONAL FEATURES

Copying a range

As well as being able to copy a single formula, some programs provide a facility to copy a range (or group) of cells. For example, it might be necessary to copy all the formulae in one column into the next eleven columns for the following months. Thus, it may be possible to specify a range of cells to be copied from a source to a destination. The destination might be specified as a range of cells which are the first cells of the target areas for the sets of formulae to be copied to. Provision might also be made to copy a rectangular block.

Graphics

The extent to which graphical output is available varies considerably. Some allow simple histograms to be made up of asterisks (*), so that, instead of displaying a number, a cell displays the number of asterisks. Other spreadsheets allow sophisticated graphics such as those normally associated with specialist graphics packages, providing bar charts, pie charts and line graphs using values in specified cells.

Sorting

Some spreadsheets provide routines which allow rows to be sorted into order according to the values in a particular column. This could be useful, for example, in producing a list of sales figures in descending order. Such manipulation will usually depend on the formulae being relative rather than absolute.

Cell locking

In order to protect cells containing complex formulae from being accidentally overwritten when data is being entered, cells can sometimes be protected. Protected cells might also contain details which the general user is not allowed access to for reasons of security. Protection can also speed data entry, as provision can be made to allow the user to move between data cells only. Individual cells or whole rows might be protected in this way. A feature is sometimes provided to lock all cells with formulae to avoid accidental changes.

Consolidation

A consolidation feature is one which allows several tables of identical type to be automatically added together, while the original data is kept intact. For example, similar statistics might be kept about each department within a company. This information might be totalled for summary purposes, but the data also held for each department for future use. Consolidation allows the totalling of the same cell in a number of different worksheets.

Goal seeking

A goal-seeking feature allows the choosing of values for various variables until a specified value is achieved for a particular cell. For this reason, it has been described as 'what if?' in reverse.

How to compare the different packages

Choice in this software area is particularly difficult and users of one particular system will advocate their choice as the best. As many spreadsheets are similar but not identical, there is a general reluctance amongst users to switch from one package to another.

In choosing an appropriate package for a particular organisation, a purchaser should first ensure that all the facilities which might be considered standard are provided. In addition, the package chosen should have the specialist features which might be desirable for the particular applications which are envisaged.

Purchasers should check that the spreadsheet under consideration runs under the operating system for the particular machine and that it is provided in the appropriate disc format. Other considerations will be the memory size required, the number of rows and columns provided and the limits on the number of cells used in any one model. For example, long thin spreadsheets might use more memory than fairly square ones.

Styles of user dialogues differ considerably between spreadsheets. Programs can be command driven or menu driven, or, most frequently, a combination of the two. The use of menus might be considered helpful by some, but to other users, the use of several levels of menus provided by some packages would be considered very tedious. It is crucial to remember that the level of user-friendliness is more important to the person entering data into the model and using the results than it is to the person who establishes the model at the very beginning. The user of a particular model will handle the worksheet over a longer timescale and may have considerable time gaps between each occasion of use.

Another important point of evaluation of spreadsheet software is to look at possible links with other software. It may be considered useful to incorporate the results of a spreadsheet calculation within a word processed report. Other spreadsheet programs contain database facilities which are a first step in the sharing within software packages of function areas which were previously considered to be distinct.

TASK

Pick three features of spreadsheet programs which you would not consider to be standard features. For each of these features, describe its implementation in a different piece of commercial software and illustrate a typical use of the feature.

13.7. CASE STUDY

A business might use a spreadsheet for its annual financial planning. The first step is to write down all the expenditure. This might be known in advance (for example, rent), or might have to be estimated (for example, telephone, salaries, purchases). Similarly, income can be estimated over various categories. Some of the amounts might not be known in advance, but very good estimates can be budgeted for based on previous experience.

A simple totalling of income and expenditure estimates might show an estimated profit over the year. This might not, however, reveal the whole picture. Depending upon how the various sums of income and expenditure fall within the year, there may be a point at which costs so far exceed income to date so that cash-flow problems will emerge. The projected cash flow can be analysed by drawing up a worksheet with the months as the columns and the categories of income and expenditure as the various rows. By placing income and expenditure within the column for which they are expected, a month-by-month picture can be prepared.

Once particular crisis points in cash flow have been identified, steps can be taken to postpone payment or bring forward receipts to cope with the situation. Such an analysis can therefore save considerable worry and probable expense for overdrafts. It can also be used as part of a business plan in discussions with bank managers, as it gives a clear picture of long-term strategy. Cash-flow analysis can also be used to minimise the amount held in a current account, so that money can be used to increase interest on investment.

13.8. WHERE TO FIND OUT MORE

As with much software, the two main sources of general information about a wide range of packages are brochures and magazines.

Many of the brochures are well produced and often include worked examples of the use of spreadsheets. These are worthy of study, even if the choice of an example renders the details of limited use in other applications. Readers should draw out general points from such material.

Specialist magazines contain reviews of new software and as new spreadsheets come on to the market, these are compared with current market leaders. Case studies in magazines might describe the benefits to be gained from the use of spreadsheet software as well as the detail of what is done and how.

Practical use of a number of different spreadsheets will help the user to appreciate both the general features of spreadsheets and the particular specialist facilities of each program used.

As it was the first on the market, there have been several books written about VisiCalc. These vary both in the background knowledge assumed of the reader and in the number of worked examples.

There have also appeared recently a number of books on the more powerful CP/M and MS-DOS based spreadsheet programs.

13.9. STUDY QUESTIONS

1 Explain the two senses in which the term **window** is used in the context of spreadsheets.
2 Why do spreadsheets have a limit on the number of rows and columns allowed?
3 How could a spreadsheet be useful in the process of costing out a potential computer system for purchase?

13.10. ASSIGNMENTS

1 Describe how each of the following people could use spreadsheets to help them to do their job:

   (a) an accountant,
   (b) a dentist,
   (c) a cricket captain.

2 Using a spreadsheet program of your choice, build a model suitable for the analysis of the following situation.

A traffic survey is carried out at a four-way junction to determine the kinds of traffic manoeuvres taking place at the junction. The initial direction of travel (into the junction), and the final direction of travel (out of the junction) are recorded. The results are tabulated as follows:

		Final direction			
		North	East	South	West
	North	x	x	x	x
Initial	East	x	x	x	x
direction	South	x	x	x	x
	West	x	x	x	x

A

450	100	0	150
140	476	97	0
0	155	444	121
100	0	160	430

B

200	140	0	170
150	210	155	0
0	154	233	167
177	0	166	250

C

370	50	0	130
122	333	65	0
0	100	322	77
88	0	100	400

(Note that nobody will do a U-turn, so some entries will be zero!) Construct a spreadsheet based on this information, and then use the information to answer the following questions.

(a) What percentage of traffic travels straight through the junction?
(b) What percentage of traffic performs right turns?
(c) What percentage of traffic initially travelling east or west performs a right turn?

Use the information to compare the traffic situations at the following three junctions.

3 What might be the benefits of the use of a spreadsheet by a leisure centre manager? (What sort of 'what if?' questions can be asked?) How might the manager of a leisure centre be persuaded of the benefits of using a spreadsheet? (A description of particular applications is not required. What should be given is a set of details of presentations to be given to convince the manager.)

14 USING GRAPHICS

We are constantly surrounded by visual images; posters, shop windows and traffic signs try to grab our attention in the street. At home we are assailed both on television and in the newspapers by what is termed 'graphics'.

In recent years, computer technology has been harnessed to aid in the presentation of images, both in commercial art and in the board rooms of companies. The old cliché that 'a picture paints a thousand words' has been applied to the often wordy area of business communication. Information can be presented to staff, shareholders and customers in a visual way to make the important facts readily digestible.

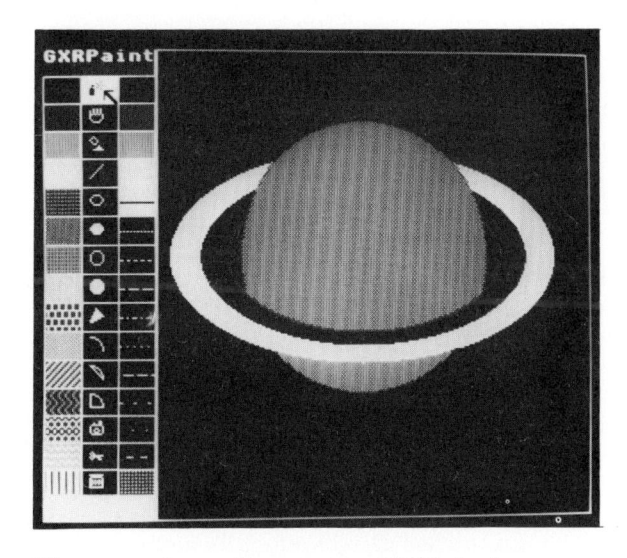

The screen of a graphics program: GXRPaint from Acornsoft

Thus customers are shown a comparison between one car and another by means of a graph, shareholders are shown a company's share of the market by showing a comparison with competitors' slices of the cake and every cartoon of a businessman seems to have a line graph on the wall as a shorthand way of telling the reader that business is booming or slumping.

14.1. TAKING A LOOK AT GRAPHICS

A clearer picture emerges of the way in which graphics are used in business when the applications are broken down into three main areas. Software providing graphics can be:

(a) analytical,
(b) an aid to drawing,
(c) an aid to presentation.

These three areas will now be discussed in more detail.

Graphics in analysis

Graphics packages have enabled the development of extensions to commercial packages such as spreadsheets. A number of graphical forms of display such as pie charts and bar charts are now provided by many spreadsheet programs. A computation is performed on a series of numbers in a table and from this a table of results is drawn up. Such summaries can be more readily understood and more meaningfully illustrated visually. Thus a graphics aspect to a spreadsheet might be described as a 'user interface' for the analysis; the primary purpose of the software, however, remains that analysis.

When the original data is changed in such circumstances, all the graphics will be redrawn. This can save significant work if the analysis is complex.

Graphical drawing aids

The use of computers as a tool in design work has made rapid steps forward in recent years. Computer aided design has many applications in engineering, where designs may have to be redrawn or adapted. The work in making major or minor changes to a specification, which used to take a skilled draughtsman a few days, can now be completed in a matter of minutes. This has opened up the potential in design for people to ask 'what if?' questions and hence to experiment with and evaluate a number of possibilities.

In a similar way, computerised design tools are used in architecture and town planning, so that projected schemes can be viewed from a number of angles, using three-dimensional techniques. Designs can be adapted and reworked when this is considered useful. Buildings can be demolished, erected or redesigned – all on the computer screen.

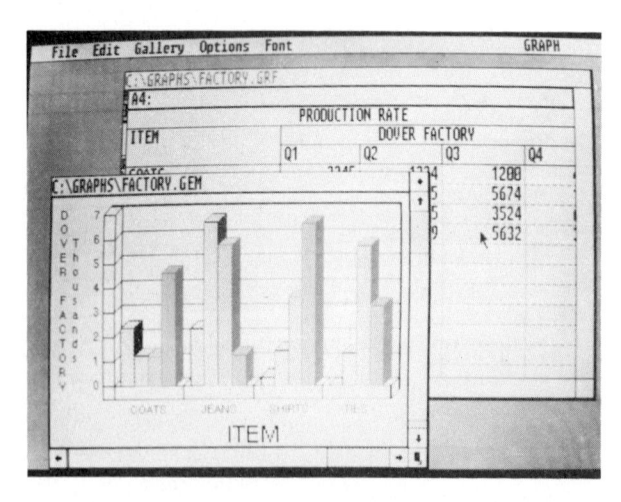

A multiple bar chart and the data which lies behind it: GEM Graph from Digital Research

Such drawing aids find a wide range of applications, each having its own specialised terminology and software. Thus design programs exist for piping design, map drawing and so on.

Presentation graphics

Computer graphics can also be used to present data in a way which grabs the attention. Thus, on television, graphics are increasingly used for the news, the weather and current affairs programmes. In many companies, computerised techniques are being used to present data in a clear and unambiguous form. A good visual presentation can be used to attract customers, to inform managers or shareholders or to train staff.

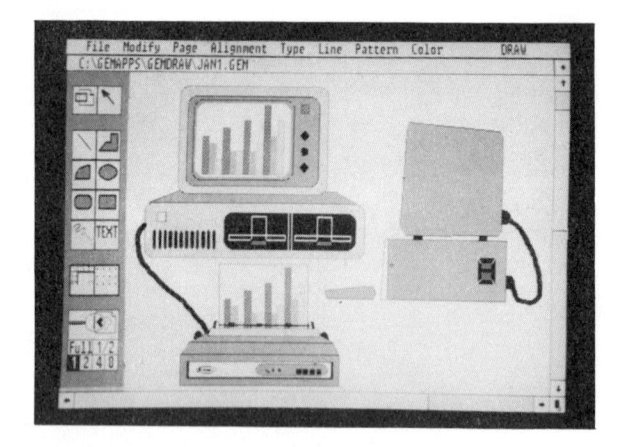

A drawing package, which can be used to create plans, layouts and diagrams: GEM Draw from Digital Research

The presentation of information within a business organisation can go well beyond that of numeric data. Diagrams can be used to show how parts of an organisation relate together, or how a project is planned over a period of time, and can make use of colour to show how a situation will change over time.

When a business presentation is to be given, programs can be provided which allow a series of displays to be put up on a large screen. Alternatively, specialised devices can be used to make transparency slides from computer displays, which provides a more portable resource for presentations.

A visual presentation of information can be useful to give an overall impression of a situation, which the presenter of a talk or report can then draw on in filling in the detail. Alternatively, graphics can be used to get information across which, because of a mass of detail, is difficult to absorb. A typical illustration is the use of a pie chart in preference to a table of figures. It is easier to see that a slice is small than it is to work out that a numerical value is small, particularly if the number has several decimal places.

The advantages of the use of design programs for presentation graphics over the previous use of commercial artists include the speed with which up-to-date information can be turned into a slide and the ease with which different ideas (such as the colours or sizes to be used) can be experimented with.

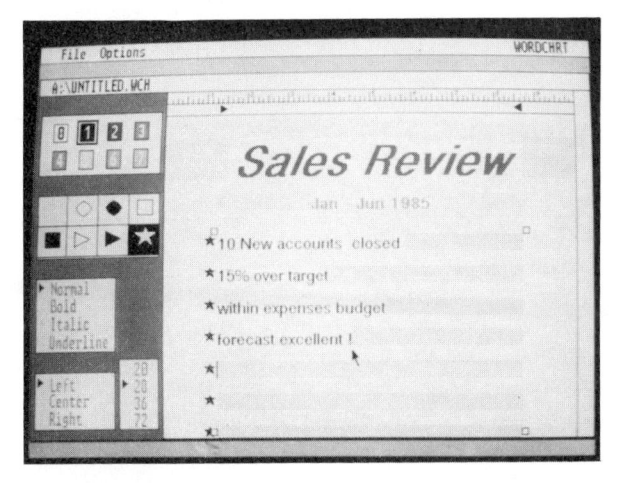

A package for producing professional-looking slides: GEM Wordchart from Digital Research

TASK

Analyse the features of three graphics packages of which you can get details. Work out which of the three categories the packages fall under or whether they cover parts of more than one of the functions.

14.2. A PICTURE OF WHAT CAN BE DONE

The image of graphics has always been that it is a specialised area with its own jargon and complex calculations separate from the mainstream of computer usage. This, if it were ever true, does not need to be the case any longer. The processing which lies behind the specification of a curve sketching program or a three-dimensional rotation might be complex, but the statement of a particular situation to be analysed need not be. Thus, while what is done is complex, saying what is wanted can be made simple.

These claims are particularly true when it comes to using light pens, graphics tablets and mice. These are all simple to operate, even if sophisticated techniques are needed to use their inputs within programs.

The term 'image processing' has been coined to cover all the areas of graphics handling and manipulation. This draws out an analogy with word processing, which can be pursued further when thinking about 'cut and paste' techniques, the re-use of identical material, and the adaptation of several drafts of an idea. These concepts apply equally to image processing and word processing.

Of the many forms of images which can be produced on a computer screen most can be used in each of the three areas already sketched above. The techniques and styles of presentation can be applied where appropriate.

Histograms, bar charts and pictograms

For statistical presentation, there are a number of standard types of diagram, which have for many years been produced by hand. **Histograms** and **bar charts** use strips, the length of which represents the value of that particular category. It is usual to make the strips different colours for clarity. Histograms and bar charts are useful for spotting

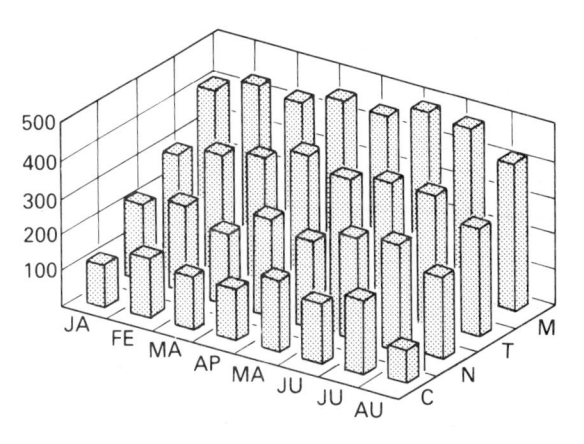

A simple three-dimensional bar graph, showing sales over eight months in each of four areas: Open Access from Software Products International

exceptions to the norm, as it is easy to see comparative sizes. There is a technical difference between the two techniques. A histogram represents by the area of a bar the amount recorded within the range indicated along the bottom axis, whereas a bar chart is used where there are only a limited number of possible values along the horizontal axis. In other words, the bar chart is used for a discrete variable rather than a continuous one.

A variation on the bar chart is the **pictogram**, where a set of pictures of objects of the same size is placed in a line, the number of the objects for each category representing the value. Both bar charts and pictograms can be used either horizontally or vertically. A **stacked bar chart** or **component bar chart** is one in which each bar is made up of a set number of clearly distinguished parts. In this case, colour or a variety of forms of shading must be used.

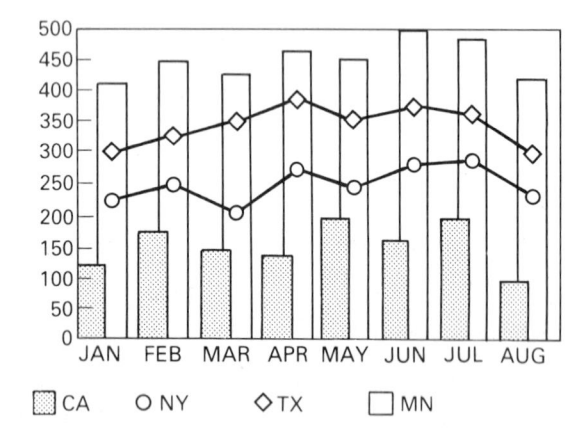

A combined line and bar graph: Open Access from Software Products International

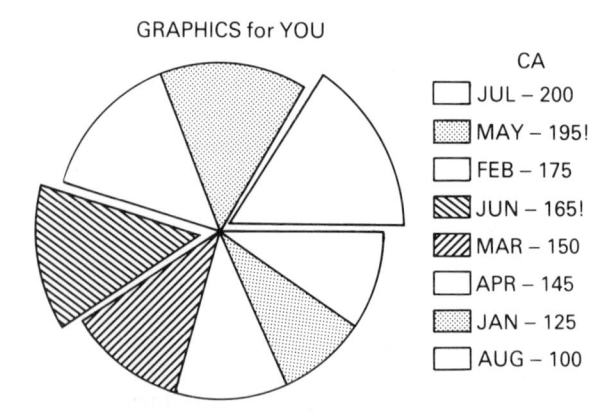

An exploded pie chart: Open Access from Software Products International

Pie charts

A **pie chart** is used to represent data where the proportion of something to the whole is important. A circular pie is drawn, and is cut up into slices, each slice representing a category. Each slice is labelled appropriately. An **exploded pie chart** is one in which one slice, normally the largest, is slightly removed from the pie for emphasis. A **solid pie chart** is one in which the pie is presented in three dimensions, although the thickness of the pie is constant and is simply included to improve presentation.

Line graphs and scatter graphs

A **line graph** is based on the traditional $x-y$ graph. The horizontal (x) axis is often used to denote the passage of time. The values of the variable along the vertical (y) axis are used to determine the position at which a point should be plotted. These points are then joined up by straight lines. From such a graph, it is easy to spot a trend. It is also common to show several line graphs on common set of axes, each line being a different colour. A **compound line graph** is used to show a breakdown of the total being plotted on the vertical axis into a number of categories. In other words, there are several y values for each x value. In this case, the areas between lines can be shaded to emphasise the totals within each category. Another variation is the **high–low chart**, which has a vertical line at each position across the horizontal axis. This can be used to represent the range of possibilities at each point, that is, a line showing the values beteen the most optimistic and the most pessimistic possibilities.

Scatter graphs present a set of pairs of variable values, plotted as points. From such a drawing, any correlation between the two variables can be spotted or investigated. Some packages which have a statistical emphasis will provide a facility for drawing the best straight line through the points. In a similar manner, packages of a more mathematical nature provide a feature which will plot the best curve of a particular type through a set of points.

Library pictures

When drawings are to be made, whether of buildings or of electronic circuits or a host of other things, complex pictures are often built out of a number of standard elements, different in each case. Thus many image processing programs allow the building up of a library of commonly used images or symbols, which can then be selected and placed as appropriate. Much software is issued with a standard library of such pictures, sometimes called a chartbook of designs. This can then be added to. Many libraries of pictures are produced for sale, either by the software manufacturer or by a third party. These libraries might contain anything from detailed street maps of major towns to a range of views of office furniture. The more flexible software allows such images to be copied and moved around the screen to suit circumstances.

A change of image

Parts of pictures can be changed and adapted using graphics software, so that an area of a picture can be magnified or reduced and placed on another part of the screen. Pictures can be rotated about a point or reflected in a line or moved horizontally and vertically. Interesting and useful effects can be achieved by magnifying part of a picture in one direction more than another, and even shearing a copy by distorting vertical lines away from the vertical.

Many of these image manipulation processes are based on the programs looking on the area of an existing picture simply as a set of points which are then mapped through the manipulation on to points on a new area. Thus direct copies, rotations, magnifications and so on are all done by a painstaking examination of the source area for the image, a more or less complicated calculation, and an amendment of the memory corresponding to the target area.

Another common feature is **rubber banding**, which shows a line from the last point plotted to the current cursor position. This line then moves as the cursor moves, so that in a new position it will join the new cursor point to the last point plotted. This can be useful when moving the cursor to a particular spot, as it shows what a line will look like before it is permanently plotted.

Three-dimensional drawing

Much of the software for drawing three-dimensional shapes uses a technique known as **wire-frame**. Using this method, shapes are shown with a line representing each edge. To represent a curved surface or some other surface which is not flat, extra lines are drawn in to give an overall impression of the shape. Lines which represent surfaces which cannot be seen by the viewer are still shown. Software can be obtained which provides a **hidden line** feature to obliterate such surfaces, or which introduces **shading** to emphasise a three-dimensional shape, but these techniques will tend to be slower and more expensive. To gain an overall impression of a view, wire-framing may be sufficient. Much software also provides features which allow **perspective** drawing, which is essential for most serious drawing work.

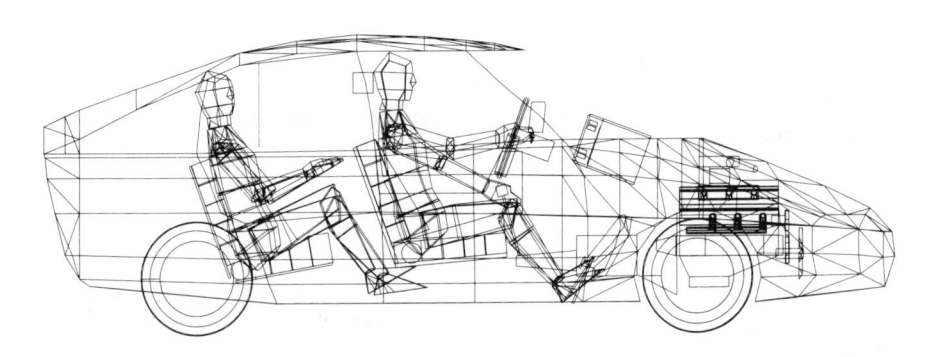

A wire-frame diagram produced using SAMMIE, a human factors CAD system from Prime Computers Inc

Colour filling

Within diagrams, shapes might be filled with colour. The methods for this sometimes work on an ink-blot principle, with colour spreading out from a point which the user specifies until it reaches lines (not necessarily straight ones) on all sides. Alternatively, every point on the screen is tested to see if it is within the shape, in which case the shape is filled from the top.

Chart drawing

Visual methods are also used in a number of specialist forms, such as flowcharts and project planning charts. Such uses usually call for specialist software, or at least the purchase of a specialised library of symbols.

Text on diagrams

All good diagrams are improved with text and a key to explain them, particularly in the case of pie charts and bar charts. Graphics software will allow the user to specify text in a number of different sizes and fonts (typestyles), with different letter spacing and at different angles to the horizontal. This can be particularly useful when labelling the vertical axis. Different sizes, styles and colours of letters can be used to associate groups of words together.

TASK
Write down a list of desirable features of a graphics program for use by an accountant who deals with the finances of six different departments of a local authority.

14.3. A GRAPHIC DESCRIPTION OF WHAT TO DO

A typical graphical package will have to receive the data which is to be represented. This might be input in one of three ways:

(a) directly from the keyboard,
(b) from a file which is output from another package (there are a number of standard formats for this which many packages will accept),
(c) as a result of another part of the package which is providing a number of other features (such as an integrated package).

Data entry from the keyboard might enable the user to specify a number of variables (typically up to 12) and a number of 'points' which have values for each variable (typically up to 60). It will then be possible to plot any variable against any other variable.

It can be very inconvenient if data cannot be amended within a package. A particular frustration occurs when data is transferred from another package and is found to be slightly incorrect. It is very wasteful if the only means of changing the data is to go back to the original package to alter the data to create a new file to be read in again once the graphics program has been re-loaded!

Packages might provide a number of features for layout, such as being able to specify the location on the screen for the origin of a graph and being able to choose a scale. Alternatively, the user can request that this is done automatically for each picture. The choice of units in which axes are marked and the multiple use of axes for bar charts and line graphs might also be catered for.

Packages can vary considerably in their processing speed. A good test of speed is to monitor the time which a package takes to change a display in one graphical format to a different one when the figures remain the same.

TASK
For a graphics program of your own choice, write down all the features which you feel could be usefully added, giving reasons and examples of their possible use.

14.4. THE TOOLS TO DRAW ON

The user-friendliness of software has improved in leaps and bounds with the widespread availability of the mouse. This hand-held device can be moved around a table and software can be made to reflect this movement with a marker on the screen, often an arrow. One or more buttons is provided on the mouse so that facilities can be chosen from a list, or in the case of a graphics program, a point can be specified. Through combinations of operations on the buttons, a user is able to draw lines and curves as required.

Similar claims are also made for the use of light pens, which are pointed at the screen and for touch screens which can be used for selection. Light pens have the advantage that parts of a drawing can be pointed to by the user very quickly and accurately. Critics point out that the movement of the body required to use light pens and touch screens is clumsy and can become stressful.

The VDU screens used in any form of graphics work would normally have to be of the high resolution type, so that pictures are crisp and clear. Lines must be easily distinguished and curved lines must be very smooth to produce a pleasant appearance. Many audiences will react unfavourably if artwork appears to be computer generated. It is interesting to note the reverse effect, that when artwork is to be produced to appear 'computer like', some programs will simply produce too good a product to have the desired effect. It must also be remembered that high resolution means that larger quantities of computer memory are used to store the picture and that files containing data for pictures will consequently be bigger as well.

TASK
Explain why a high-resolution display needs more computer memory.

When considering the use of a graphics system in a business, it is also important to consider the form of hard copy which is to be produced. In some instances monochrome dot matrix output will be sufficient. In other cases, colour printers might be used or ink jet printers can be considered on the grounds of the noise level. For large-scale accurate drawing, plotters have been and continue to be very popular. Pictures might be printed sideways on a matrix printer, as the need is often for a picture with landscape rather than portrait layout, as this echoes the shape of the screen.

TASK
Explain why it might be helpful to print a draft diagram on a matrix printer, but to then produce a final copy using a different peripheral.

In some cases, the printout will be a bit-by-bit dump of the contents of the screen, but this need not be the case. Some software both stores and prints a drawing as a set of 'logical objects', remembering how the shape was originally formed. Thus a circle will be remembered not as a set of points of a particular colour, but as data representing its centre, its radius and its colour. The recording of shapes and text in this form can enable the hard copy output generated to reflect more accurately what was required than the screen can represent with its fixed resolution.

14.5. A LINE MUST BE DRAWN

It is a very common temptation among users of image processing software to attempt to use every available feature in every piece of work. There are limits to the amount that the viewer will be able to take in and thus special effects must be used with caution, lest familiarity breeds contempt. A many-coloured screen with several colours of flashing text and boxes full of lots of interesting information will become too much. Techniques should be chosen carefully.

Particular colours have been found to go together well, such as yellow with blue. A limited number of colours ought to be used, a maximum of seven may be best – the colours of the rainbow have been found to produce an appealing and creative contrast. Users should avoid the temptation to show off every time that their machine can display sixteen different colours at once.

The eye finds it relatively more difficult to pick up thin lines drawn in blue or yellow; these colours are more suitable for blocks of colour. In choosing colours, it is worth bearing in mind that a significant proportion of people are colour blind, confusing particularly red and green. Having said this, however, it is sometimes useful to exploit the natural association of red for danger and green for positive. Stronger, more eye-catching colours can be used to encourage users to pick out particular significant details. This might be used effectively, for instance, to highlight particular items within a set of accounts on a screen. Accounts can be shown to be literally 'in the red'!

Statistics are treated with suspicion by many people and this is often based on their experience of the distortion of the presentation of statistics. The use of computers to present statistics is not immune from such distortion. Indeed, the user of computerised statistical presentations should be aware that the use of a computer can give extra credibility to the figures in the minds of members of an audience. At times, this can degenerate into the listeners being 'blinded by science'.

Typical distortions of presentation can include the use of non-zero base-lines to graphs and the use of non-linear scales. Both of these techniques are valid, and can be useful, but they should be pointed out clearly. Some diagrams depend on the comparison of areas, which can give a deceptive impression. Other presentations give all the different rivals' information in a single dull dolour and then one particular firm's in an eye-catching colour, such as red. Another deliberate distortion is to present too much information for people to take in in the hope that attention will be captured by part of the display which is subtly highlighted in some way.

TASK

Suggest some advantages and disadvantages for a graphics package of:

(a) being menu-driven,
(b) having a 'help' feature.

14.6. CASE STUDY

'Energraphics' is a menu-driven graphics package for the IBM PC and compatibles, as well as Wang and Texas models. It combines business graphics facilities with 2D graphics design and 3D CAD (computer aided design). It supports a wide range or printers and plotters and can be used in conjunction with the 'Polaroid Palette' system to produce 35 mm transparencies and prints in twenty seconds.

The manufacturers claim that the software can combine a number of the features generally associated with different graphics applications. 'Energraphics' can be used by marketing and communications staff to illustrate presentations and to personalise business graphics, using logos and so on. Engineers, architects and programmers can improve productivity in drawing applications, from circuit diagrams to mechanical design to organisation charts. Statisticians, technical authors and artists can also find features of particular benefit to them.

For a basic price of under £500 (1987 rates), which includes software to drive plotters, the user gets a package capable of drawing pie charts with up to fifteen slices. Several of these can be exploded if necessary and the slices can include percentage indicators. Line charts can contain up to 200 points per line, and up to ten lines per chart. Up to four y scales can be included on a graph, and curves can be fitted through points. Linear and polynomial regression can be carried out, up to order 10. Additional features are provisions for the use of log scaling and of scatter graphs.

Bar chart features include the drawing of 2D or 3D charts, either horizontally or vertically. Charts can be multiple (showing several bars in each position starting at the base), or stacked (where several categories are compounded at each position). Up to ten graphs can be shown on one set of scales, and up to four y scales can be used.

As well as receiving data from the keyboard, it can also be accepted from files output in the DIF format produced by such packages as Visicalc, Lotus 1-2-3 and Multiplan.

The 2D drawing feature allows objects to be drawn using function keys for cursor movement as a drawing tool. Scaling and rotation and line thickness can also be controlled using the keyboard. Symbols for a library of up to 2280 shapes can be generated on a dot matrix grid.

The 3D features are described as being 'state of the art' CAD, including features of zooming, rotating, hidden line removal and duplication. Shapes can have up to twenty thousand points. Planes can be translated, revolved and rotation about an axis of revolution can be achieved.

The package includes an A5 manual (fast becoming an industry standard), a tutorial, some sample data, and is supported by a regular newsletter.

TASK

Read through brochures for three commonly available packages, one from each of the areas of analytical graphics, drawing aids and presentation graphics. Draw up a table contrasting aspects of the packages such as hardware requirements, cost, add-on facilities, ideas about the market that the brochures are aimed at, main features provided and any other details which you consider relevant.

Run a graphics package to which you have access and use it to present some of the features of the packages which you identified.

14.7. WHERE TO FIND OUT MORE

The needs of one user of graphics software can differ greatly from the next person's. In this way, image processing differs significantly from word processing. In seemingly very different applications, users of word processors often have remarkably similar needs, as all are dealing with words. In the image processing field, however, users require very different kinds of images. Some will want to be able to specify and draw a wide range of geometric shapes, others will want to draw free-hand and others still will want large libraries of standard pictures. Thus graphics software must be chosen very carefully, with a limited number of applications in mind.

Thus, one user might give glowing reports of a particular package's use, but if it does not suit the particular needs of another situation, it may be far from ideal. In some specialist areas, such as computer aided design (CAD), there are a number of specialist magazines on the market, which give details of the features of many of the CAD packages.

A number of firms specialise in the sale of both hardware and software for the preparation of presentation graphics, such as slide shows. Their products include cameras as well as computers. Literature from such firms is interesting and well presented (not surprisingly).

A number of the modern 'do it all' integrated packages, which combine several software tasks, are beginning to incorporate several graphical output features. These again are worthy of a closer look.

14.8. STUDY QUESTIONS

1   In what ways might the graphics provided by analytical software differ from that in presentation software?
2   In what circumstances would a pie chart be preferable to a bar chart for a presentation?
3   When the points on a line graph are joined up, what do the intermediate points between the plotted points represent?
4   Why might the shading of a large area on a screen take a considerable time?
5   Why can a plotter draw a circle more accurately than it can be displayed on a screen?

14.9. ASSIGNMENTS

1   How could cartoonists make use of graphics packages? Write a report detailing the criteria which a cartoonist could use when choosing a graphics package.
2   Write a report on the changes that the use of computer aided drawing has made to engineering firms, in particular describing the effect on the range of products produced, the size of production runs, profitability and so on.
3   As a computer consultant, you have been asked to write a report on image processing by a landscape gardener, whose job it is to suggest possible designs for laying out formal gardens for parks and stately homes in consultation with their owners. Your report should be presented with a formal structure and should recommend three packages which the landscape gardener could consider.

15 INTEGRATED SOFTWARE

15.1. THE PURPOSE OF INTEGRATED PACKAGES

The idea of an integrated package is that it provides a number of functions normally associated with separate packages, such as a spreadsheet, a database and a word processor, all as part of a single product.

15.2. 'LET'S PUT IT ALL TOGETHER'

Integrated packages have thus been marketed by their manufacturers as 'the only program you will ever need'. Among the advantages of linking of packages in this way are:

(a) a reduction in cost to the purchaser,
(b) the use of similar styles in different parts of the package,
(c) the transfer of data from one application to another.

Such packages are competitively priced compared to buying a number of separate packages, though are usually somewhat more expensive than one package carrying out a single function.

The uniformity of command styles, such as the use of similar menus and wording in different parts of a program can aid users in widening the range of software that they can use. However, a user does not have to learn all the commands before starting to use part of the package. The transfer of data between application areas reduces the problems and frustration involved in attempting to transfer material from, say, a spreadsheet into a word processed document.

15.3. EXAMPLES OF INTEGRATED PACKAGES

One of the earliest integrated packages was Lotus 1-2-3. This brought together the functions of a spreadsheet, a database and graphics. At first sight, it looks like a spreadsheet, but it is possible to treat rows as records in a database, with the columns representing the fields. Data can also be converted into display graphics. The speed of calculation is impressive; all the data is held in internal memory.

Recent trends in integrated software design have been:

(a) combining more features traditionally associated with separate packages,
(b) providing more options within these parts,
(c) enabling more flexible links between the parts of the package.

Though it was rightly hailed as a major breakthrough at the time, 1-2-3 lacks a word processing feature. Lotus put this right with the launch of Symphony, which has more features than 1-2-3 in each of the application areas, plus word

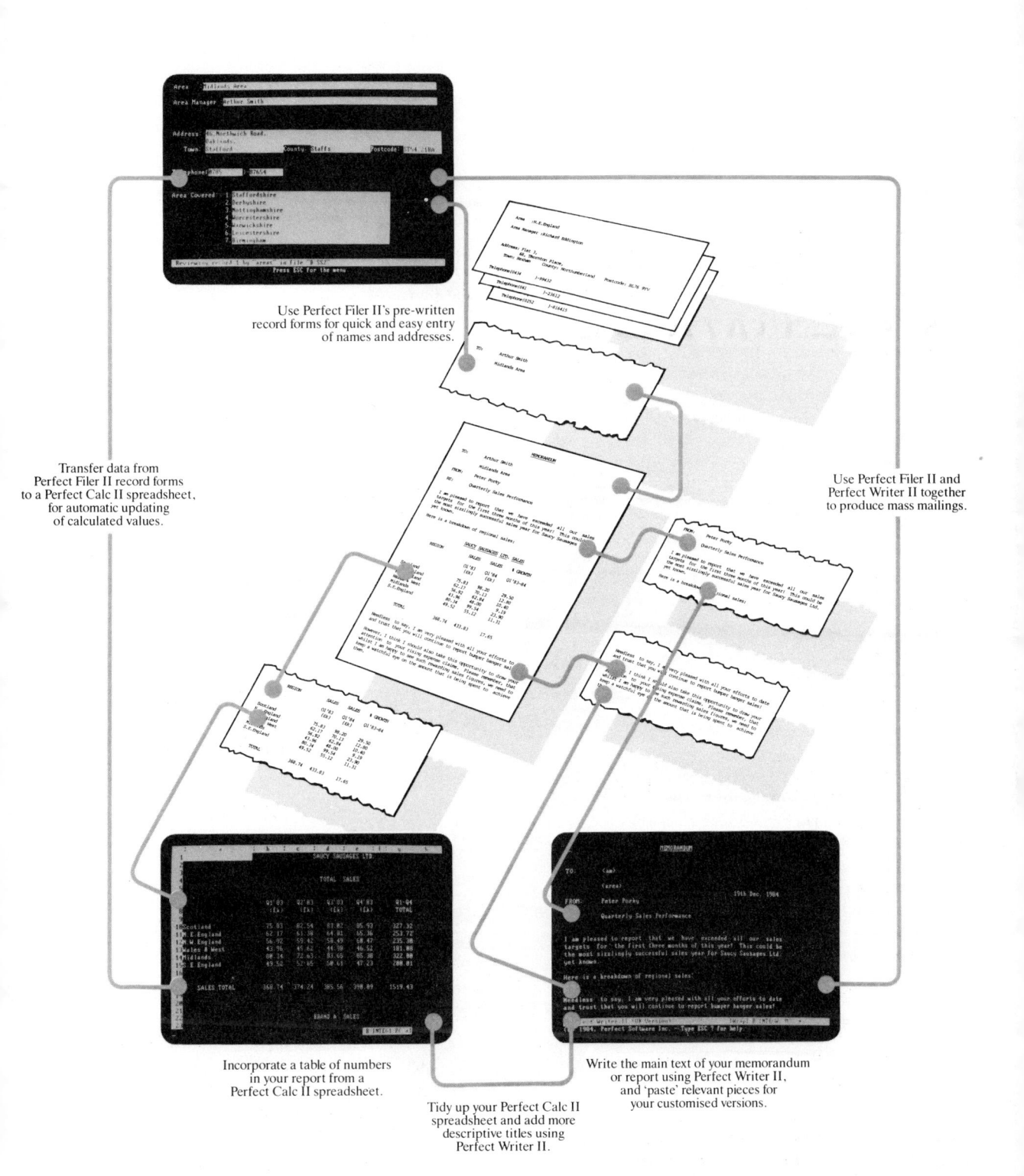

Use Perfect Filer II's pre-written record forms for quick and easy entry of names and addresses.

Transfer data from Perfect Filer II record forms to a Perfect Calc II spreadsheet, for automatic updating of calculated values.

Use Perfect Filer II and Perfect Writer II together to produce mass mailings.

Incorporate a table of numbers in your report from a Perfect Calc II spreadsheet.

Tidy up your Perfect Calc II spreadsheet and add more descriptive titles using Perfect Writer II.

Write the main text of your memorandum or report using Perfect Writer II, and 'paste' relevant pieces for your customised versions.

Links between database, spreadsheet and word processor: Perfect Filer II, Perfect Calc II and Perfect Writer II from Thorn EMI Computer Software

processing and facilities for communications from the computer to other computers, through a communications window.

Other integrated packages incorporate databases which can handle several files at once, spreadsheets which include a 'goal seeking' feature, 3D graphics, and time management (diary-like) features.

15.4. FEATURES OF INTEGRATED PACKAGES

Manufacturers have continued to add further, previously separate software functions to integrated packages. This is an attempt to provide a more comprehensive service to users (so that it is more likely to be the only software you will ever need) and to provide a unique product in a quickly expanding and competitive market-place.

Features which are 'essential'

In a fast-changing area of the market, definitions change quickly as well. Thus some computer practitioners would claim that there are four essential features of an integrated package. These are a spreadsheet, a database, graphics and word processing. It is true that many modern packages include these four areas, but from the continuing high sales of Lotus 1-2-3 it is clear that to many people its three features are sufficient. Attempts at rigid definitions of what constitutes an integrated package are not very fruitful. They say nothing of the quality of the individual parts of the package, which, combined with the flexibility of links between the parts, is what matters to users.

Other desirable features

Extra features beyond what is considered a minimum are desirable if they will be used and exploited. If they are not used, they are simply an unnecessary overhead in terms of cost, speed of operation, disc space and memory space. In choosing a package in this area more than in any other, it is important to be very clear as to what the precise requirements are.

Features which can be included in integrated packages are:

(a) **A spreadsheet** incorporating some or all of the features of modern spreadsheets.

(b) **A database** with features previously described under the heading 'databases', plus an ability to transfer data, to, say, a spreadsheet.

(c) **Business graphics** in their own right or as a means of displaying the results of spreadsheet calculations.

(d) **Word processing** with many typical word processing commands and features allowing the incorporation of output from spreadsheets, databases or graphics into reports.

(e) **Time management** allowing the entry of details of meetings or jobs to be done, which can be sorted in time or priority order, displayed by the month, by the week or by the day. Regular appointments can be included by a single entry. Charges for time spent on work for particular clients might be calculated from this data.

(f) **Statistics** allowing a range of 'number crunching' features for the analysis of data.

(g) **Communications** allowing the computer to link with other machines by a process known as terminal emulation. This ensures that the machine receiving messages gets them in the format (or protocol) which it expects and that its signals back can also be interpreted. Thus information can be transferred in or out of the package. This can be used for anything from electronic mail to looking up data on share prices. A communications module might also incorporate auto-dialling features, providing a means of remembering telephone numbers so that numbers can be called repeatedly until a line is free. This could include sending messages overnight, even when an operator is not present.

TASK

Draw up lists of features which you might expect to find in a typical word processor, a typical spreadsheet and so on. Choose an integrated package, preferably one that you can try out on a computer. Check off the lists of features to see whether the integrated package provides all the features in each part that you might expect.

15.5. TYPES OF INTEGRATED PACKAGES

There are two main forms which integration takes:

(a) Some integrated packages consist of one large 'monolothic' program with a large range of features which is held permanently in memory.
(b) Other integrated packages consist of a series of separate but related programs called 'modules', which are loaded from the discs when particular features are needed. The user will be prompted to change discs when it is necessary.

Those who favour monolithic programs argue that disc swapping can be tiresome, particularly if a program is spread over six discs. One problem with the large program, however, is the huge amount of internal memory required to hold both the program and the data.

An advantage of the modular approach is that the parts of the package might be sold as a series of separate modules, which can be acquired and linked together as they are needed. This means that an organisation need buy only those elements of a system which are appropriate to its processing requirements or its financial commitments.

Other paths towards linking packages

In other circumstances, any integration which is necessary is achieved through an operating system which allows such features as windowing. Some computer practitioners believe that this path will be more fruitful in the long term, as it allows the user to choose to link particular favourite or suitable packages. Another path towards linking different packages is through common file formats, so that one program can read the files produced by another program. Examples of such file conventions are DIF (used by Visicalc) and SYLK (used in Microsoft products). Indeed, some packages are now available which will read 'most' common formats and will produce results in 'most' formats.

TASK

Set up a simple application in an integrated package, for example, having a spreadsheet accessing data from 20 different records in a database. Then alter a single entry in the database and measure the time taken for the change to be reflected in the spreadsheet. If possible, compare the performance of an all-in-one package, a family set of programs and an arrangement of separate packages using common file formats. Include in your calculations the time it takes you to swap discs.

15.6. WHAT INTEGRATED PACKAGES DO BETTER

Integrated packages are particularly useful for linking features which are normally associated with different software areas. Thus, for example, a set of names and addresses and other details about clients can be held in a database format. This database can then be used, with selection and sorting as appropriate, and linked to a word processed document. Thus, all the selected clients get a personalised letter, which could include details of their current account status from the database. This links the power of database manipulation to the flexibility of a mailing list feature.

Another example of linking separate functions is the reading in of up-to-date currency rates from a central computer service and the linking of these values to spreadsheet calculations for an accurate and up-to-date picture. If such links are made permanent, this data can be updated daily or even more regularly, with the only effort being that of initiating the transfer each time.

Avoiding duplication of effort

On the most straightforward level, the linking of separate software areas avoids the need for re-entry of data, say from a spreadsheet into a word processed document. Re-entry has the drawback that there is a waste of time and duplication of effort. It is also possible that errors and inconsistencies will be introduced, even with copy typing. The linking of software areas has the positive advantage that permanent links might be arranged. This will then mean that when the spreadsheet, for example, is changed, the word processed document is changed to reflect this.

It is also possible with integrated packages to establish a common style of layout for reports. Conventions can be established for the use of headings, page titles, page length, page width, page numbering and so on. With separate packages, this would all have to be done at least once for each package, perhaps in quite different ways each time.

From this point of view, from that point of view

Integrated packages can allow the user to have a number of different views of the same data, which can be very useful when data has to be manipulated in a number of different ways. One minute it can be viewed as a row of a spreadsheet for a complex calculation, the next as a record in a database for a selection test and the next as a line in a word processed document for a spelling check.

Many integrated packages allow the same data to be viewed in more than one way at the same time, by use of windows. Thus a pie chart can be produced which shows diagrammatically the result of complex spreadsheet calculations and this can be included in a word processed report with some of the important figures. When the figures on which this calculation is based are altered, this change can be reflected in the appropriate parts of the report. By using windows on the screen this change can take place 'before your very eyes'.

15.7. WHERE INTEGRATED PACKAGES ARE CRITICISED

When choosing software which is linked in this way, it is important to investigate what is actually provided in the system. It is easy for the purchaser, particularly the first-time user, to be impressed by a bombardment of different features of the ways in which an integrated package links various parts together. Integrated packages differ considerably in the links which can be made between various parts.

Thus, it may be possible to link from the database into the spreadsheet, but can the spreadsheet be linked into the database? In order to get graphics output from data held within the database, can this be done directly, or must data first be transferred to the spreadsheet? With the large range of features available in each previously separate software areas, the number of potential links between them is huge. Potential purchasers should consider very carefully to what uses the software is to be put, and therefore what links are needed.

TASK

Give three examples of the way that the linking of data from a database into a spreadsheet could be used by a small business.

15.8. FEATURES WITHIN EACH PART

Some would describe an integrated package as a 'jack of all trades'. Others quote back the other half of the proverb and say that it is 'master of none'. When evaluating an integrated package, it is important to look at the quality of the individual parts. Thus it may be that the ideal word processor for an application would have a number of other features, that a spreadsheet with more financial functions is needed and that the database has not really got all the reporting features which are desirable. The compromises which have to be reached may be acceptable or they may not; what is important is that the pros and cons are considered.

It might well be the case that an integrated package has graphics, and not 3D graphics. It might have word processing, but not a spelling checker. It might have a database, but not a feature allowing more than one file to be open at once and so on. For reasons of speed, cost and size, integrated packages do not always have all the possible features in all the parts. Thus, if the needs of any organisation are specialised, such as printing three columns to a page in word processing, then many integrated packages will not be appropriate.

Another possible drawback of integrated packages is that an organisation may be paying for

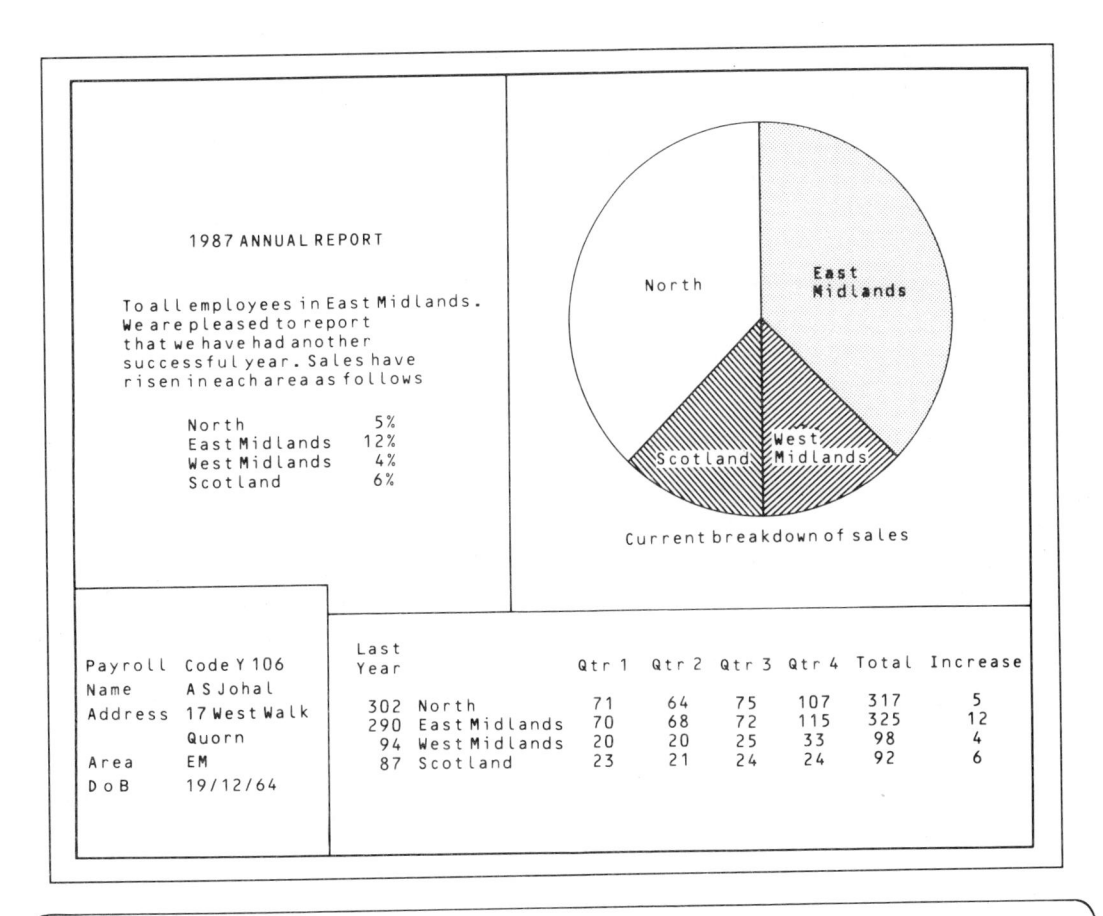

```
1987 ANNUAL REPORT

To all employees in East Midlands.
We are pleased to report
that we have had another
successful year. Sales have
risen in each area as follows

    North            5%
    East Midlands   12%
    West Midlands    4%
    Scotland         6%
```

```
                                                                        Current breakdown of sales
```

```
              Last
Payroll  Code Y106    Year                Qtr 1  Qtr 2  Qtr 3  Qtr 4  Total  Increase
Name     A S Johal
Address  17 West Walk  302  North           71    64     75    107    317      5
         Quorn         290  East Midlands   70    68     72    115    325     12
Area     EM             94  West Midlands   20    20     25     33     98      4
DoB      19/12/64       87  Scotland        23    21     24     24     92      6
```

Links between the elements of an integrated package

features which it does not wish to have. Perhaps only four out of the six features are wanted. Others would argue that the saving is worth it anyway and that a single integrated package may well cost less than four individual packages.

When considering all the different parts there will be a large number of commands for the user to learn. This can be a particular problem for the occasional user. In most integrated packages, however, the command structure is designed to be simple and similar in the different parts.

15.9. OPEN STRUCTURE

The designers of some integrated software have made details of their file formats public knowledge. They hope that in this way they can encourage other, often smaller, companies to bring out software which uses files in the particular format. Such 'third party' software is available to provide utilities which were not implemented in the original versions of software, such as a spelling checker or extra graphics facilities, or additional communications features. The purpose of this 'open' approach to software design is clearly to encourage sales of the original product by allowing it to be enhanced. It also helps to develop particular file formats into 'standards'. Smaller companies are often better geared to producing specialised add-on software than large companies and the financial benefits of the risk might be greater to them.

15.10. PROGRAMMABILITY

Integrated packages differ considerably in their capacity for remembering a series of commands. At the simplest level, a series of keystrokes can be remembered and recalled by pressing a function key. This is sometimes implemented by the inclusion of a 'learn mode' option, so that, once this feature is on, all commands are recorded until it is switched off.

In a more wide-reaching way, a whole series of commands can be remembered as a program and stored in a file. This is similar in manner to the way in which a database can be programmed. Such programming within an integrated package could include full program structuring, with repeat . . . until, do . . . while loops and so on.

TASK

Outline the benefits of having an integrated package which is programmable.

15.11. CASE STUDY: HOW DO YOU CHOOSE?

Choosing an integrated package is a process full of compromise. The first step might be to make a list of all the features, under the headings of database, word processor, spreadsheet and so on, which are considered essential for the particular applications. This list will form the minimum standard in the selection.

This first list might then be subdivided into features that it would be expected that nearly all integrated packages have and features which only some will have. Thus, if the handling of more than one file at once in the database is considered essential, then this, being in the category that 'only some will have', can be used to eliminate some possible packages.

Then, a second list of features could be made which it is important for the packages to do well. Thus if high-precision arithmetic would be valuable, this would be put in the list. If high resolution of printed graphics is important, that is added to the list. If proportionally spaced, right justified text is important, that is noted and so on. A shortlist should be drawn up of packages which meet the minimum criteria. The desirable features can then be put in a priority order and a package which provides the highest proportion of the features in the early part of this list can be chosen. A more sophisticated weighted ranking system as used in general systems analysis might be used if a more rigorous approach is needed.

15.12. STUDY QUESTIONS

1 Is an integrated package the only piece of software you will ever need?
2 The brochure for a new integrated package states that it will read a number of standard file formats, such as DIF and SYLK. You consider this useful, as you have existing packages, and you want to use the files from them, so you buy the package. When you have used it for a while, you discover that, though it can read other file formats, your existing software cannot use the files from your new package. Why might this be?

15.13. ASSIGNMENTS

1 Write a discussion paper outlining the developments which you consider might take place in the next five years in the integration of separate software areas into common programs. Do you think there will be more parts in each package, or better features within each part? Will additional applications areas be added? Or will users be more demanding of software features and demand the best in each application area?
2 Imagine that you are employed as a junior office worker in an office stationery company which employs about a dozen people. With your computing background, you have been asked by the managing director to suggest what software the firm should buy for the IBM PC which is arriving next week. No software has so far been ordered. This is the first time that computers will have been used within the company. Describe the process that you would go through to decide whether an integrated package would be useful and what features it would require. (You may wish to be critical of the way that the matter has been dealt with so far by the company, but remember your junior position.) Suggest the jobs that such software would not do adequately and outline other applications packages it would be necessary to buy. Point out any ways in which data from the applications could be transferred in to the integrated package.

16 THE MONEY PROGRAMS

16.1. HANDLING ACCOUNTS

At the heart of all businesses and many other organisations is the handling of money. Regardless of the sources of the finance or its ultimate destination, an organisation has a responsibility to record all its financial transactions, and to present them, that is, to give an **account** of its business.

16.2. THE TASK

Methods of recording accounts, evolved over hundreds of years, are available to ensure that all transactions are properly recorded, that mistakes are rarely made and that when they are, they can be rectified by checking back through the records. It is unfortunate if, in the description of these methods to successive generations of accounts clerks, the temptation has been to say 'this is what must be done', rather than to explain the reasons. With a computer, however, the repetitive following of procedures is its greatest asset.

Keeping accounts using a computer enables technology to aid an existing process. In this respect, this application is rather different from many other computer applications, where the computer opens up whole new areas of tasks which can be carried out, for example by the use of databases and spreadsheets. Though tasks done by databases and spreadsheets may have been done by hand before, the keeping of accounts must have been done before.

On the one hand, it is a great benefit to computerise an essential business task. On the other hand, there are obvious dangers in making a job which is essential for the functioning of the firm dependent on a computer system. Provision must clearly be made for the possibilities of hardware breakdown. Also an individual organisation might need to adapt its methods of accounting to conform to what a particular accounting package provides. While computerisation provides for a wide range of reports to be produced within the system, assembling reports which are not specified as part of the system will be more difficult or even impossible.

All accounting programs reflect the tried and tested methods by which organisations currently transact their finance. Thus, the computer is being used as a tool to assist within the process. Serious questions must be asked if an organisation is going to need to make major changes in accounting processes in order to adopt computer-based techniques.

16.3. THE BENEFITS

It is unlikely that, within a small business, there will be major savings in staffing costs when handling accounts by computer. However, computerised accounts will:

(a) ensure that invoices are sent out promptly,
(b) allow the chasing of debtors quickly (so that money is not left outstanding for too long, which possibly then has to be written off),
(c) enable an organisation to make best use of discount terms when paying other people,
(d) allow the extraction of information from the basic data in order to produce reports to help in determining company policy,
(e) give greater accuracy (the cross checking of arithmetic by hand can be dispensed with),
(f) allow better financial control through having more up-to-date information,
(g) change the auditor's job considerably (this may or may not be considered a benefit, depending on the quality of the computerised system and its use).

16.4. THE JARGON

As with many other specialist areas, accounting abounds with technical terms. To make accurate and efficient use of any of the software, a member of staff requires an understanding of the jargon, and more importantly, the concepts which lie behind the jargon. Because of the technical nature of bookkeeping, accounts programs will normally be used by some staff as a major part of their work. Very few staff will make casual use of such software.

Modern accounting uses a method known as **double entry bookkeeping**. This is based on the principle that all transactions have two aspects. For instance, if a company sells goods to a customer, this increases the amount of cash held, but decreases the value of the goods in stock by the same amount. An organisation has **assets**, which are resources on which financial value can be put. It also has **liabilities**, which are the debts caused by the acquisition of the assets. All transactions fall into one of the four categories below.

First action	Compensating action	Example
Increase assets	Increase liabilities	Buying goods on credit (we now possess goods which have a value, but we owe for them)
Decrease assets	Decrease liabilities	Paying for goods previously bought on credit in cash (we use the asset of money to reduce our debt)
Increase assets	Decrease assets	Buying goods for cash (we exchange the asset of money for the asset of goods)
Increase liabilities	Decrease liabilities	Paying for goods previously bought on credit by credit card (we exchange a debt to one person for a debt to another)

A bookkeeping program will maintain a series of accounts showing an organisation's transactions with its **debtors** (people who owe money to the organisation) and **creditors** (people to whom the organisation owes money). Accounts will also be maintained for other items of expenditure such as wages and insurance, and money spent is charged against appropriate headings called **accounts**. Thus all income and expenditure is categorised according to the account to which it belongs. In a manual accounting system, each of these accounts might be held on a separate page of a book, which is called a **ledger**. Each transaction has the two aspects of debiting one account and crediting another account with the same amount.

The ledgers

In an accounting system of any appreciable size, it is useful to break the complete ledger into three smaller ledgers:

(a) the **sales ledger**;
(b) the **purchases ledger**,
(c) the **nominal ledger**.

Sales is the term used to describe those goods sold which were bought or manufactured for the primary intention of resale, and thus are part of the main trading of the organisation. This is a rather narrower definition than in everyday English. Thus the second-hand sale of a van which has been used for deliveries is not termed a sale in this sense, as it was bought for use rather than sale. The **sales ledger** consists of an account for every customer who buys on credit and an account for cash sales. Entries are made into customer accounts when a sale on credit is made and when a payment is made by the customer.

Purchases are those items bought with the primary intention of resale, perhaps after reprocessing. Again, this technical use of the word

```
12/11/85              Sales Ledger Invoice
Account ID        Name                          Line No.
<A123   >         <Test Run              >         1
                                           . Option [A ]
Part ID        <         >
Description    <AAAAAAAAAA         >
Analysis No.   <  1> LADIES BIKES
Analysis Gr. 2 < 0>
Analysis Gr. 3 < 0>
Vat code       <0>
Price          <         50.00>
Quantity       <          2.00>
Discount       < 0.00>
Total                   100.00>
Grand Total    <        100.00>    Quantity         Total
1              AAAAAAAAAAAA          2.00          100.00

A to add, R to remove, C to change, U to scroll up, D to scroll down or END
```

A sales ledger screen, entry of invoice details: TABS III

differs from everyday language. For example, furniture bought for use in the office would not be considered as a purchase, as it is not primarily bought for resale. The **purchases ledger** has an account for each of an organisation's suppliers which is similarly adjusted when purchases and payments are made.

The distilling of the two major areas of sales and purchases into separate ledgers leaves the **nominal ledger**, which contains all other transactions, relatively less cluttered. A **sales account** is included in the nominal ledger to show all the income from sales, and a **purchases account** is included to show all expenditure in this form. The use of the other two ledgers allows the nominal ledger to hold only summary figures, with detailed breakdowns of the amounts being held in the other

```
11/11/85           Purchase Ledger : Assign Payments
Account ID          Name
[      ]            <                                >

Unpaid Invoices    <    0>
Total of Invoices  <         0.00>
Unassigned Debit   <         0.00>

Item    <   0>    Date           <01/01/79>
                  Invoice Number <    0>

                  Invoice Value  <        0.00>
                  Outstanding    <        0.00>

                  Assign         <        0.00>
```

A purchases ledger screen, assigning payments to invoices: TABS III

two ledgers. The double-entry system is still used with the three ledgers, which should still balance.

The idea of a journal system

All transactions which take place must be entered into the system. Each time a cheque is received or a purchase is made or a sale takes place, the fact must be recorded. In a manual system, such data would not be entered into the double-entry bookkeeping system immediately, but would be entered by way of a **journal** system. Another name for the journal is a **day book**.

The transactions recorded in the journal are carried over to the ledger at regular intervals into the relevant accounts. Each transaction will have a debit and a credit effect. The entries for one side of the double entry are the recording of each amount against the individual account; the other side of the double entry is completed by carrying over a total, as a sales account or purchases account.

At the point at which the transaction is entered or **posted** to the appropriate ledgers, an entry is made on the journal giving it a reference number. This allows all transactions to be traced back from the ledger to their point of entry to the system. For these reasons, the journal is known as a **book of original entry**. The recording of all transactions in the journal and the ledgers is helpful in tracking down errors, accidental or otherwise.

Cross checking

In a manual system, the process of posting transactions from the journal to the ledgers is a painstaking task. Opportunities for mistakes abound and so the process of posting is checked by a system of **control accounts** to ensure that the total of sales ledger debtors does indeed equal the balance on the sales account reflected in the nominal ledger. The processes of journal entry and ledger entry are combined into one process by computer bookkeeping. At a transaction's point of entry, it is recorded in a journal which is printed and used for audit purposes. The aim of the journal in the computerised system is not as a back-up to check arithmetic errors, which often occur in manual systems, but to ensure that all entries are made and that all entries can be traced back to their origin.

TASK

Make a list of reasons why all entries to an accounting system must be traceable.

Because in a computerised system there is not such a need to check that all postings from the journal have been carried out without transcription or arithmetic errors, the system of control accounts is not necessary. Strict checks must, however, be made to ensure that **all** source information is in fact included in the computer 'journals' used for audit purposes.

Thus, all entries to the system are printed out, either immediately, at the end of a batch of entries or at the end of a period. For obvious reasons, it is important that entries cannot be made into the system without their point of entry being traceable. Thus all pages of the journal will be numbered consecutively and will include the identity of the person entering the transactions. All systems which are to be used by more than one person must have unique identifying codes for users.

The journals

At the single point of entry of a transaction to a computerised system, details must be given of the points to which transactions are to be posted. This process is somewhat simplified by splitting the journal into parts, one for all transactions involving the passing of money (by cheque or cash), called the **cash book**, and three other journals reflecting the three ledgers.

The **sales journal** will contain details of all the sales on credit, allocated to the appropriate account. The value of all the sales will be included in the nominal ledger balancing the entries against the individual customers' accounts. The **purchases journal** will contain details of all the acquisitions on credit, allocated to the appropriate expenditure heading or account. Other transactions, such as account adjustments, are made through what is termed the **journal proper**. Thus there are four books of original entry, though in some cases, the cash book is divided into a cash received book and a cheques issued book, making the total five.

The splitting of the journals means that details of only one side of the double entry need be given for a sale or a purchase. In the case of a sale, the details of the account against which the sale is charged must be recorded. The other half of the double entry process is completed when totals are carried across at regular intervals, in order to record the income on the sales account in the nominal ledger. In a manual system, the important task of ensuring that the nominal ledger is kept in balance can be very time consuming.

It is normal practice that only the totals from the sales journals are entered without being itemised into the sales account in the nominal ledger, with a description such as 'credit sales for the month', thus keeping down considerably the number of entries. In a manual system it is normal for the total of a page to be transferred at a time. In a similar way, only totals from the purchases journal are transferred into the purchases account in the nominal ledger. This transfer will be done from time to time at the end of what is called the accounting period, typically a month. Until this transfer takes place, the accounts will not balance according to the rules of double entry.

Journals often include information regarding cash transactions as well as credit transactions. This enables sales invoices for example to be entered in numerical order to ensure that all are included, which is vital for checking purposes.

The cash book, too, is often split into a 'main' cash book (which itself may be subdivided into cash received and cheques issued), and a petty cash book, which allows small sums to be summarised.

The summaries

In order that an organisation's financial status can be assessed at a particular time, either at the end of an accounting period or at the end of a year, a list must be made of all the accounts with their current status. This list, a summary of all transactions, is called a **trial balance**. It is easiest to understand this as consisting of all transactions, though in reality only the balances of each account are used. Because of the principle of double-entry bookkeeping, these lists should balance (hence the name). In a manual system, there is a high probability that it will not balance because of copying errors from the journal to the ledgers and because of arithmetic errors. In a computerised system, the chance of this sort of error is virtually eliminated.

Following the drawing-up of a trial balance at the end of an accounting period, additional entries will be made to give a true picture for the period. Transactions relating to the period which have not been completed, such as debtors, creditors, accruals (money now owing to other people but not yet invoiced, such as gas and electricity) and prepayments (payment in advance for goods or services not yet received, such as rent) must be included. Similarly, the depreciation of assets (which is a cost, though it does not appear as a payment out), the disposal of assets and the stock in hand must be estimated. Once these adjusting entries have been made, a closing trial balance can be produced. It is from this more complete picture of the financial status of the organisation that financial reports are drawn up.

These reports include the **trading and profit and loss account** and the **balance sheet**. The details of these processes are outlined in all good accounting books, where rules are given as to what should be included and the form in which these reports should be presented. Within a computerised system, as all the data is present from which these reports are drawn up, these can be supplied when requested without further operator intervention.

The inputs

The design of data entry for accounts programs has to strike a balance between ease of data entry and checks against errors. When sales are to be charged against a particular customer, details to identify the customer must be entered. The briefest way of doing this is by using an account number, rather than using names, which tend to be longer, and may not be unique. A good accounts package will allow a user to correct obvious mistakes as data is entered. Thus if details of an invoice are incorrectly entered and the user spots this, an on-screen editor is used before the transaction is processed.

The entry of transactions, particularly for sales and purchases ledger is often batch based. This entails a series of similar transactions being entered one after the other. This enables more checking to take place to ensure that all transactions are entered and that typing errors are reduced. At the end of the entry of a batch of data, cross checks can be made against manually calculated totals and corrective action can be taken if appropriate. Systems differ in their capacity to correct transactions already entered as part of a batch.

When using some of the worst packages, the user might detect a data entry as soon as a line is entered and yet have to take several steps to correct the error. Without a screen editor, an error in a line which has been entered cannot be altered. Without a facility to abort the entry of a batch, the details of all the rest of the batch have to be entered and then, at the end, the user must state that the batch is not acceptable, ensuring that the batch is rejected. Then data entry of the whole batch has to start again. This is not a very helpful approach, as it entails a lot of frustrating extra work, particularly when a similar error is made at the second attempt. Such packages are to be avoided.

TASK

Describe the advantages and disadvantages of an accounting program being transaction-driven, rather than batch based.

The detail

There are two main styles of sales ledgers available. In the **open item** method, the details of all unpaid invoices are carried over from one accounting period to the next. Thus statements can include details of all unpaid invoices. This system uses substantial storage space, as each account might have several invoices outstanding, and the details of these will be included in the individual account, possibly for several months. The alternative method is the **balance forward** method, where only the total sum outstanding is carried from one period to the next.

It is clearly advantageous to be able to give a breakdown of a customer's debt. In order to know which invoices are outstanding, details must be entered as each payment is made stating which invoice or invoices they relate to. This gives the user the task of matching all payments to the corresponding invoices. Complications also occur when customers make part payments, or when cash cannot be clearly identified with particular invoices.

A major disadvantage of the balance forward method is that statements will only include previous debts as 'balance owing at end of last month', with no explanation of how this amount is made up. The amount may, for instance, include charges for goods which have been found to be unsatisfactory and are therefore the subject of a disputed bill.

An organisation may feel that a major advantage of a computerised sales ledger is the ability of the computer to do the tedious job of highlighting disputed and unpaid invoices. Within an open item system, the computer can do this on demand; with a balance forward method, this can only be done by hand by going through accounts for several months previous.

On the purchasing side, it is useful to be able to print a **remittance advice note**, identifying which of a supplier's invoices are to be paid. This would be sent off with the cheque. This helps the supplier keep an accurate picture in a sales ledger. A remittance advice note helps a company in cross checking the cash book with the purchases ledger, both for audit purposes and for checking future queries. A useful facility within a purchases ledger is to be able to pay all the invoices for a given supplier. This is far quicker than having to identify one at a time the invoices to be paid. For this purpose it is useful to be able to have displayed on the screen at one time all the outstanding details for a supplier.

```
                    STATEMENT

TO                            FROM
A. CUSTOMER                   A. SUPPLIER
69 CONNAUGHT GARDENS          33 RADFORD BOULEVARD
NOTTINGHAM                    NOTTINGHAM

              ACCOUNT NO  1234    DATE 30.04.87
                                       PAGE 1 OF 1

OUR REF    DATE      YOUR REF    TRANSACTIONS
                                  DR       CR
                     BROUGHT
                     FORWARD    265.00
2764      07.04.87      -       196.90
  -       14.04.87    CHQ                165.00
2910      15.04.87      -       100.80
  -       24.04.87    CHQ                196.90

                    TOTAL NOW DUE  200.80
```

```
                    STATEMENT

TO                            FROM
A. CUSTOMER                   A. SUPPLIER
69 CONNAUGHT GARDENS          33 RADFORD BOULEVARD
NOTTINGHAM                    NOTTINGHAM

              ACCOUNT NO  1234    DATE 30.04.87
                                       PAGE 1 OF 1

OUR REF    DATE      YOUR REF    TRANSACTIONS
                                  DR       CR
1017      16.02.87              100.00
1462      21.03.87              165.00
2764      07.04.87              196.90
  -       14.04.87    CHQ                165.00
2910      15.04.87              100.80
  -       24.04.87    CHQ                196.90

                    TOTAL NOW DUE  200.80

AMOUNT DUE       1 MONTH      2 MONTHS     3 MONTHS OR MORE
CURRENT MONTH    OVERDUE      OVERDUE      OVERDUE
  100.80          0.00         100.00       0.00
```

Statements using the balance forward method (left) and the open item system (right)

TABS Limited

[SAL]	SALES LEDGER ACCOUNT LISTING					Date: 04/04/86	Time: 14:18
UNNASSIGN	BALANCE	YEAR TOT	CURRENT	OVER 30	OVER 60	OVER 90	OVER 120
BIKES1	The Bike Shop				0912 334455		
166.17	19201.34	21816.40	19367.51	0.00	0.00	0.00	0.00
BOBJA1	Bob Jackson Cycles				0835 864334		
0.00	0.00	2933.60	0.00	0.00	0.00	0.00	0.00
CAMDE1	Camden Bikes Ltd				01 485 1424		
1033.93	3701.73	6541.00	0.00	2047.36	0.00	2688.30	0.00
ENGL1	English Cycles Ltd				0563 78532		
0.00	98.40	12275.00	98.40	0.00	0.00	0.00	0.00
HARR1	Harris & Sons Ltd				0722 342587		
105.50	1519.50	6542.00	1052.00	395 00	0.00	178.00	0.00
M&BCY1	M&B Cycles				0246 412850		
0.00	1267.36	1109.29	500.00	267.36	0.00	0.00	500.00
REGEN1	Regent Cycles				01 643 9646		
0.00	2488.09	2782.57	0.00	1652.21	276.48	559.40	0.00
RADCL1	Radcliff UK Ltd				0706 54305		
1960.20	2000.60	5460.80	460.80	2000.00	0.00	1500.00	0.00
TRISK1	Triskell Bike Shop				0225 316743		
0.00	196.62	3333.10	196.62	0.00	0.00	0.00	0.00
	TOTALS						
3265.80	30473.64	62793.76	21675.33	6361.93	276.48	4925.70	500.00

An aged debtors report showing amounts outstanding for the current period, amounts which have been owing over 30 days, and for longer periods (60, 90 and 120 days): TABS III

It is also useful to be able to pay all invoices from a supplier posted by a certain date. For example, invoices might be paid at the end of the month following the one in which an invoice was posted. For this reason, an ageing facility is useful for cash-flow predictions.

In some systems, the individual accounts on the purchases ledger are updated when the remittance advice note is printed; in others, they are only updated when the cheque has actually been sent. Both systems have their merits and the choice depends on the amount of cross checking required and on the individual company's style of working.

TASK

Outline the benefits of a remittance advice within an accounting system (whether computerised or not):

(a) to you as a supplier,
(b) to you as a customer.

16.5. THE REPORTS

The two main types of reports are:

(a) reports which are available on demand as required,
(b) reports which are produced as part of the regular cycle, at the end of an accounting period.

It can be very useful to produce from the sales ledger a list of all outstanding debts. Such a report is most useful if it identifies how long each of the amounts has been outstanding. This is known as an **aged debtors report**. The ability to generate such a list for some or all of the customers is a valuable tool in controlling and chasing debts, which is in turn useful for reducing the number of bad debts. The production of such a report is possible within a manual system, but it would be a long drawn out process.

TASK

State the advantages in being able to generate a list of aged debtors.

Similarly, it is useful to produce customer statements, regularly or on demand, either on screen or in printed form, so that details can be discussed with individual customers.

The format of reports can have a critical effect on the methods of a business. A particular item of detail which should be investigated is the width in characters of the printouts. Eighty-column printouts can be rather cramped and difficult to read, so a width of 132 characters is more common. Some printers have switchable width and can attain 132 columns in condensed print. Manual accounts were traditionally drawn up with two columns, one marked DR for debit, and the other CR for credit. With the introduction of computer accounting systems, it is now general practice to use a single column, marking entries as + or −, or using brackets to indicate negative amounts. Serious questions have to be asked by an organisation before deciding whether this style is acceptable.

TASK

Examine a bank statement. Describe how such a statement might differ in its appearance and its generation if it were produced by hand rather than by computer.

Reports can take a considerable time to print and a user may not wish to wait until one report is produced before performing other transactions, perhaps requesting another report. For this reason, some packages incorporate spooling, which allows the report to be sent to disc awaiting printing at a later, more convenient time.

16.6. CUSTOMISING

Accounting programs can be adapted or customised to suit the individual style of accounting, as well as the type and number of accounts of an organisation. Programs also have to be adapted to particular computer configurations, such as memory capacities and printer used. This flexibility has its penalty, because all the details of the system have to be specified before the actual work of using the system can begin. This work, and the initial entry of data to start the system, is a considerable overhead in terms of time and money. It is also clearly very important to specify precisely what is needed from a system when it is established, otherwise considerable extra work is necessary to put problems right.

The maximum sizes have to be set for the length of account titles, names, addresses and narratives to identify transactions. Another important value or parameter which has to be set is the length of the

accounting period. This determines the frequency with which accounts are balanced off and reports are generated. Making changes to the accounting period once the system is in operation might pose considerable difficulties. In choosing accounting software, it is important to ensure that an organisation's precise needs can be catered for. For example, some firms split the year into thirteen four-week periods rather than twelve months. Not all packages take well to this method.

TASK
Write a list of factors which should be considered when deciding on an organisation's accounting period.

For the production of reports which analyse finance according to the different accounts to which they relate, there has to be a careful analysis of the means of specifying the grouping of accounts.

A typical approach, for example, is to allocate accounts numbers which are made up of a series of aspects which describe the source of the account. For example, an account code might be 2034178. The 2 might represent region 2, the 03 might represent a particular member of the sales staff within that area. Thus, to analyse sales region by region, the program must look at all accounts beginning with a 1, then all those beginning with a 2, and so on. Similarly, the performance of different members of the sales staff can be measured by analysing data according to the first three characters.

Once a set of account numbers is allocated, the forms of reports which can be generated can be limited by the style in which the codes are made up. With any accounts package, it must be possible to add additional headings (for instance a new region), but the extent to which this will be possible varies from system to system.

When the system is initially set up, the user will be able to determine the layout of the various printouts, the details necessary to give a posting, and possibly choose the style of dialogue and amount of help given to the user. In this, the speed that data can be entered will be determined, but the quicker data entry is made, the more problems might occur with data entry errors or confusion of the user.

The amount of detail required at data entry will determine the types of reports and their level of detail when the package is in regular use.

16.7. THE ROUTINE

At the end of each accounting period, whether it be four weeks, a month or any other length of time, a number of routine tasks will have to be performed. The totals of sales and purchases ledgers if not regularly carried over as part of the daily routine will be posted to the nominal ledger, to make the double-entry system correct before the trial balance is worked out.

Other entries to the nominal ledger may be made either at regular intervals during the accounting period, or at the end. Such transactions will include all those which do not involve sales or purchases on credit, for example payment of salaries or acquisition of assets. There might also be the writing off of bad debts or allowances for depreciation of assets. Any such entries which are to refer to a particular accounting period should be completed so that the accounts can be balanced off in order for the various reports to be prepared.

Different accounting arrangements are made by different organisations to allow for transactions which take place in one accounting period but actually refer to another, such as the payment of rent in advance. These must also be allowed for by a computerised system. Some packages also have a feature which allows entries for one period to be made before the previous period is completed, otherwise no new work can be done while period-end accounts are being drawn up.

In order that regular charges can be made against accounts, such as the costs of depreciation, standing orders can sometimes be established as part of the regular end-of-period routine. Another useful feature is the entry of transactions temporarily at the end of an accounting period so that accounts can be drawn up. These can then be reversed before moving on to the next period. This might be particularly useful for the preparation of mid-year accounts.

When trial balances are being drawn up, some packages will include all the transactions, which can be useful for getting the precise picture. Other packages only include the balances of accounts, as this might give a clearer overall picture by leaving out detail which is not essential. Some packages allow the user to choose which way the trial balance will be drawn up.

At the end of an accounting period, it is usual for the accounts to be reduced simply to those transactions which are still outstanding or **live**. Thus, where a sale has taken place and the appoiriate money has been paid, these details are removed from the individual account, leaving only details of unpaid invoices. At this point, it is important to keep a back-up copy of the files and to have an audit trail printed if this has not been done before. Most instruction manuals will emphasise the importance of this; users ignore the advice at their peril.

At the end-of-period some reports are produced automatically, others can be requested. Accounts might be listed in full, or in selected parts. Some reports might be for the period which has just ended. Others might be for the year to date.

16.8. THE SPECIALS

Additional reports are provided by some systems. For example, facilities might be available to compare the current figures with a budget. A similar exercise might be carried out in comparison with the previous year's figures. Other reports might produce ratios of actual spending to target spending in each category, or calculate percentages of the total within each category.

In all such reports, it is clear that any target figures or previous year's figures must be present within the system for them to be used. Relevant data might be saved from one period to the next or one year to the next if this is required, but figures such as targets will have to be entered, possibly at the start of the year.

The details of the figures and calculations needed for reports will either have to be established as a routine for each period (perhaps at the customising stage) or some scope may be included to define reports on request. For any report to be produced, however, it is obviously essential that the relevant data is present.

16.9. THE DANGERS

It is easy to get carried away with the possibilities of computerisation, particularly when it comes to the large scale and repetitive work of keeping accounts. It is vitally important, however, to remember that a package must be suitable for an organisation's needs.

There are two important groups of people who must be consulted before the process of computerising accounts goes too far. The first group to be consulted should be the auditors. The role of the auditor is to ensure that the accounts presented by an organisation give a true and fair view. The **external auditor** has the job of ensuring that the accounts which are published genuinely reflect the current status and trading over the period of the organisation. It is the concern of the **internal auditor** to monitor the financial transactions of the organisation and to ensure that the business has been conducted properly, and to detect any mistakes or fraud.

Thus when a cheque has been paid out, the external auditor is only interested in the fact that it has been paid out and that the money has been deducted from the account. The internal auditor wants to see evidence that the cheque was paid for a legitimate expense and wants to know that what the money was paid out for is reflected in the accounts. Both the internal and external auditors have to be satisfied, when computerisation is mooted, that they will be able to carry out their task effectively.

The second group of people to be consulted are the **VAT inspectors**. Organisations must ensure that the outputs produced and the records which are kept are sufficient to satisfy the regulations of VAT in their particular circumstances.

As with all computer applications, prospective purchasers of systems must ensure that the capacity of the system under consideration is sufficient to cope with current and future needs. The theoretical maximum and the practical maximum data which can be dealt with might differ, as the constant swopping of discs to interchange programs and data can be a major handicap in the functioning of a system.

In summary, an accounts package must fit very precisely the essential tasks which an organisation wants to carry out. If some operations are cumbersome, then this may be acceptable, but it will be a limiting factor on the amount that can be achieved in a given time; this can be particularly important if the system is working at a level approaching its maximum. When a shortlist of potential packages is being drawn up, there will be many features which will be considered essential. This contrasts strongly with areas like word processing, where the inability of a package to provide a particular feature might be regrettable, but the main task of producing a document can still be done without it.

16.10. THE ADD-ONS

Beyond the basic system of the three ledgers, a number of additional features can be added to extend accounting outwards from these core activities. These features include:

(a) the production of invoices,
(b) stock control,
(c) order processing,
(d) payroll.

Invoicing

When customers are to be charged for goods, the total amount which they are to pay must be calculated. The sales ledger already described will simply record the total of each invoice. Information can be provided to the sales ledger package either by manual input after the invoice total has been calculated (either by hand or using a computer) or the total can be passed from an invoicing package.

An invoicing package, whether linked to the sales ledger or not, will require details of all goods available and the charges for them. When an order is input, the totals can be calculated. Thus the computer is being used to perform a considerable amount of arithmetic – a task for which it is ideally suited. Details will be kept of price lists, and clearly an essential feature is that it must be easy to amend the price list.

Stock control

Stock control is the recording by an organisation of the types and numbers of goods held. This information is useful in attempting to minimise the number of times when orders cannot be fulfilled because the organisation is out of stock. Thus when stock of an item gets sufficiently low, before it reaches zero, goods can be reordered. On the other hand, from a financial point of view, an organisation wants to keep to a minimum the amount of capital tied up in goods which are simply sitting in a warehouse. This problem is compounded if the goods are to a greater or lesser extent perishable or seasonal.

Whatever the policy, however, it is clearly useful for the out-of-stock or low stock condition to be detected as soon as possible. It would be wasteful to prepare an invoice for goods which could then not be sent; it would be disastrous to send such an invoice. The linking of invoicing with stock control ensures that orders are checked as soon as possible and that current stock levels are also updated quickly.

```
16/09/85                    New Item
    Part ID                       Description
    <A123      >         1st  <Test run              >
                         2nd  <                      >
                         3rd  <                      >
                         4th  <                      >
Number of decimal places in:  Price  <2>   Quantity  <3>

                Current Stock level  <        0.000>

               Reserved Stock level  <        0.000>

                           VAT Code  <1>

Analysis Codes:     Sales    Ledger  <  1>
                    Purchase Ledger  <  2>

Enter next action |  |  (C)ontinue, (S)ave & finish, (R)e-do, (A)bandon
```

A stock control screen, creation of new stock item: TABS III

Once the basic data regarding stock levels is held on computer, it is possible for the current value of the stock to be assessed. This **stock valuation** might be at the actual prices at which the goods were purchased or at the current purchase price.

It will still be essential from time to time to check the actual stock in the warehouse with the stock figures as recorded on the computer. This is a precaution against loss, wastage or pilfering. The availability of stock figures held within the computer does, however, mean that stock valuations are available on demand, a task which would previously have required a complete stock-taking in the warehouse.

It is possible for stock-control systems to function independently of invoicing, but linking them works to mutual benefit.

TASK

Suggest the benefits of the use of good stock control procedures by a local chemist's shop.

Order processing

The recording of stock levels is also useful in the detection of circumstances where an order cannot be fulfilled on the (hopefully) infrequent occasions when, despite all precautions, stock does run too low. It is most likely that, when this occurs, most of the order can be fulfilled. In this case, companies should have a policy whether part of an order should be sent and invoiced for, with a note being sent stating that the rest of the goods will follow.

An order processing system allows a customer's requests to be matched to the stock available. When an order is for a number of items, the user will be able to decide on appropriate action for items for which the order cannot be fulfilled. When an order cannot be completed, an order processing system might keep details until the order can be completed, or the order is changed because of the circumstances (in consultation with the customer!), or the order is cancelled.

It will then be possible to obtain reports on the orders outstanding for each customer, or the orders outstanding for any particular item.

Payroll

In many businesses, the computerisation of the payroll has been the first major application. This has been because of its large scale and repetitive nature. Many successful payroll programs function entirely independently of other uses of the computer. Many packages are available to perform this role and much literature exists on the subject. A more recent development, however, has been for the payroll to be linked with other accounting features. For example, when payments are generated from the payroll, they can be charged against a particular budget in the accounts.

All payrolls will deal with overtime, bonus payments, statutory sick pay, national insurance and tax. The Inland Revenue has particular specifications for the records which must be kept.

```
28/11/85    Employee Pay & Tax Details - Head Office MONTHLY

Record Number      <    1>
Surname            <            >    N.I. Number     <           >
Forenames          <            >    Works Number    <           >

Tax code prefix    <  >              Scheme no. pre-tax  <0>
Tax code number    <  0>             Scheme no. post-tax <0>
Tax code suffix    <  >              Bonus 2         <    0.00>
                                     Other           <    0.00>
N.I. Contracted I/O   <I>            Pre/A           <    0.00>
N.I. M-W rate Y/N     <N>            W/O             <    0.00>
N.I. Calculation letter <  >         Post/A          <    0.00>
Gross to-date pre. emp.  <    0.00>  Scheme item 1   <    0.00>
Tax to-date pre. emp.    <    0.00>  Scheme item 2   <    0.00>
                                     Scheme item 3   <    0.00>
Rate of pay           <    0.00>
Pay method            <  >           Analysis number <  0>
Is sick pay field used <N>           Job Costing Number <  >
```

A payroll screen entry of an employee's pay and tax details: TABS III

Records of employees can be linked to particular cost centres, so that the total wages bill can be analysed. An extension of this is to relate the labour costs of particular jobs to the charges to be made to customers, either directly, where labour is a service which the firm sells, or indirectly, through the pricing policy for goods.

16.11. INTEGRATION

When some or all of the functions described are combined either into a single program or into a series of modules, the term **integrated accounts** is used. This emphasises that data which relates to a number of different business functions has only to be entered into the computer once. Thus when an order is entered, a system may check whether the order can be fulfilled and will ask for the operator's decision if it cannot. If items then become too low in stock, a reorder could be generated. The creditworthiness of the customer could be checked, to ensure that orders are not sent allowing a customer's credit to advance beyond a defined point. The invoice could be produced for sending and the details entered in the sales ledger against the particular customer – and all this comes from the single entry of an order.

Where accounting systems are produced and sold in a modular form, they can be bought a few modules at a time. This might be useful to phase the cost or the process of computerisation over a period. It is also possible with a modular system to mix and match only those particular functions which an organisation requires.

TASK

A company holds details of all its customers on an integrated accounting system. If, for some reason, the company has a cash-flow crisis and needs to get hold of cash quickly, in what ways would the system help?

16.12. CASE STUDY

TABS III, produced by TABS Limited, is described as a 'fully integrated business accounting suite', running on a number of microcomputers using MS-DOS and PC-DOS.

It consists of 8 modules: sales ledger, purchases ledger, nominal ledger, stock control, sales order

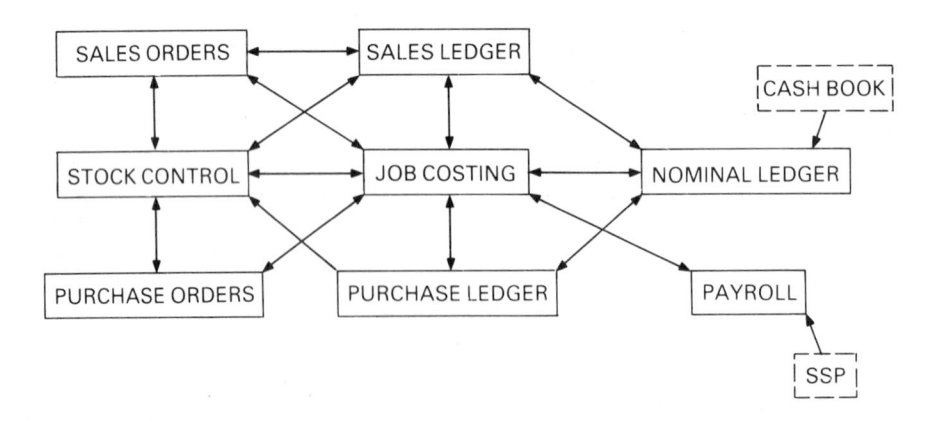

Integrated accounting: links between modules in TABS III

processing, purchases order processing, job costing and payroll. Each module can be used separately or can be linked to other modules bought, so a user can choose the appropriate modules and links for a particular situation.

Updated information on one module can automatically update information on related modules. This ensures that the information is kept up-to-date and accurate and avoids the types of errors that occur when information is entered twice into separate modules. During installation, a number of options can be set to enable the end user to tailor the system to a company's requirements with the entry of appropriate values.

The sales ledger allows three types of account:

(a) a simple balance forward method, which clears transaction details at the end of a month, but allows ageing of the balances;
(b) reconcile accounts, where every transaction is held open item until the user 'ticks' it as paid or written off;
(c) assign accounts, where payments can be posted as invoices are created, which is useful for cash with order accounts.

The stationery can either be pre-printed or plain paper and the layout can be defined, which clearly involves a lot of detail. At the end of period, six reports can be produced. These are the day book (or journal), the cash book, adjustments, sales analysis, VAT analysis and customer ledger cards. Though these reports can be bypassed, this is not recommended. Sales can be analysed in three groups, with a hundred categories in each group. For example, a sales analysis can be established by product type, by outlet and by area.

The purchases ledger has three types of account:

(a) a balance forward method, where the user does not have to worry about the assignment of payments;
(b) reconcilable accounts, where all transactions on an account are kept open until the entries balance, when they are marked for removal at the end of period;
(c) assignable accounts, which allow part payment of any invoices.

Payment can be made for all accounts before a given date, accounts can be 'held' if there is some dispute about a bill, and there is a feature allowing the user to choose which bills to pay from a list of those outstanding. Facilities are provided to print remittance advice notes and cheques.

The entry of transactions is controlled by a 'batch entry' system, which allows entries to be stored in a batch file until the user chooses to post them.

Modules in TABS III can be linked in various ways in addition to the obvious links of the sales ledger and purchases ledger into the nominal ledger. Job costing, for example, can be related to all the other seven modules. When a detailed quote for a job is prepared, this can take into account labour costs (through the payroll module) and the anticipated material costs (through the stock control module). Through links with the sales and purchases ledgers, invoices relating to the job can be posted; through the corresponding order processing modules, effective control can be carried out over the processing from the initial enquiry to satisfactory payment for the job. Budget control is aided by the inclusion of management accounts in the nominal ledger.

16.13. WHERE TO FIND OUT MORE

It cannot be stressed too often that the advice of accounting specialists should be sought when considering using computers for accounts. Only those with a detailed understanding of accounting procedures will be able to discern whether the facilities provided by a package will meet the needs of a company.

In order to be able to read the product literature with understanding, some basic knowledge of accounting is helpful. Two useful introductory books are *Book-keeping and Accounts* by Frank Wood (Longman 1981), and *Keep Account* by John Etor and Mike Muspratt (Pan Breakthrough Series 1982). In simple terms and considerable detail, these books explain the jargon and the ideas which lie behind it.

The serious business computer magazines frequently have reviews of financial software. Such reviews are interesting even if the particular package is not chosen, because they give pointers to features to look for in any package. Once a shortlist of possible packages has been drawn up, reviews can be located by looking through indexes of previous editions.

The best impression of an accounts package can be gained by its actual use. Suppliers may be able to provide demonstration data. This is useful, as it avoids the cumbersome task of system generation, the quality of which should not be a primary consideration in the choice of a package.

Potential users should be careful, however, to ensure that they are not misled about the speed of operation by a demonstration set of data which is only very small.

16.14. STUDY QUESTIONS

1 What are the benefits of performing an essential business task by computer? In other words, if you have to do it, why do it by computer?
2 What details of a transaction will be needed to enter a purchase? Where does the other half of the double entry go?
3 Why do trial balances only need to include the balances on each account rather than all the transactions? How does this work?

16.15. ASSIGNMENTS

1 Using the text of this chapter and any other relevant material, make a list of ways in which accounting packages differ. Using this table contrast the facilities in three commercial packages of your choice, either through reading manufacturers' literature or (better) by using the packages.
2 Imagine that you are the manager of a medium-sized department store and are to have a meeting with all the managers of the departments. What information would you require to be able to discuss sales performance and staffing in an informed way? How might such information be produced?
3 Design and describe the screen dialogue which would be needed for a sales ledger program using the open item method. This should include the creation of new accounts, the entry of invoice details and the production of end of period statements.
4 Imagine that you are a computer consultant for a small newsagent's shop employing three people. Write a report describing the advantages of the integration of accounting functions for your client.

SECTION D

OTHER CONSIDERATIONS

17 OPERATING SYSTEMS

17.1. WHY OS?

Typical single instructions within a computer are 'read the contents of memory location number 3572', or 'test whether the printer has sent a signal to say it has received the last character', or 'if the locations X and Y contain the same numbers, then skip the next instruction'. This is the stuff of which all programs are made. The form of these instructions will depend on the particular machine being used and what is called its architecture of memory access and manipulation. No program will run on a machine without such instructions.

Help is, however, at hand. Programs have been written to shield the everyday user from the intricacies of the machine's internal workings. There are commercially available programs which will load another program from a disc. This will include looking up the position of a file on the disc from a directory, moving the head to the correct position, waiting for the disc to rotate to the correct position and so on. This program will work by interpreting signals received from the disc drive. The directory of files on the disc will have to be updated every time a file is added or deleted. A program must do this also. When a user wants to run a word processing package, for example, control must be passed to it and control must be taken back when the user has finished the editing, or when an error occurs, such as a disc fault.

It is usual for many of the features of peripheral control and computer memory management to be provided in a single piece of software, which is known as the **operating system**.

An **operating system** can be described as a program or set of programs designed to supervise the running of other programs. It is these other programs for which the computer is bought. The aim is then to simplify and standardise the form in which those other programs are written and presented. Thus, an operating system provides a large number of standard features for the convenience of the computer user directly, or of other programs. Thus, in some sense, the operating system is a means to an end rather than an end in itself. Other programs carry out the tasks which are required, and so they are known as **applications packages**. The operating system performs much more of a service role, and indeed, may be so much in the background that the user may be unaware of its existence.

17.2. TYPES OF OPERATING SYSTEM

As computers became popular, manufacturers of mainframes had to ensure that users were provided with a wide range of useful facilities. Indeed, beyond basic features of size, power and reliability, the quality of the operating system on machines became a major means of distinguishing between them. It became common to produce a range of machines which all used the same operating system, which meant that users could move up the range of a particular manufacturer's models. A switch to another manufacturer, however, would require retraining in a new operating system.

When minicomputers and later microcomputers came along, manufacturers had to work very hard to provide a good range of features within an operating system without using up so much of the computer's memory that there was too little space for applications programs. The competition was intense and again operating systems were a major selling point for particular machines. The less work that it took the purchaser to produce a running program, the better. Perhaps of even greater significance was the effect that the less work it took to write programs, the more commercial packages came available.

These individual operating systems could be provided in one of two ways. An operating system could be provided on a chip which was built in to the computer. Alternatively, it could be provided on disc and read in each time it was used and a simple chip capable of loading the instructions from the disc would then be included (this is called a bootstrap loader because of its simplicity – the analogy being 'picking yourself up by your own bootstraps'). The disadvantage of the operating system having to be loaded from disc every time the machine is used has to be balanced against the advantage gained by the ease with which the program on disc can be replaced by a new one with more features as an upgrade to the system. A chip is more difficult to replace.

A further development took place when an operating system was designed to be general purpose and was implemented on several computers. This meant that, though the computers were completely different inside, through the use of the same operating system, they could appear remarkably similar to users. This general purpose operating system was called CP/M, from Digital Research, and it rapidly gained popularity because of its portability. Users who were familiar with the use of CP/M on one machine had no difficulty using a seemingly very different machine which also used CP/M. This in turn led to a large number of packages being designed to run using CP/M, and hence the popularity snowballed and more manufacturers produced CP/M for their machines. CP/M was written for the Z80 chip and it became extremely common for Z80-based computers to run using CP/M.

The basic philosophy of a portable operating system is to provide a core of commands for the user, which look the same to the user whatever machine is being used. The actual implementation, however, is different when it comes to handling different types of disc drives or different forms of sending signals to the printer and back. This is done by placing instructions within the body of the operating system program which call routines held in other parts of memory. The program that is actually held in other parts of memory then depends on the particular machine. This design

Typical operating system commands

CP/M	Meaning	BBC DFS
DIR	List of all files	*CAT
STAT *.*	Details of all files	*INFO *.*
PIP B:=FILE	Copy FILE from one disc to another	*COPY 0 1 FILE
REN TWO=ONE	Change the name of file ONE to TWO	*RENAME ONE TWO
SUBMIT COMMAND.SUB	Run the operating system commands held in the appropriate COMMAND file	*EXEC COMMAND
B:	Future commands will refer to alternative disc drive	*DRIVE 1

feature meant that only part of CP/M had to be rewritten for each new machine which came out based on the Z80 chip.

Having identified and cornered the lucrative 8-bit market, it was clear that CP/M would have competitors as the new 16-bit microcomputers developed. CP/M was adapted, with many more features added, and the 16-bit CP/M has sold well, but its sales have been outstripped by MS-DOS, from Microsoft. In another form, this is called PC-DOS, and is used on the IBM PC range.

17.3. WHAT IS UTILITY SOFTWARE?

The phrase 'utility software' has been coined to describe programs which have been written to carry out frequently-required tasks which users find themselves faced with. This can include such operations as copying a disc or 'dumping' a precise copy of what is currently on the screen on to the printer or tidying up unused areas of the disc by putting all unused space together. Some of these features may well be provided already within some operating systems. There is much confusion about the distinction between an operating system feature and a utility. The distinction is purely based on what is sold as part of the operating system and what is bought as an add-on. Indeed, in many cases, the most successful add-ons of one generation become the standard features of the next generation. As it happens, because of the small size into which CP/M was designed to fit within a microcomputer, a number of its standard facilities are provided as programs which are loaded and run from disc, just as any other program (such as a compiler, editor or utility) would be.

17.4. THE JOBS TO DO

There are many tasks which a user would wish to carry out with a computer as a background to those tasks for which the computer and its applications software were purchased. The distinction between the operating system and utility programs is somewhat blurred and the general heading under which all such programs come is 'systems software'.

17.5. FEATURES WHICH ARE ALMOST ESSENTIAL

When considering purchasing a computer system, it is important to discover how a number of housekeeping routines have to be carried out. The way that such tasks differ from one operating system to another will not be discussed in detail in this text, what is important to the purchaser is whether a system provides the features at all. Computer users would rarely agree exactly on the list of tasks that it is essential for an operating system to carry out. Here is a suggested list of 'essential tasks':

(a) If each individual disc has to be **formatted** (as most general-purpose discs do), how is this done?
(b) Is it possible for a disc to be checked (**verified**) to see whether it has been corrupted?
(c) Is the operating system to be copied onto the disc (for a disc-based system)? If it is, how is this done? Can discs be used without a copy of the operating system on them in order to save having multiple copies?
(d) How is a list obtained of all the files on the disc (the **directory**)? Is it possible to get details of file sizes, the dates and times that the files were created or any other details?
(e) How is a file copied from one disc to another? (Methods can be very different if there is only one disc drive, as the discs will have to be swopped over perhaps a number of times.) Some software, of course, is protected by manufacturers from copying in the normal way, in an attempt to reduce piracy.
(f) How can the name of a file be changed?
(g) Is it possible to make an extra copy of a file on the same disc, with a different name?
(h) Can two or more files be combined into a single file? (This is sometimes called **merging**.)
(i) How are files deleted, and when the user issues a request to delete a file, is a question asked so that the user has to confirm the deletion?
(j) If a file has been erased, but the disc has not had any other files recorded on it since, can the erased file be recovered? (Sometimes referred to as **unerase**, this is an extremely useful way of recovering from accidents.)

(k) Is it possible for an operation to be carried out on a series of files, by specifying a group of names, such as all files with the extension .LGP or all files with names beginning with an 'F'?
(l) Can a file be **locked**, so that it cannot be accidentally deleted or overwritten? (If a lock feature exists, an unlock feature must also be there!)
(m) Can a command be given to lock a whole disc in a similar way, so that it cannot be written to at all?
(n) If there is more than one disc drive, how does the user specify which drive a command refers to? If the discs are double sided, does the operating system refer to the separate sides by separate codes?
(o) Is it possible to display or print the contents of a file as a series of character codes? Can the actual characters be displayed? If a file consists purely of text, can this be displayed?

17.6. FEATURES WHICH MIGHT WELL BE USEFUL

(a) Can the previous command issued be recalled for re-execution? Can it be edited? (This is particularly useful when the user makes a simple typing error in a long command.)
(b) Can a series of operating system commands be stored in a file for later execution? Can a file be created which can be automatically run when a disc is loaded? (This makes use easy for an inexperienced operator.) If so, how easy is it for such commands to be edited?
(c) Does the operating system maintain a calendar and a clock? (Usually these are set each time the machine is switched on.) This can be useful in dating reports, invoices, files and so on.

TASK

Choose an operating system with which you are reasonably familiar. For each of the tasks under the headings 'Features which are essential' and 'Features which might well be useful' above write down how they are implemented in your chosen operating system, or whether they are not available.

17.7. PRINTER UTILITIES

A number of utilities might be available for use with a printer. The choice and availability of such software depends on both the computer and the printer which are to be used. It is sometimes only possible to purchase printer utilities for use from a popular computer to a popular printer.

Software can be purchased which will dump the contents of the screen on to a printer. These programs come in two types:

(a) those which will dump only text.
(b) those which will dump the complete screen, including any graphics (**graphics dumps**).

17.8. PROGRAMMING AIDS AND OTHER MAJOR SYSTEMS SOFTWARE

Other software which comes under the 'utility' heading includes tools for programmers, such as a 'trace' facility, which will monitor the running of a program so that problems in its execution can be tracked down. Programmers also use test data generators which can be used to create large amounts of data for testing at the development stage of a program. The extent to which this type of utility software is needed, of course, will depend on the amount of programming which will be done on a system. In many cases, this will be very little.

A 'dump and restart' facility allows the execution of a program to be halted and the contents of the memory at that point remembered, so that the program can be reloaded and execution can begin again at the point at which it had been left off. One way in which this can be useful is if processing is taking a long time and other jobs have to take priority, for example for user applications, or for systems administration, such as making back-up copies. Another important use of the dump and restart is in the case where the computer detects an imminent power cut – there may be just enough time to save the current status.

Other frequently required tasks in a business context are the sorting and merging of files. Such standard features can be supplied as part of an operating system or as a utility.

Many operating systems will include an editor, whereby the contents of a text file can be altered. This can enable users to change data files or program files. Files containing machine code instructions are not usually edited in this way. The range of features for editing provided with an operating system vary greatly. If sophisticated features are required, it is advisable to use an editor provided as an application program designed to run from the operating system.

17.9. THE HIDDEN AGENDA OF OPERATING SYSTEMS

There are some features of operating systems, particularly those on the more powerful microcomputers or minicomputers, which can carry on in the background without the user being aware of them. An example of this is the logging of computer use on a minicomputer system; this can be used for charging purposes and for allocating job priority. On a single-user system, such accounting features are rarely needed.

From the system point of view, the purpose of the operating system is to protect hardware, software and data from the user. Thus, the user does not normally have access to the disc direct, but always goes by way of the operating system. As well as the obvious advantage of the simplicity of this arrangement for the user, it has the less obvious advantage of being able to filter out commands which could be harmful (such as attempting to write on track 81 on an 80 track disc). Thus, as the operating system forms a link between the two, it is sometimes described as an 'interface' between the user and the machine.

In a similar way, an operating system may present to a user a simplified view of the hardware, so that the user can specify operations to be carried out. For example, the user may be allowed to have the impression that the machine is larger than it actually is, so that large programs can be run, or large amounts of data can be handled. The operating system will contain features to control this situation and to swap the appropriate parts in and out of memory. The theoretical machine which the user views is known as the 'virtual machine'. Similar techniques can be used to give each person operating a multi-user system the impression of having sole use of the whole machine.

Users can similarly be one stage removed from using a printer, so that when they issue commands to send something to the printer, the data to be printed is actually sent to a disc file and a separate program handles the actual printout when the printer is available. This provides a buffer between the user and, in this case, the printer. This idea is known as **spooling**. It is useful when a user wants to send several documents to the printer, but would like to get on with other work once the command has been issued, not wanting to wait for the printer to finish. Spooling is essential for a multi-user system.

TASK
Make a list of the advantages of controlling access to hardware such as a printer and disc drives through the operating system, rather than the user having direct access to them.

17.10. HOUSEKEEPING

When discs have been used for some time, the information on them may become organised in a haphazard and inefficient manner for file access. This is because lots of creations and deletions of files mean that each file has contents which are widespread over the disc, although all data can still be retrieved. From time to time, the disc will have to be reorganised either within itself or by copying on to another disc first. This can lead to more efficient processing in the future. The nature of this tidying-up process has led it to be called **housekeeping**.

When a fixed hard disc is used, regular back-up copies of its contents should be made. Thus the contents of the disc will have to be copied to a tape, exchangeable hard disc or floppy discs. The operating system should provide features to do this. It will save considerable time for copies to be made only of files which have changed since the last back-up copy was made. It would be wasteful to be making regular copies of systems software or applications programs. An ability to copy only some files is called selective back-up.

Responsibility for many such housekeeping tasks need not be the concern of most users. Some sort of administrator should be given the responsibility for carrying out such jobs.

Users have a habit of keeping more files on a disc than they really need, particularly if they are tempted by the large amount of space which might be initially available. Users themselves must be encouraged to delete files which really are no longer necessary. They will take such requests more seriously if they have confidence in the back-up system.

17.11. THE MARKET LEADERS

CP/M

CP/M (which stands for Control Program for Microcomputers), was designed for microcomputers with the Z80 chip. Although initially it was only written as a series of utility programs, its author discovered that, as personal computers became cheaper and therefore more accessible, users wanted to buy his programs. CP/M was and is sold by Digital Research. Its design enabled implementations of CP/M to be prepared efficiently as new machines also based on the Z80 chip came on to the market.

CP/M is designed so that it consists of a number of standard elements. One of the sections of coding handles all the input and output, which are very machine-dependent. This section is called the BIOS (Basic Input Output System). All of the other code is generally portable between machines and makes calls to BIOS for input and output.

MS-DOS

The market leader in 16-bit operating systems, on the other hand, has been MS-DOS, from Microsoft. It has been implemented on a wide range of 16-bit computers, and was adopted by IBM for their personal computers with the name of PC-DOS.

A number of features were incorporated into MS-DOS which had not been present in the early versions of CP/M. These included additional commands, greater standardisation of command format and choice of more meaningful command names.

Unix

Unix was developed by Bell Laboratories for DEC PDP minicomputers. It is designed in a series of layers, the innermost layer being the kernel, the next the shell, and the outermost layer consists of utilities. A user can carry out many tasks without requiring an understanding of features of inner layers, in a sense, working from the outside in as his or her skills develop.

Unix has been implemented on the IBM PC, and so has developed 'down' to 16-bit microcomputers from minicomputers, rather than 'up' from 8-bit microcomputers.

TASK

This exercise is a practical test of competence in using an operating system. You should carry it out on a machine to which you have access. If possible, carry out the following tasks; if these tasks are not possible, state that they cannot be achieved on your particular system.

(a) Create a new file (using an editor or word processor for example).
(b) Copy the file to another disc.
(c) Lock the original file.
(d) Change the name of the copied file.
(e) Copy this file to the original disc.
(f) Combine the original (now locked) file and the copied file into a single file, with a third name.
(g) Erase the original file.
(h) Bring that file back (that is, restore it in the directory).
(i) Build a file of commands to be executed, which will take two named files and will swap their names (note the files may be locked).

17.12. THE NEW GENERATION OF OPERATING SYSTEMS: USER-FRIENDLINESS

One impact of the spreading of computer use from the specialist to the ordinary office worker or manager, is that concern has been expressed about how difficult traditional operating systems are to use for the novice or irregular user. This has led to the development of a new breed of operating systems which give the user more help and prompts. Rather than being purely command-driven and expecting the user to know what to type next, the latest generation uses menus to offer the range of options and uses pictures to represent features. This new generation of software is known as **WIMPs**, which stands for Windows, Icon and Mouse-driven Programs.

The idea of a **window** is that the screen can be divided up into a number of areas, so that in each part a task can be represented. Thus on part of the screen the user may be writing a document using a word processor, in another window a directory of the files on the disc can be displayed and in a third a spreadsheet can be displayed. The user can switch between applications to make a different one of the windows active. This is achieved by moving the hand-held **mouse** device around the desk. The ability to move around is useful, for example, when writing a document, having to leave off to perform a calculation, and then coming back to the original document at the point that it was left. The area on the screen allocated to each activity can be altered by dragging the areas around with the mouse. Old features can be discarded or new ones activated using the mouse for selection. This is known as closing and opening windows.

An **icon** is a small picture to represent a function which can be carried out by the computer. So an icon can represent a feature which is normally regarded as part of the operating system, such as a dustbin to represent 'scrap' a file. This would be used by pointing to the appropriate file name with the mouse, and dragging the name over the screen to the dustbin. When a document is to be saved to or retrieved from a file, an icon representing a filing cabinet is used. The use of pictures rather than words saves considerable reading and is more pleasant to the eye. Individual programs can be given icons so that they can be accessed in this manner. Thus a picture of a calculator can be used to access a calculator program, a clock to represent a program which displays the current time, a painter's canvas to represent a graphics program and so on.

Pull-down menus

The move towards making operating systems easier to use by making the screen look something like a desk-top has led to the use of the term 'operating environment' to denote something more than a pure operating system. Products like MS-Windows are designed as an interface between the user and MS-DOS, and in this sense are loaded 'on top of' the operating system, shielding users from the precise syntax of MS-DOS. A similar approach is taken in GEM from Digital Research.

In order for software such as MS-Windows to be used as software through which other commercial packages are viewed, a file (called a parameter file) must be created so that standard facts about the package can be recorded, such as the memory space needed, and the way the program handles the keyboard and the screen. For many of the popular packages such parameter files are readily available; for some packages the file might have to be specially set up.

17.13. MORE THAN ONE THING AT ONCE

Some operating systems allow more than one program to be running apparently at the same time within the computer, by means of memory management techniques and giving each use a portion of time (**timeslicing**). This could occur either with a system with a number of terminals or, increasingly, with a powerful microcomputer where a single user has some tasks working away in the background while another is being carried out in the foreground (**multitasking**). For example, a user might wish to check the spelling of the words in a document. Rather than wait for the whole document to be checked a word at a time, the user

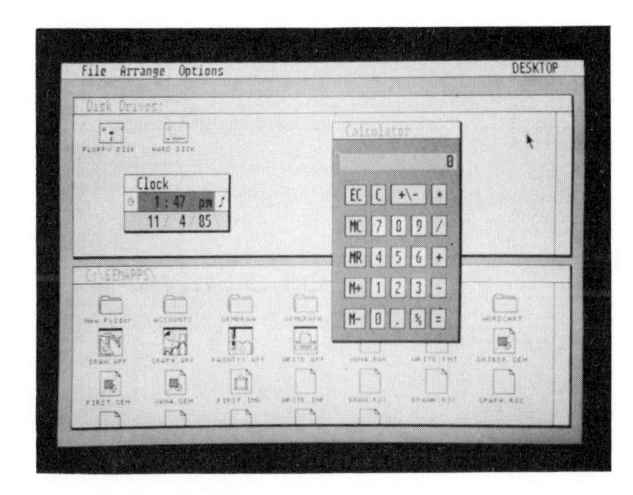

An operating environment where the user doesn't have to enter text-based keyboard commands, but instead refers to icons by using a mouse and a pointer on the screen: GEM from Digital Research

can initiate another task, such as the entry of data into a spreadsheet. The computer will service the user's needs to process inputs from the keyboard, but any other unused time can be allocated in slices to the job of spelling checking. This makes more efficient use of the computer's and the user's time.

Multitasking is often presented in a windowed style, so that different tasks which are (apparently) running at the same time are presented on different parts of the screen. It is usual for the primary ('active') task which the user is carrying out to be 'zoomed', that is, it will take up most of the screen area, whereas the background tasks use smaller parts of the screen. The selection and manipulation of different tasks is normally achieved by use of the mouse.

17.14. WHERE TO FIND OUT MORE

The choice of an operating system becomes an increasingly more important part of choosing a computer system. This is because, as the hardware develops with more and more sophisticated features, the user needs to have ways of exploiting them. This is usually done by way of the operating system. Beyond the basic physical features of a machine, then, the choice of operating system is crucial. In particular, much commercial software has been designed only to run under a limited number of operating systems.

Reviews regularly appear in the top of the market business computing magazines of new or of tried-and-tested operating systems. The comments of reviewers and of other regular users of particular operating systems or operating environments are worthy of attention.

Similarly, magazine articles might explain more advanced features of operating systems, or describe how to carry out tasks more efficiently. Such hints and tips can be useful, even to the most seasoned users of an operating system. It should always be remembered that the mere fact that some tasks are made easy by an operating system (such as making back-up copies of files) does not mean that all users will exploit them to best effect. All users can continue to develop techniques in their use of an operating system.

17.15. STUDY QUESTIONS

1 What are the advantages and disadvantages of operating systems designed by manufacturers for specific model ranges, such as Primos for PRIME computers?
2 What are the advantages and disadvantages to manufacturers of publishing an 'open architecture' for an operating system to enable other companies to provide add-on features for the operating system, such as additional commands?
3 Why is spooling essential for a multi-user system?

17.16. ASSIGNMENTS

1 For an operating system that you know, design a set of guidelines for users which outline conventions for naming files, for making backup copies of files, for erasing unwanted out-of-date files and any other features of good practice which you consider would be useful. Include instructions on how each of these tasks is carried out.
2 The ease of use of operating systems has made it easy for users to copy software. This is often very useful for adequate security for an installation. However, it can also make the illegal copying (pirating) of programs easier as well. Find out some of the ways in which security features have been built in to commercial software and describe what you can find out about them.

18 HARD CHOICES

18.1. TAKING A HARD LOOK AT EQUIPMENT

Much has been said and written about computer equipment. Different machines and new models are reviewed in computer magazines and Sunday newspapers; they are advertised on television. The development of computers in their capacity and their speed has been breathtaking. Each year, for about six years, memory sizes of microcomputers have doubled **and** the price of any particular category of computer has almost halved. Against this background of the wizardry of technology, it is often difficult to hold fast to the philosophy that it is the **software** which should be chosen before the hardware.

Many new features are being made available in the competitive world of computer manufacture, but this is of little value if the software used on the equipment does not exploit the features available.

This text will not attempt detailed descriptions of how hardware works. There are many computer studies texts which will give a more detailed description. There are many magazines which will give more up-to-the-minute information. This text looks at how some of the main features of current computer technology can be used. References to detailed descriptions are given at the end of the chapter.

18.2. THE NAMING OF THE PARTS

It is traditional to think of data processing as consisting of three stages; input, process and output. Computer equipment can also be considered under these three headings, with the additional consideration of backing storage devices for keeping files and intermediate results.

18.3. PROCESSING: THE MAIN COMPUTER

Some computer practitioners have a tendency to describe computer equipment in very technical terms. They talk about a 4 megahertz chip, or a 256 kilobyte RAM, and about handshaking and communications protocols; yet, for most users, these terms mean very little and users realise they do not have to understand them to use the equipment. In many ways, this is similar to the car driver, who need not understand the operation of an overhead camshaft, and indeed, can be a successful driver without even knowing that a car has an overhead camshaft. Some might argue that some detailed knowledge might help somebody be a **better** driver, or computer user, but this will usually come after the basic skills have been mastered.

TASK

Give examples of ways in which having a technical knowledge of how computer equipment works would help you to be a better user.

In buying computers, as with many other things, it is said that 'you gets what you pays for'. In any particular price range, whether it be around £500, £1000, or £10 000, the features of the main computer (often called the **central processing unit**, or **CPU**), will be broadly similar. Some of the aspects which it might be fruitful to examine when contrasting broadly similar machines are:

(a) memory size,
(b) the length of data items processed by the CPU (measured in bits),
(c) the operating systems supported,
(d) the types of printer supported,
(e) the number of colours available (the importance of this will depend on the applications being considered),
(f) the size and types of screen display output which it can provide,
(g) any feature enabling the computer to run more than one program at once,
(h) speed (though this is best compared, not on manufacturer's published internal clock speeds, but on the time taken in the sort of processing for the applications being considered).

18.4. OUTPUT

Monitors

Some computers come with a display monitor included as part of the standard price, in other cases purchasers can choose their own. The inclusion of a monitor by the manufacturer can exploit the features of the main computer to the full and the features of many displays form a prominent part of the advertising material. Manufacturers may include anti-glare screens, which cut out annoying reflections, screens which can tilt and twist for the user's own convenience and which may be in colours which are restful for the eyes.

When choosing monitors, there are many aspects which can be examined. Monochrome monitors display text in a single colour and there is a wide choice of different monochrome monitors. As well as the traditional white on black, there is also green on black, and amber on chocolate, which many consider better. Appearance also plays its part in the choice of a monitor. What is important, however, is to ensure that the monitor being bought can be used with the particular computer. This will mean that appropriate leads will have to be bought to carry the signals in an appropriate way; on other occasions, links are simply not possible for technical reasons.

Monitors are normally described as being of a particular 'resolution', such as high- or medium-resolution. This refers to the clarity of the picture displayed. Purpose-designed monitors give a much sharper picture than a domestic television; the quality of monitor that is needed will depend on the user, the application and the computer. It is worth pointing out, however, that the display on the monitor can only be as good as the signals that the computer sends out. Most obviously, if the computer only sends out monochrome signals for display, the most expensive colour monitor will not be able to display the results in full colour. Similarly, much software is only designed to run in monochrome.

Printers

When choosing a printer, it is important not only to consider what features particular printers have, but also which of those features matter **for the particular application**. The features available fall into two main areas. There are those features which are to do with the quality of the finished product and there are those to do with the speed of getting that product. Both these areas can be important – they are not just about convenience. The quality of printed material will particularly affect the company image; the speed of printing will affect staffing levels, and, indeed, whether work can be completed on time.

Impact printers

The printing method has a major impact on the quality of the finished product. A number of methods depend on striking a ribbon on to the

The features of the Epson LX–80 explained and illustrated

EPSON

THE EPSON LX-80
A MORE PROFESSIONAL PERSONAL PRINTER

Despite its handsome, low profile looks, the LX-80 is packed with powerful, professional features you'd expect to find only in a printer costing far more - setting new standards of versatility and quality, for low cost printing.

Near Letter Quality, Built-In. And Quick Draft Printing in a Variety of Styles
Roman for correspondence, Pica and Elite for drafting, at 100cps in all the normal styles: Enlarged, Condensed, Emphasized, Double Strike, Italics, Sub and Super Script.

Easy Type Selection
In addition to all the fonts and typestyles available through software control, each of the LX-80's resident typefonts can be summoned at the touch of a 'Selectype' key on the printer itself. You can also select condensed and emphasized from the front panel.

Plus Word Processing Functions
To help you to put its type style versatility to full use, the LX-80 offers word processing functions - text justification and centring which are software controlled.

Easy to change Ribbon Cartridges
When the time comes to change your ribbon all you have to do is snap a new cartridge cleanly into place.

Versatile Paper Handling
For letter headings, individual sheets and many word processing applications, the LX-80 is equipped with a friction paper feed.

An optional cut sheet feeder is available, and an optional tractor feeder enables the LX-80 to handle anything from pre-printed forms to self-adhesive labels just 3" wide.

Powerful Graphics TOO!
Charts and diagrams can be combined with text to illustrate financial information, sales statistics or mathematical concepts with graphic precision.

EPSON LX-80
More printer for your money.
Prices: LX-80 £255 : Sheet Feeder £55 : Tractor £20 : Excl. VAT
Epson UK Ltd. Dorland House, 388 High Road, Wembley, Middlx. Tel.: 01-902 8892

piece of paper, leaving a mark. Such so-called **impact** printing methods include **matrix** printers, which form the characters from a series of dots, and **daisywheel** printers, where a wheel contains a different character form on each spoke. The quality of the characters formed with a matrix printer varies considerably and improvements continue to be made. The term **near letter quality (nlq)** has been coined to describe those matrix printers with many dots per character, where the output is almost as good as the results that a daisywheel produces.

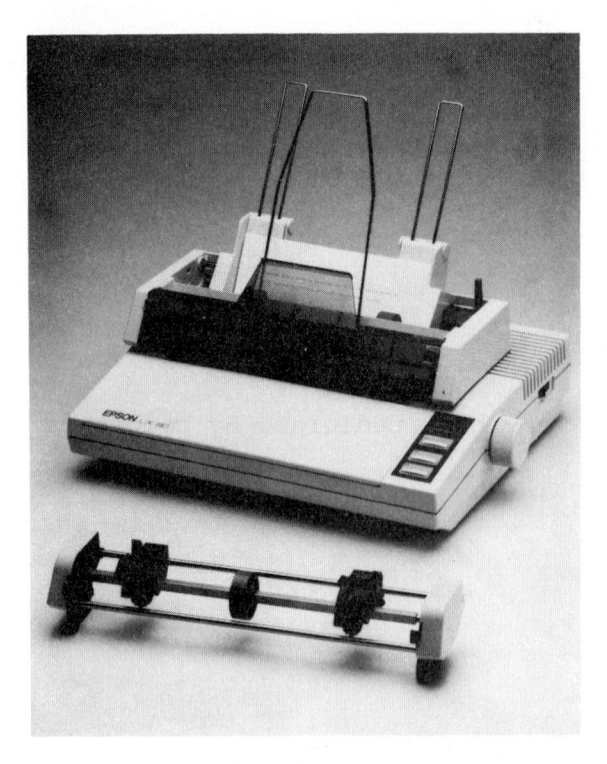

A matrix printer with near-letter-quality (NLQ) output and a choice of single sheet feeder, friction and tractor feed: the Epson LX–80

The Brother Twinriter combines both matrix printing for speed and graphics, and daisywheel printing for quality printing

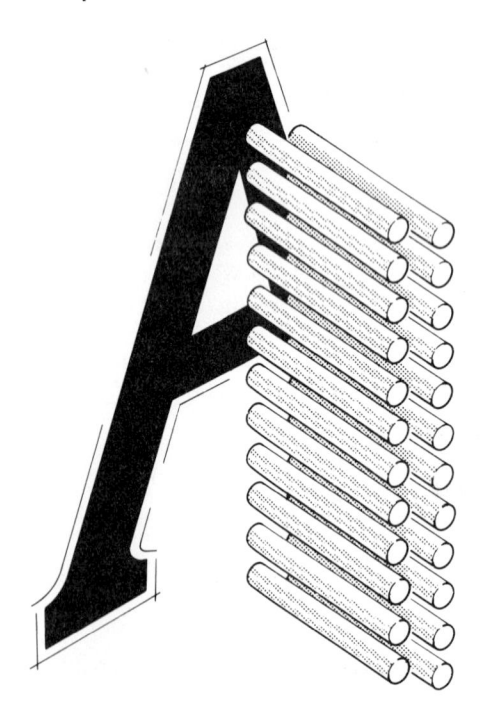

Printers in the Epson LQ range use a print head consisting of 24 fine pins in 2 lines of 12 to give a higher concentration of smaller dots

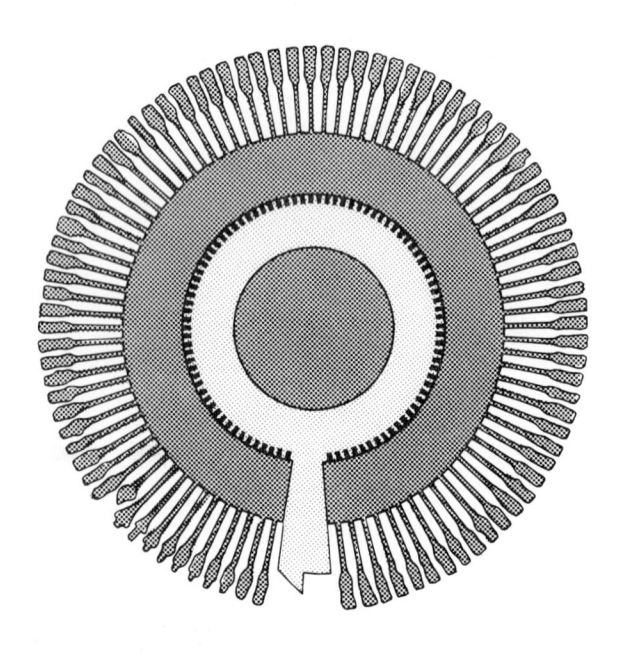

A daisywheel is used to produce high quality printout; the daisywheel can be exchanged so that different typefaces can be used

The features of the Brother Twinwriter explained and illustrated

brother

```
    Twinriter5
```

An outstanding <u>new</u> **MULTIMODE** printer from **BROTHER**
Twinriter5 is a hybrid printer of the very best pedigree. By combining
our best in **Daisy wheel** technology with our expertise in **Dot matrix**
we have produced a printer that offers the very best of both worlds.

Characters not on the Daisy wheel can be printed by NLQ dot matrix

IBM 8 bit extended character set.

üéâäàåçêëèïîìÄÅÉæÆôöòûùÿÖÜ¢£¥₧ƒáíóúñÑªº¿⌐¬½¼¡«»
αßΓπΣσμτΦΘΩδ∞ØЄ∩≡±≥≤⌠⌡÷≈°··√ⁿ²■

Bit image characters and graphics characters can be printed

   IBM Graphics
   ▓│┤╡╢╖╕╣║╗╝╜╛┐└┴┬├─┼╞╟╚╔╩╦╠═╬╧╨╤╥╙╘╒╓╫╪┘┌█▄▌▐▀♥♦♣♠

By using all the features together we can produce the following.

              ****   EXAMPLE APPLICATION ****

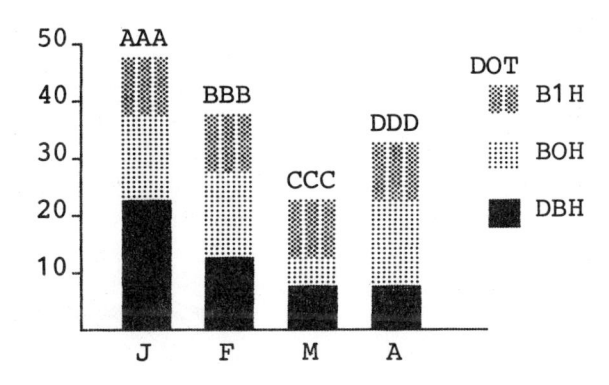

[bar chart showing months J, F, M, A with values approximately 48, 38, 23, 33; legend: DOT, B1H, BOH, DBH; bars labeled AAA, BBB, CCC, DDD]

       For further details contact.

              BROTHER OFFICE EQUIPMENT DIV.
                    SHEPLEY STREET
                     GUIDE BRIDGE
                     061 330 6531
                      MANCHESTER

Non-impact printers

Some other printer technologies do not rely on impact methods, and are therefore much quieter in operation. Ink-jet printers spray charged ink particles through a nozzle. These are then deflected by electrostatic plates to position them on the paper. Laser printers use a rotating mirror to direct a laser beam on to a rotating belt or drum which has a photoconductor surface. The image attracts a toner, like that used in a photocopier, which enables the image to be transferred to paper. The image is made permanent on the paper by heating it. Non-impact printers are not able to produce several copies at once using multi-part stationery.

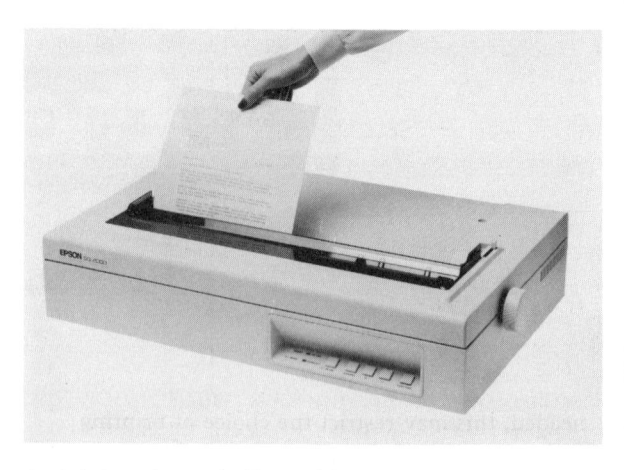

An ink jet printer: the Epson SQ-200

Sample output from the Epson SQ-200 ink jet printer

DRAFT PICA
ABCDEFGHIJKLMNOPQRSTUVWXYZ][\abcdefghijklmnopqrstuvwxyz}¦{1234567890

CONDENSED DRAFT PICA
ABCDEFGHIJKLMNOPQRSTUVWXYZ][\abcdefghijklmnopqrstuvwxyz}¦{1234567890

EMPHASISED DRAFT PICA
ABCDEFGHIJKLMNOPQRSTUVWXYZ][\abcdefghijklmnopqrstuvwxyz}¦{1234567890

DRAFT ENLARGED
ABCDEFGHIJKLMNOPQRSTUVWXYZ][\abcdefghijklmnopqrstuvwxyz}¦{1234567890

DRAFT ELITE
ABCDEFGHIJKLMNOPQRSTUVWXYZ][\abcdefghijklmnopqrstuvwxyz}¦{1234567890

DOUBLESTRIKE DRAFT ELITE
ABCDEFGHIJKLMNOPQRSTUVWXYZ][\abcdefghijklmnopqrstuvwxyz}¦{1234567890

ITALIC DOUBLESTRIKE DRAFT ELITE
ABCDEFGHIJKLMNOPQRSTUVWXYZ][\abcdefghijklmnopqrstuvwxyz}¦{1234567890

ENLARGED ITALIC DOUBLESTRIKE DRAFT ELITE
ABCDEFGHIJKL]\[abcdefghijkl}{¦1234567890

LETTER QUALITY

LQ
ABCDEFGHIJKLMNOPQRSTUVWXYZ][\abcdefghijklmnopqrstuvwxyz}¦{1234567890

EMPHASISED LQ
ABCDEFGHIJKLMNOPQRSTUVWXYZ][\abcdefghijklmnopqrstuvwxyz}¦{1234567890

ENLARGED LQ
ABCDEFGHIJK][\abcdefghijk}{¦123456789C

SUPERSCRIPT LQ
ABCDEFGHIJKLMNOPQRSTUVWXYZ][\abcdefghijklmnopqrstuvwxyz}¦{1234567890

Other differences

Other ways in which the output quality differs between pieces of equipment include the different **print pitches** which are available. This is the term used to describe the spacing between letters in the text. The commonly available pitches are 10, 12 and 15 characters per inch. **Proportional spacing** allows each character to take up a width according to its size; thus 'm' and 'w' are allowed more space than 'i' and 'l'.

If there are particular uses for which a printer is needed, this may restrict the choice of printing formats. A daisywheel printer, for example, is not suitable for printing graphics output, but is very good for cutting a stencil for use on a duplicator.

Paper feeding

There are two main ways that paper is fed through a printer. The first, called **friction feed** pulls paper through around a roller, pinching the paper against the roller as in a conventional typewriter. The other common feeding mechanism is the **tractor feed** which uses the sprocket holes on the sides of computer paper to pull or push the paper through. Friction feed is more suited to printing on individual sheets of paper than to using continuous stationery.

Speed considerations

The speed of printing is affected by the particular printing technology used (daisywheel printing being much slower, as there is much more physical movement of parts), but speed also depends on a number of other inbuilt features which printers may have. A **bi-directional** printer will print one line with the head travelling from left to right, then the next with the head travelling from right to left. This reduces the delay between lines. A **logic seeking** printer only moves the head as far forwards or backwards after printing a line as will be needed to print the next line. A **buffered** printer contains a memory (typically of 4000 characters) into which characters for printing can be sent by the computer prior to being printed. This may enable the computer to complete the sending out of data to be printed, so that the computer can be used for some other task while the printer completes the printing.

A printer has to be linked to a computer by means of an interface. This enables one piece of equipment to interpret signals from another. There are many styles of interface, some of which are described as 'standards'. The most frequently used are the **Centronics** interface and the **RS232** interface. The Centronics is a parallel method (several wires are used at once), the RS232 is a serial method, sending one signal at a time. Some printers will accept output in either form. What will matter to a purchaser will be whether a particular computer can be used with a *particular* printer.

Modern developments in printer technology are enabling the manufacture of **colour printers** at prices which more people can afford. Colour output might be particularly useful when using graphics and drawing packages. Similarly, graphics **plotters** can be used in this way.

TASK

List the factors which should be taken into consideration when choosing a printer for a busy office.

18.5. INPUT

The keyboard

Virtually all computers have the 26 letters of the alphabet laid out in the way which was developed for typewriters from the earliest days. This is known as the QWERTY layout, as these are the first six letters on the top row of the keyboard.

The placement of the alphabetical characters, however, is the only universal standard for computer keyboards. Numeric keys are normally in one of two places. They are either directly above the alphabetical keys forming an additional row, or they form a separate area on the keyboard, sometimes called a key-pad, with the digits 1 to 9 forming a 3 by 3 square and the 0 being conveniently placed adjacent to this. The numeric key-pad is most useful when large amounts of numeric data are to be entered. Some machines have both a row of digits and a numeric key-pad for maximum convenience.

A SHIFT button is used in conjunction with other keys, firstly to provide capital letters in addition to lower case letters and secondly to provide punctuation and other symbols, such as ? $ & £. In many systems, there is a SHIFT LOCK facility, which will enable the user to get capital or shifted letters without constantly holding down the SHIFT key. In some cases, SHIFT LOCK is automatically on when the machine is switched on.

Other important keys are the RETURN key (alternatively called ENTER), which is used when data is being entered to denote that the entry of the item is complete. A DELETE key is usually provided so that errors which are spotted in time can be corrected before data is entered. The key labelled CTRL (or sometimes ALT), is only used in conjunction with other keys. These combinations usually provide special features via the operating system. In addition to these keys, separate keys can be provided for movement of the cursor around the screen, to clear the screen, and to stop the program. Keys labelled ESCAPE and BREAK have specialised uses which should be explained in a manual. These operations can involve the loss of data or programs.

Special 'function' keys are provided on many of the more recent machines and these can be given a specialised function by each program which is run.

TASK

Suggest ways in which the competence of a person is using a keyboard could be measured. Outline some methods of keyboard training.

The mouse

An increasingly popular input device is the **mouse**. This hand-held device can be moved around the desk and as it moves, signals are sent down a wire into the computer. Programs are designed to respond to the mouse movement. There are up to three buttons on the mouse and signals are also sent when these buttons are pressed.

The mouse is very useful for input which does not consist of text or numbers. When a user is being asked to select from a list of options, a mouse can be used. The user simply has to move the mouse across the table. This movement is shown on the screen by the movement of some symbol (such as an arrow) reflecting the mouse position, until the symbol is over the appropriate user choice. The user then presses one of the buttons to select that option. The advantage of all this is that the user can look at the screen throughout the process. The use of keyboard input for a user who is not a keyboard expert can involve searching for a number of characters on the keyboard and glancing up at the screen several times in between.

The mouse can have an important role to play with applications such as word processing and image processing, where a section (of text or drawing) is to be moved or copied; this process is sometimes known as 'cut and paste'. The mouse can be used both to indicate what to move and where to move it to. It is possible to move a pointer around more quickly using a mouse than it is using cursor control keys on the keyboard.

Other input devices

A number of other devices are available to bypass users' inexperience with the keyboard. These methods often have particular applications for which they are especially useful. Such methods include **bar code readers**, **light pens** and **touch screens**. **Joysticks** can be used for the input of a two-directional movement and additional information can be input by rotating the joystick itself. Developments in **voice input** may well enable users to bypass the keyboard, usually when a limited vocabulary is required. Other special devices include the **graphics tablet**, where a puck is moved around a flat drawing area. These can be used for detailed drawing, with the puck having a pair of crossed wires for accurate positioning.

Each of these hardware innovations has its place, but purchasers should always bear in mind that the hardware is only of benefit when used with powerful applications software written to use such devices to advantage.

TASK

Outline some of the alternatives to keyboards that can be used for input by business executives.

18.6. STORAGE DEVICES

Magnetic discs are used for the storage of data. They work by using a disc drive both to record digital information on the disc in a magnetic form and to read the data back when required, using a read/write head on the disc drive.

There are three main types of discs used in this way:

A range of magnetic media: 3M products

(a) **5¼ inch floppy discs**, which have been in use for many years are common to computers as varied as the BBC, the IBM PC and the Victor. The disc itself is circular and made of a polyester film, with a fine coating of magnetic particles. It is housed in a flexible square plastic case, known as a jacket, with a small window so that part of the surface is exposed for recording data and reading it back. The jacket is lined with a fabric which very gently removes dust which has gathered on the exposed surface. Discs have to be handled gently, so that the exposed surface is not touched and the case is not creased. A typical such floppy disc might hold between 100 000 and 200 000 characters of information.

The various features of a five-and-a-quarter inch disc (diagram courtesy of 3M United Kingdom plc)

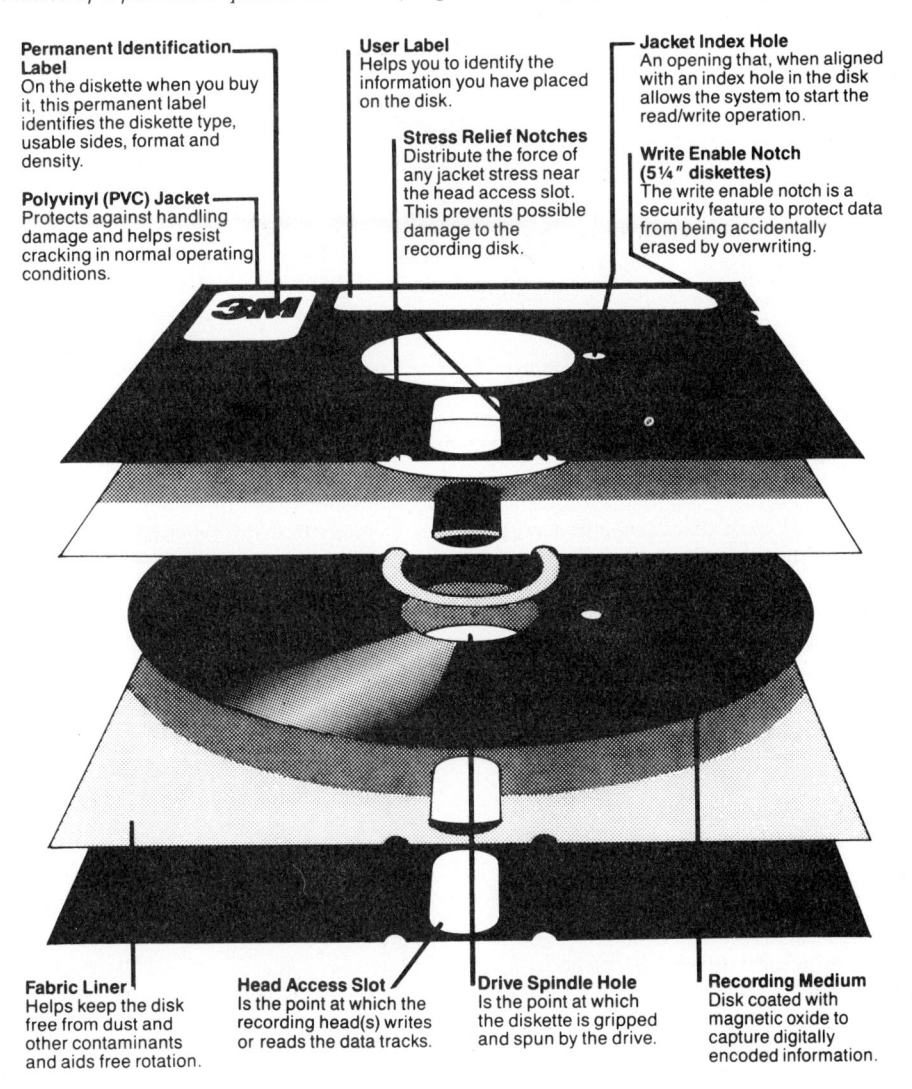

Permanent Identification Label
On the diskette when you buy it, this permanent label identifies the diskette type, usable sides, format and density.

Polyvinyl (PVC) Jacket
Protects against handling damage and helps resist cracking in normal operating conditions.

User Label
Helps you to identify the information you have placed on the disk.

Stress Relief Notches
Distribute the force of any jacket stress near the head access slot. This prevents possible damage to the recording disk.

Jacket Index Hole
An opening that, when aligned with an index hole in the disk allows the system to start the read/write operation.

Write Enable Notch (5¼" diskettes)
The write enable notch is a security feature to protect data from being accidentally erased by overwriting.

Fabric Liner
Helps keep the disk free from dust and other contaminants and aids free rotation.

Head Access Slot
Is the point at which the recording head(s) writes or reads the data tracks.

Drive Spindle Hole
Is the point at which the diskette is gripped and spun by the drive.

Recording Medium
Disk coated with magnetic oxide to capture digitally encoded information.

The various features of a three-and-a-half inch disc (diagram courtesy of 3M United Kingdom plc)

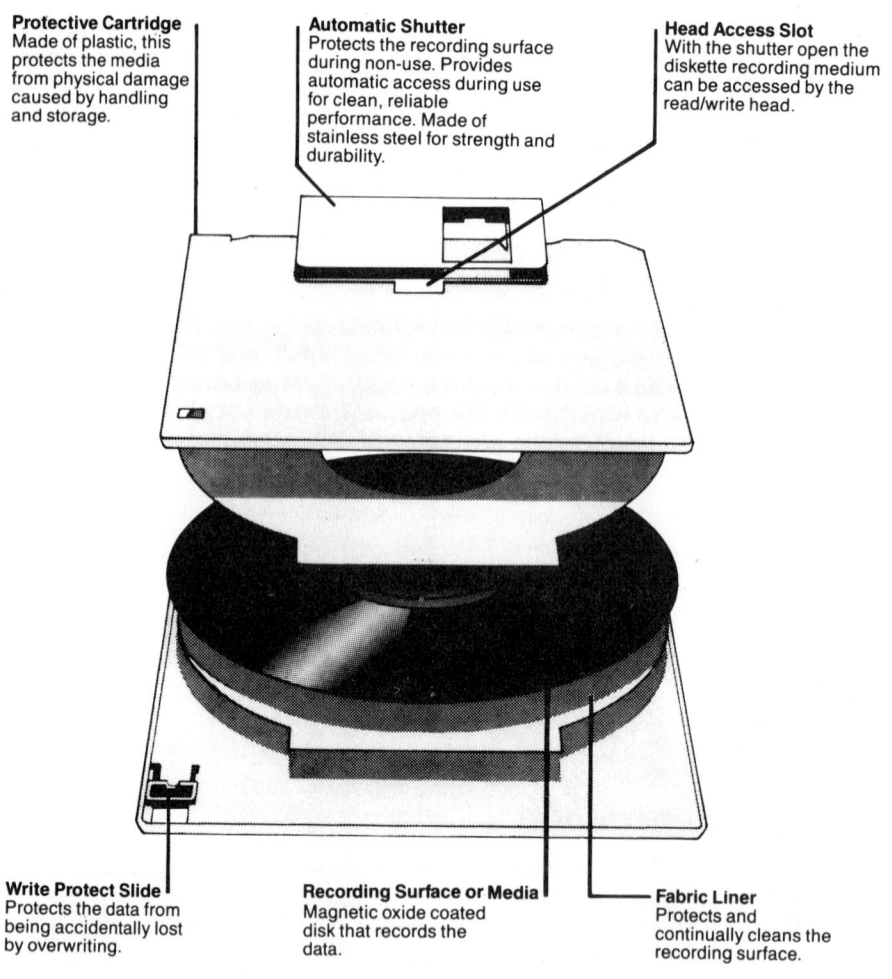

Protective Cartridge
Made of plastic, this protects the media from physical damage caused by handling and storage.

Automatic Shutter
Protects the recording surface during non-use. Provides automatic access during use for clean, reliable performance. Made of stainless steel for strength and durability.

Head Access Slot
With the shutter open the diskette recording medium can be accessed by the read/write head.

Write Protect Slide
Protects the data from being accidentally lost by overwriting.

Recording Surface or Media
Magnetic oxide coated disk that records the data.

Fabric Liner
Protects and continually cleans the recording surface.

(b) **3 inch and the 3½ inch discs** come in a **rigid** plastic case. In the case of the 3½ inch disc, a metal shutter covers the window on to the surface, which slides back when the disc is inside the drive. The case and the shutter provide additional security for the data and enable the recording to be much more densely packed on the surface. Thus they normally have a higher storage capacity than the larger 5¼ inch floppy discs, typically half a million characters.

(c) **Hard discs** are fixed in a sealed unit. As the unit is free from contamination, the recording on the disc can be more densely packed and thus a typical Winchester disc, as they are often called, will hold 40 million characters of data. The Winchester disc drive will often come inbuilt within the casing of a computer. Because the disc cannot be exchanged in the way that floppy discs can be, there is an upper limit to the capacity, but with good disciplined use of files this should not be too much of a problem.

In most business applications, it is vital to have a computer with two disc drives. This makes the copying of files from one disc to another straightforward. While files can be copied on a computer with a single drive, this can be very time-consuming, which is frustrating, as file copying is essential, but is usually not productive work.

Discs which are **soft sectored** must be formatted to lay out the sectors on the recording tracks before use. Other terms which are used in describing the various discs available on the market include single or double density, single or double sided, and a specification of the number of tracks per inch (TPI).

Users need not worry about these terms, but should discover at the outset what quality of discs is necessary for a particular system.

18.7. OTHER EQUIPMENT

When choosing computer equipment, it is important not to overlook the additional purchases needed as well as the basic hardware, as the costs of these might be considerable. A number of cables may be needed to link pieces of equipment together. These can cost between £10 and £20 each.

Often new furniture will have to be bought. This might include typist chairs, desks, monitor stands, printer stands and special desk lamps depending on the siting of equipment within a room.

On the electrical side, special wiring will probably be needed so that the supply is 'clean', and several adaptors may be required.

Another part of the initial cost of a computer system will be an initial stock of paper, ribbons, daisywheels, floppy discs and so on. Boxes will also be necessary for the safe storage of discs, including back-up copies of important files in a different place from the discs in daily use. Storage boxes with locks are available.

18.8. MAKING THE LINK

It is increasingly important in business data processing to be able to link together several microcomputers in a network. This is an alternative to the more established multi-user systems, where a single computer has a number of terminals. Linking up in these ways enables information to be available for access or alteration from several sites at the same time.

18.9. NETWORKS

A network consists of a number of microcomputers linked in such a way that data can be passed between them. The term **local area network (LAN)** is used to describe the linking of several devices within a restricted geographical area, usually within one building. Thus, permanent links, normally via cabling, are maintained between devices, whether in use or not. There are a number of ways in which links can be formed in a LAN, including the **ring**, the **star** and the **bus** methods.

Each shape of linking up is known as a **topology**.

A **star** has a central point, called the controller, which is linked to each of the workstations, at the points of the star. This system is clearly vulnerable, as if the controller develops a fault, the whole network will go down.

In a **ring** network, all the devices are connected to a ring of cable. The data moves round the ring in one direction. When it reaches its destination, it is taken off. Because a lot of the development work was done at Cambridge, the ring is sometimes known as the **Cambridge Ring**.

In a **bus** topology, all the devices are linked to a single cable which has terminators at each end. Each device is given an address. Messages are broadcast on the network, but only the device with the correct address picks it up. One of the early networks with this style was **Ethernet**, on which many bus systems are still based.

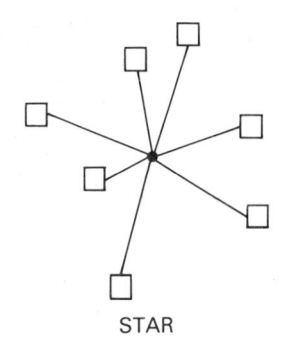

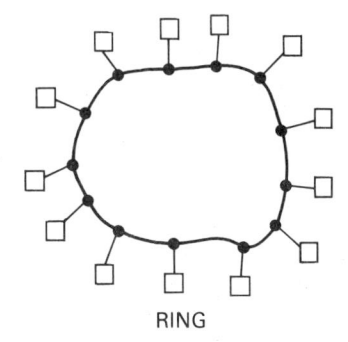

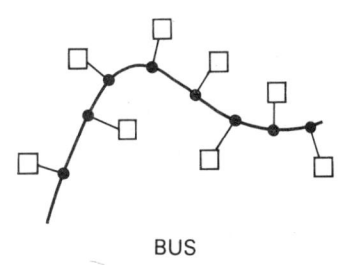

STAR

RING

BUS

Three types of ring topologies: Star, Ring and Bus

Sending messages

Messages can be passed round a network in a number of forms, called **protocols**.

Token passing involves the circulation of empty 'tokens'. When a device wishes to send a message, it grabs an empty token, places the data in it and sends it back around the network. When a device detects a token addressed to it, it accepts the token and removes the data.

In some systems, each device is allocated a **time slot** in turn, during which it can transmit data. If this system is not used, and all devices can transmit at any time, then there is a possibility of a collision. This has to be dealt with by a method known as carrier sense multiple access with collision detection (**CSMA/CD**), to prevent two devices sending messages simultaneously, which would mean that the messages would be corrupted.

The linking of devices over larger distances, and the linking of different LANs together is achieved by means of a **wide area network (WAN)**, which will use telecommunications lines or other forms of transmission.

In order that digital devices such as computers and terminals can be linked using the analogue telephone lines in Britain, the digital signals must be converted. The device which achieves this is called a **modem** (modulator/demodulator). Modulation is the process of loading the digital signal on to an analogue carrier wave, demodulation is the stripping of the digital signal back off. British Telecom is in the process of installing a system of digital telephone exchanges, known as System X. With the use of local PABXs (private automatic branch exchanges), this will supersede the need for modems. A **multiplexor** allows several low-speed terminals to share a single high-speed transmission line. This can represent a substantial cost saving.

The benefits of networks

A network provides a link-up with each workstation being a microcomputer in its own right, thus having its own processing power, but also allowing the passing and sharing of data. One reason for the popularity of networks has been that they are built around existing microcomputers and users may already be familiar with the hardware, an operating system and applications software.

A network system: the 16-bit RM Nimbus Network from Research Machines Limited

When data has been received at a workstation, it can be manipulated purely locally. Within a network, the processing power is distributed and this means that a local copy of any operating software must be available. This is usually down-loaded into the microcomputer from the network.

Separate licensing arrangements usually operate when software is acquired for a network. The charge is usually something between the charge for a copy runnning only a stand-alone system and the charge for acquiring a copy for each of the workstations.

18.10. MULTI-USER SYSTEMS

A **multi-user system** will allow several users to be carrying out a variety of tasks simultaneously. A true multi-user system will also allow several people to carry out the same task on the same files on the same machine at the same time. This is generally achieved by having a centralised computer with access by means of a number of terminals. A good multi-user system will be powerful enough that users will not notice a reduction in the response time despite sharing a resource; in other words, they can be unaware of other users.

A multi-user system is very useful in situations where access to the same files is required by several people at the same time. Such people might be in the same place, such as several clerks in an accounts department or in a number of widely different locations, such as occurs in an airline booking system. In such situations, it is important that the software ensures that only one user has access to files or records during the actual time that the data is being changed. This is known as **locking**. If such a facility were not provided, two users might amend the data in different ways simultaneously and it might become internally inconsistent. Neither user would know how to restore the data. Indeed, the users might not even be aware that there was a problem.

18.11. ADVANTAGES OF LINKED SYSTEMS

Linked systems, either networks or multi-user systems, are useful where there is a regular need to transfer files from one place to another. They can also be useful for resource sharing. In this way, a number of users can share hard disc storage, or a top quality printer, to which they do not need sole access, but would find very useful from time to time.

The ability to link computers or terminals also introduces more flexibility to a system's development. New microcomputers or terminals can be linked into the system as and when they are needed and the money is available. Users sometimes find that a new mainframe system is under-used for the first year or two of its life.

Setting up a local area network can open up the possibility of linking with other networks.

One additional benefit of deciding to network within a diversified organisation is that it opens up the possibility of putting an individual in charge of coordination, which can lead to more widespread compatibility of equipment. It can be a move away from the style typified by one organisation where it was claimed that Noah had decided the computer purchasing policy, because there were two of everything!

TASK

Describe the ways in which the use of a local area network could be used to hold data to be used within a large hospital, with terminals available in wards, theatres, reception, the pharmacy and other departments.

18.12. VIEWDATA

Businesses can also make creative use of computer based information systems, such as **Prestel**. Information within the system is provided by a number of government bodies, travel firms, financial services and other businesses. Users of the system can select pages of information through a microcomputer or handset linked with a screen and a telephone line. Users are charged a rental for the Prestel service, the cost of the telephone call, and during the day a charge is made for the Prestel computer time.

In addition, information providers may charge for each screen of data. Thus, the service is not particularly cheap, but for access to up-to-date information on stocks, shares or currency rates, or information which is valuable for some other reason, many businesses consider the system worthwhile. The tourism industry in particular makes great use of Prestel.

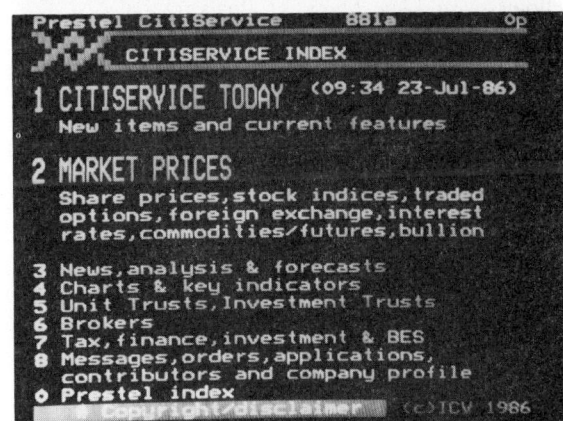

Prestel screens (courtesy of British Telecom)

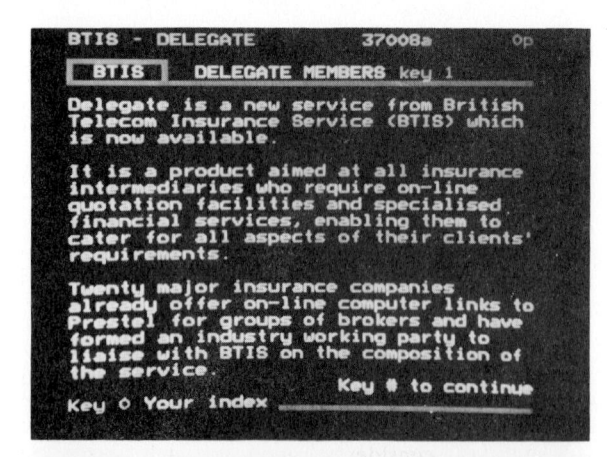

Prestel screens (courtesy of British Telecom)

Prestel can be used to request further information, or to order goods, by using what are called response frames. In this way Prestel differs from the Ceefax and Oracle services, the teletext services provided by the television companies, which only communicate one way. Prestel can be used as a means to access data within international databases as well.

Private viewdata systems have also been established by some firms or groups of organisations as an efficient and fast means of communication.

18.13. MORE NEW TECHNOLOGY IN THE OFFICE

Electronic mail allows the sending and collection of messages, with a host computer system holding a message until the recipient next logs on to the system. The user can retain the message for longer if this is required. Such systems can allow the passing of the same message to different locations very swiftly, including the possibility of sending to others copies of messages received. **Facsimile transmission (fax)** allows the sending of a copy of a document by way of telecommunications. With a fax machine at each end of a line, the original document is placed in the device at one end, and a copy is produced on paper at the other, as if by a photocopier. This is done by the translation of the document into digital form for it to be sent. The document to be sent does not have to be text, it could be a map or a drawing. For some organisations, their information needs are such that this service is cost-effective.

The term '**information technology**' has been coined as a general term for computers, microelectronics and telecommunications which are used to obtain, produce, store, process and send information in the form of pictures, words and numbers. The technology has developed rapidly. It is the uses which come in the wake of that technology, however, that are having the major impact on businesses, and, through them, ordinary people. Campaigns like 'Information Technology Year' in 1982 have rightly begun to put the emphasis on to the impact of the use of the tools we now have available to meet our information needs.

18.14. WHERE TO FIND OUT MORE

In the last few years, many books have been published in the computing field. A substantial number of these include detailed descriptions of how computer hardware works, in some cases even when this is not essential to the rest of the book.

Among the most precise and concise descriptions are those given in text books designed for schools and colleges, up to A-Level standard. These textbooks often reflect the heavy emphasis within some academic computing qualifications on a detailed study of the equipment.

Useful textbooks for this include: *Comprehensive Computer Studies*, 2nd edn, by Peter Bishop (Nelson 1982), *Computer Studies – A First Course*, 2nd edn, by John Shelley and Roger Hunt (Pitman 1984), *Computer Science* by Carl French (DP Publications 1984), *Mastering Computers* by G. G. L. Wright (Macmillan 1982).

By their nature, books do not contain up-to-the-minute information (we shall have to wait for electronic books to appear for that!). Current information on developments of equipment, and of the use of that equipment, can be found in magazines (such as *Micro Decision* and *Which Computer?*), and in the computer trade press (publications such as *What's New in Computing?*, *PC Week*, *Computer Weekly* and *Computing*). By far the best way of getting to know about computer equipment, however, is to **use** it.

18.15. STUDY QUESTIONS

1 Why are there **so many** different sizes, makes and models of microcomputers?
2 What value have computer games in encouraging people to become familiar with computers?

18.16. ASSIGNMENTS

1 How might an estate agent make use of information technology? How would this affect:

   (a) the partners in the firm,
   (b) the clerical staff,
   (c) the customers,
   (d) rival firms?

(You might think about the ways in which details of houses for sale are stored, and how they are copied in appropriate numbers. You might also consider the ways in which people looking for particular kinds of houses might be matched to houses for sale).

2 Write a report on how political parties are making use of computers. Choose one party on which to focus. Describe the hardware they have, how it is organised (centralised or decentralised), who uses the equipment and what the party considers to be the benefit. (Articles about this appear in the press from time to time. Particular use of computers seems to be made at by-elections.)

3 Write a report on the use of Prestel and other on-line information services in the travel trade. Find out what firms do and how much it costs. Describe also the training which staff undergo. How much do they understand about how the equipment works?

19 JOIN THE PROFESSIONALS

19.1. PROFESSIONAL BEHAVIOUR

High standards of behaviour are expected of trained computing personnel. In order to do a job properly, staff must work with a degree of honesty and integrity, particularly when put in a position of responsibility or trust by an employer or client. All professionals should have a particular set of values. The practical ways in which these values influence everyday working situations are known as **ethics**.

Doctors, lawyers and a host of other long-standing professions have evolved codes of conduct or standards which all new entrants to the profession should set themselves. This body of corporate behaviour is passed on from one generation to the next and is refined in the light of new circumstances, such as the advent of kidney transplants. The computing profession has grown up in such a rapid and haphazard way that it is only in fairly recent years that its professional bodies have begun to think about codes of conduct. A number of bodies, such as the British Computer Society, and notably in the United States, the Association of Computing Machinery (ACM), have discussed and issued guidelines about professional conduct.

The ACM has chosen to present its ideas as professional ideals (which are termed Ethical Considerations) and mandatory rules (termed Disciplinary Rules). The Ethical Considerations are more general, are couched in terms of encouragement and suggestion and are not binding. The Disciplinary Rules are more direct and clear-cut and failure to observe them can be the cause of suspension or expulsion from the Association. These rules are drawn up in such a way that a breach of them is clearly a serious misdemeanour. There is no suggestion that merely avoiding breaches of the rules makes somebody a caring professional.

Clearly it is difficult to draw up hard and fast rules of action to cover all possible circumstances which could occur. Many claim that a person's ethics are hammered out in the hundred-and-one judgements one is called upon to make in the situations which occur every day. This has led to the consideration of situation ethics – considering how a person would react in particular situations. For this reason, a number of broad areas of concern within modern computing are examined to lay the groundwork of our ethical framework. This will be followed by a series of situations, where you will have to decide, after discussion with others if necessary, what **you** would do in the particular circumstances. No 'right answers' are offered – you decide for yourself.

19.2. THE LAW

One obvious starting point as a yardstick in deciding what is and is not acceptable behaviour is to look to the law for guidance. This might at least determine some guidelines beyond which computer practitioners should not stray. To understand the basis on which computing law is based, it is important to look at the forms of damage that can be perpetrated by use of a computer system.

Privacy, security and integrity

Three important areas in the protection of data are those of **privacy**, **security** and **integrity**. These are distinct ideas, but they overlap and have their impact on each other.

Privacy

is the right of an individual citizen to determine what personal information to share with others. It is common practice for organisations to sell mailing lists to others. Thus when people buy new cars, a firm which sells anti-theft devices might like to send them a catalogue. Firms can get names and addresses from the garage and put a catalogue in the post. To what extent is this reasonable business practice? Is it helpful to the customer or is too much junk mail a nuisance? The individual's rights have to be balanced against the organisation's needs.

An added dimension to the sale of data, which is what such business information is, is the possibility of errors creeping into the data. From time to time, cases come to the attention of the press, where some 'computer error' has lead to an innocent person being refused a job or security clearance. Many other cases may well go undetected. The individual must clearly be protected against the sale of false information

The parallel to individual privacy is the confidentiality of an organisation's information. Some legislation exists to ensure that some information about organisations cannot be kept secret, such as the publication of financial results of a public company. There is a lot of very valuable information which a company will not wish to disclose, particularly to competitors.

Security

is the overall term to describe the protection of data from being accessed, changed or destroyed in an unauthorised way. This may come about because of malicious attack or failure of a system's hardware or software.

Thus, the breaking in to a computer system to alter the total in a personal bank account, to read Prince Philip's private mailbox, or simply 'because it's there' are all breaches of security. Much effort in large organisations is expended in ensuring an appropriate level of security. There is no way to guarantee absolute security, a balance has to be struck between the costs and benefits of different levels of security, so that the appropriate level can be chosen. In smaller businesses, it is all too easy to neglect these aspects of computing.

In cases where information is held about an individual and there is a failure in security terms, whether malicious or accidental, the loss, access or corruption of personal data in this way can also be a breach of privacy.

Integrity

is the keeping of data up to date, accurate, complete and consistent. Ways that this is achieved include steps to ensure that all transactions are processed, all data is validated and that all transactions are monitored. Databases have often been introduced to improve the consistency of files, in that only one copy of an address is held rather than holding it in several files, risking the updating of some but not all files when the address changes. Out-of-date data and inaccurate data can bring about a breach of privacy. When data is not accurate or up to date, security failures can become more serious, where data is more difficult or impossible to reconstruct.

Why is there a problem?

In principle, the holding of data in electronic form is no less vulnerable than written data. A magnetic disc and a file of papers can both be stolen, both can be copied without leaving any obvious signs, both can be destroyed by fire. The differences come, however, in scale and speed. A single disc is easier to transport than the 100 sides of paper which its represents. It can be copied more quickly in electronic form than by use of a photocopier. A bank can be robbed of £1000 by changing a few magnetic recordings, rather than lugging a holdall of used fivers. Because computer crime is so swift and leaves so few signs, some people feel that the punishments handed out to offenders are far too lenient compared with other 'conventional' crimes.

Until the passing of the Data Protection Act in 1984, Britain had no legislation which acknowledged the new medium of computers, and the need for specific legislation concerning computers. Thus, for example, program copyright was covered only by the 1956 Copyright Act, drawn up when most of the present difficulties were not envisaged. Interpretation of the law has come from rulings given in particular cases which rulings given in particular cases which have arisen.

To copy somebody else's work, whether it be a computer program, a symphony or a novel, and to sell it for financial advantage without the writer's permission is clearly an offence. It is clear, however, that much copying goes on using home computers, and is therefore very difficult to trace or stop, in the same way that photocopying has opened up new areas of problems. An additional problem with software is that a legitimate purchaser might wish to improve a program in order to make better use of it within an organisation. When substantial changes have been made, should the person amending the program then be able to copy it, or even sell it? In British law, it is not possible to have copyright on an idea.

The Data Protection Act

Britain was the last country in Western Europe to bring in legislation to protect the individual's rights over data about themselves. This enabled Britain to sign the Council of Europe's Convention on Data Protection. Some countries with stringent data protection laws had previously prevented the export of data about its citizens to Britain, as the data would not be protected by law once it arrived. Thus one motive in passing the British Act was an anxiety not to lose trade.

Under the Act, a Data Protection Registrar is appointed to ensure that its terms are adhered to. All 'data users' and computer bureaux are required to be registered. Registration involves the declaration of what data they hold, for what purpose and to whom they provide information. There are a number of bodies who are exempt for security reasons. 'Data subjects' (people about whom data is held) are able to apply for a copy of any data held about them.

A number of principles about the holding and use of data are either implicit or explicit in the law. These ten principles were put forward by the Younger Committee in 1970. It can be argued, and this is where the mere requirement of law and wider ethical considerations interplay, that computer practitioners should abide by the principles of Younger, whether forced to by law or not.

The principles of Younger are:

(a) Data should be held for a specific purpose and should not be used for any other purpose without permission.
(b) Data should only be available to those authorised to use it for the purpose for which it was supplied.
(c) Only the minimum data necessary for the specified purpose should be collected.
(d) When data is collected for statistical purposes, the identities of the individuals should be separated from the rest of the data.
(e) There should be a means by which any individuals can be informed about the information held about themselves.
(f) The level of security of the data should be specified in advance and should include precautions against the abuse and misuse of the data.
(g) The system should be monitored to detect any breach of security.
(h) The data should only be held for a specified time.
(i) Data should be accurate, and there should be means for correcting and updating information.
(j) Where opinions or value judgements are included, great care should be taken in their compilation.

19.3. THE COMPUTER AS THE ROOT OF ALL EVIL

Because of the widespread lack of knowledge about computers, it has become commonplace to blame computers for numerous difficulties within a business. A customer might be told that the sending of a bill was a 'computer error', or that an answer cannot be given to a query because the answer is 'in the computer' and 'the computer is down'. To play on the lack of public knowledge can be considered harmful both to the individuals concerned and to the image of computing generally, hence perpetuating public misunderstanding.

Lack of public awareness about the capabilities of computers might also lead the computer dealer into supplying a computer for a situation in which a computer is either not necessary or where its effects can be positively harmful. The advice of a minority of people calling themselves 'computer consultants' might not always be as impartial as they would like to imply. The vast majority of computer professionals, of course, are extremely honest and straightforward, but most businesses have their sharks, and the bait of what might be seen as quick profits in the computer field has attracted more than a fair share of them.

19.4. THE IMPACT OF COMPUTERS ON SOCIETY

Wider political and moral issues are raised when considering the emotive area of the impact that new technology is having on society. There are those who claim that computerisation is the main cause of mass unemployment and that 'computers destroy jobs'. Those who resist technological change are branded by others as Luddites.

Increasingly, computer operators in large organisations have sought the collective strength of a union to seek better working conditions, fringe benefits, pay and so on. The increasing dependence of organisations, whether they be large or small, on computers has made their use a tool of industrial action. A small handful of crucial staff can have a far-reaching impact on an organisation by interfering with its ability to access or process data.

Unions also provide an effective way for management to discuss and plan with workers. Liaison with unions can be a crucial part in building up goodwill and confidence in a new computerised system. One particular area of concern and involvement of unions is through Safety Committees established under the 1974 Health and Safety at Work Act. Much concern has been expressed recently about the effect of long periods of VDU usage on staff. Evidence has been collected to suggest that considerable strain can be placed upon the eyes, the back and the wrists without the provision of appropriate equipment and proper rest periods and changes of activity. There is also considerable concern about the effect of VDUs on pregnant women.

Ergonomics

The science of ergonomics (literally 'work-study') has provided recommendations for keyboard layout, work-station and room design. From the employer's point of view, an uncomfortable or unhappy staff will give poorer value for money in their work. In any computer working environment, serious consideration must be given to potential causes of accidents. The avoidance of accidents is clearly in everybody's interests. Trailing wires which can be tripped over should be avoided; adequate lighting should be provided; precautions should be taken against static electricity, against fire and against liquids (including coffee).

Many people are also concerned that more women should .be attracted into computing and that this will only be achieved by active encouragement and even positive discrimination. Where women have been employed in the computing industry, it has tended to be at the lower wage end of the market, with relatively few women rising to managerial posts. Computing has been seen as a male preserve, some would say because of an aggressive image encouraging fierce competition, and through computer games which are more popular with boys than girls. One area in which it has been found that women are more skilled, however, has been in the assembly of chips, which takes a lot of fine and detailed work. Women are increasingly making their presence felt in all areas of computing, encouraged by the Government's WISE (Women Into Science and Engineering) Campaign.

19.5. WHAT DO YOU THINK?

In reading through the following situations, try to view the events from the point of view of each character in turn. What are the moral or legal issues involved? How should they react? How would you react?

Scenario 1

A drugs company has successfully used a database program over a number of years, most notably to analyse results of the effects of using large doses of

Vitamin C to reduce the chances of catching the common cold. Participants in the scheme were contacted annually and data was collected and collated using a commercial database package. Various reports were drawn up, but no further collection of data or analysis of results is currently planned.

The company has decided to progress and to buy a series of larger models of computers which do not run the particular database package. The old hardware is to be sold to a local estate agent. By agreement with the software company who supplied the database program, it too is sold as part of the package. The drugs company signs to say that all the rights to the program are to be transferred to the estate agent under the terms of the original software licence.

In order to avoid entering data into the new system which there are no plans to use, the estate agents agree that should the drugs company wish to access the data at any future time, then they can do, at a minimal price. To save complications, the drugs company gives the estate agents the data discs for safe keeping. Several months after the sale of the program, an employee of the drugs company finds another copy of the database program in his cupboard.

> Are the estate agents acting properly or legally in allowing the possible continued use of something which has been sold and signed away?
> Is there a breach of confidentiality in giving away the discs?
> Who would be responsible if the discs were stolen from the estate agents?
> Should the employee tell anybody about the extra copy of the program? If so, who?

Scenario 2

As part of its normal procedure, a charge card company keeps a record of all the locations at which each customer's card is used. This can be useful in detecting patterns in fraud following the theft of cards and can be useful in rectifying the occasional entry made against an account in error. (A customer may be able to prove that he or she was not at a particular place at a particular date.)

After some time, the company realises the potential of this information as a saleable commodity. It produces lists of names and addresses of card holders who visit hotels more than once a month and sells these lists to major hotel chains to aid them in their direct-mail advertising.

When the scheme is to be extended to carry out a survey of the petrol companies used by clients, the employee who is asked to write the program refuses to do so and is faced with a disciplinary hearing. The union requests that a lawyer be present at the hearing, but the management insists that the matter is purely an internal affair regarding discipline.

> Was the charge card company within its rights to sell the mailing lists, consisting purely of information legitimately gathered?
> Would a hotel chain be within its rights to sell the list to another firm, a luggage manufacturer, for instance?
> Should the employee be given an ultimatum to do the work or be sacked?
> Should the union be allowed to be present?
> Should a lawyer be present?

Scenario 3

An owner of a small but growing business has acquired a computer which currently has a substantial spare capacity and therefore decides to allow a college student to come in and use the computer one day a week, for which the student's college pays an economic fee.

The student is analysing results of a survey of local housing conditions which the residents have been told is being collected as part of a local planning exercise. Realising the potential of the data gathered, the student uses the computer to produce lists of addresses which do not already have double glazing, and attempts to sell the list to somebody who sells double glazing. When this is reported to the police, they visit the owner of the computer who is implicated in the incident.

> Is the owner of the computer responsible for how it is used?
> Does it affect the situation if the owner of the computer knew this was going on and sold the student some labels?
> Does it matter that the computer time is being paid for?
> What is the responsibility of the college?

Scenario 4

A survey has been carried out by a firm into the effects of VDUs in the office. The results have been entered into an integrated package in order that the results can be presented in a variety of ways.

A user who is trying to learn how to use the package discovers the file on the disc and decides to use the data to explore the features of the package. She therefore displays the results as a bar chart, as a pie chart, and as a pictogram, using a symbol of a VDU.

In order to see the effects of different data, she decides to change the figures, and produces some interesting effects. She prints some of the graphs out to see what they look like, but as they are not all that interesting, and as the data is not reliable, she simply throws them in the wastepaper basket.

A few days later, an emergency meeting is called by the Convenor of the Safety Committee who has received 'some very interesting facts' anonymously via the internal mail.

> Is it wrong to experiment with live data?
> Should attempts be made to track down the person who removed the papers from the wastepaper basket? If so, for what purpose? What action should be taken?

Scenario 5

A senior manager asks a programmer to establish some fictitious accounts within an accounts system. These are to be used to monitor the effectiveness of the internal auditors, with whom the manager is dissatisfied. Once the accounts are set up, the programmer is asked to generate transactions to work the accounts as if they were live and to introduce features which will cover over the creation of the new accounts, to see whether this is spotted. The major discrepancies in the accounts are not discovered for a considerable time and it is decided to reshuffle the internal auditing department.

Though the manager only asked for ten accounts to be created, it is discovered by the new auditing staff that there were clearly eleven dummy accounts created, but because of the poor record keeping, it is not clear what the eleventh account was used for. When challenged, the programmer offers to resign 'with no questions asked', on condition that the firm give him a good reference so that he can get a job with a rival firm which uses the same accounts package.

> What are the advantages and disadvantages of giving the programmer the reference?
> If, as appears likely, no evidence can be produced, does the programmer's attitude suggest some guilt?
> Would the firm be better served to accept the offer, but actually to send a very poor reference so that the programmer does not get the move?

Scenario 6

An investment consultant, who has built up a considerable reputation and a wide range of well-to-do-clients, is about to retire. She has kept details of all her client's investments over the last few years using a sophisticated integrated package. When she comes to sell the business, the prospective purchaser requests the client details in the form of files for the integrated package. As the manager of the software house which wrote the package is a client of the consultant in his personal capacity, the consultant makes one or two discreet enquiries. It is revealed that the prospective customer has never bought the package. The consultant does not tell the software company the reason for the enquiry.

> Should the consultant inform the software house of her suspicions that the prospective customer has an illegal copy of the software?
> Was it wrong of the consultant to use a business contact to check up on a customer in this way?
> In what ways can the best interests of the consultant's clients be served?

Scenario 7

In the early stages of the design of a revolutionary new software tool for managers, three analysts working for a software house are involved. They are responsible for conducting surveys amongst existing clients, discussing possible designs and presenting reports to senior management on the feasibility of the project. The report which they present concludes that the software will take at least eighteen months to complete. Reluctantly, the software house says that it will not go ahead at this stage, but will bear the project in mind next year.

One of the analysts resigns his post a few weeks later, with the intention of starting his own software company. One of the first ideas he begins working on is the idea rejected by his previous employer. He has not taken any of the written material from his previous employers, he simply reconstructs the ideas from what he remembers. He feels that with the flexibility of a smaller company, the job could be completed in twelve months. In order to bring his project to fruition, he invites his two former colleagues to resign their posts and to join him as partners in his new company.

One colleague agrees to join and offers to get copies of some vital reports. The other refuses and reports the matter to senior management.

> Has the first analyst done anything morally or legally wrong in taking away ideas in his head?
> Are the ideas which a person takes away at the end of a job just as marketable as the skills acquired?
> Would the situation be affected if copies of the reports were passed over?
> Should the offer of the reports be refused?
> What action could or should the original employer take?

Scenario 8

Plans are being discussed regarding the introduction of machine readable passports for use throughout the EEC. As well as simplifying passage through checkpoints, this would cut down on use of false passports. It would also open up possibilities to record all the international movements of each passport holder.

> Is the central recording of all one's movements an infringement of personal liberty? (Previously, when the passport was stamped, the only record kept was held by the passport holder.)
> For what purposes would it be acceptable for information so collected to be used?
> How might criminals, terrorists or repressive governments make use of the information if they were to get hold of it?
> What steps should be taken to make sure that they can't?

Scenario 9

As a result of industrial action, a vital processing run is not carried out and some vital data is not entered into an accounting system. This means that the information contained within the files is not entirely up to date; a day's transactions are missing for one day of the month. Management decides, however, to send out statements as is normal at the end of the month, realising that some will be in error. It is decided that it would be too expensive to let all the customers know about possible inaccuracies.

Accounts staff who deal with telephone enquiries are told, after the statements have been sent, that any customers who complain should be told that the problems have been caused by 'an error in the computer system'. In cases where people have sent more than they actually now owe, staff are instructed to cash the cheques in the usual way 'as a payment against the next bill'.

> What should have been the attitude of the staff who operated the computer to produce the incorrect statements?
> What approach should have been made in dealing with the customers?
> Is it acceptable to say that the problem was with the computer system?

Scenario 10

A visiting client points out to an assistant on the administrative staff that there are a number of serious hazards in the data preparation area. The floor is too slippery and the chairs move around too easily and have inadequate backrests. There is little desk space and so piles of paper are left on radiators and on the top of printers. The VDU screens are too small and rather dirty. Two of the operators are pregnant, and appear to be exposed to a lot of VDU work, including overtime.

Deeply concerned, the administrative assistant reports these matters to the administrative manager. The manager simply replies that these things are bound to happen, that the two pregnant women would be leaving soon anyway and that, because of reorganisation, it was likely that the data preparation staff would be severely cut soon.

> What action could the administrative assistant now take?
> What approaches should the management take to the different problems outlined?
> In what ways should the data preparation staff be involved in finding solutions to the problem?
> What should be the role of the unions in this?

APPENDIX A
CASE STUDY

This extended case study tries to pick out relevant issues around the subjects covered in this book. Students on the National Diploma in Computer Studies 'Small Business Computer Systems' units will find this a useful revision of the whole course. Other readers might like to use the material as a starting point for discussion and revision. The case study takes a broad-based approach to the knowledge and skills needed by a computer practitioner in a small business.

Cowslip buys a computer

Cowslip Dairies is a medium-sized business which specialises in dairy product deliveries in a small East Midlands town and the surrounding villages. Each delivery round covers a couple of hundred houses, factories and offices. There are about a dozen such rounds. As well as milk, the milkmen will also deliver cheeses, yoghurt and butter, either on a regular basis, or when requested. At peak times, such as Christmas, each customer is given a form to request additional deliveries.

Ivy Plant, the Managing Director, had been thinking for some time that computers might well help the company, but she had read so many horror stories in magazines about things going wrong with computers that she was reluctant to take the first steps. She was finally persuaded of the need for computers by the crisis over Christmas orders. A delegation of the milkmen came to her to complain about the amount of extra work involved in the Christmas rush. An agreement was reached that, provided the system would be improved for next year, the milkmen would work the old procedure one last time. This was the spur for Ivy to pursue computerisation actively.

Nobody at Cowslip had any experience of computers, and so Ivy contacted the local Small Firms Advisory Service, who suggested that she should bring in a consultant and they sent her a list of local ones. Knowing that both hardware and software are important in deciding on a system, Ivy chose the name of somebody who had experience of a number of different makes of computer, Cactus Computer Consultants of Meadow Lane.

When Mr Reed made a preliminary call, Ivy was most impressed. He wanted to seek the opinions of a number of the staff. He had a chat with Holly Bush, the office supervisor, and although she was rather negative at first, he won her round with his descriptions of some other firms with which he had worked. Before signing a contract, Holly and Ivy paid a visit with Mr Reed to one of his other clients, Flora Fertilisers, who talked about their early teething troubles, but their eventual satisfaction with a system.

The contract signed, Mr Reed got to work, asking to see all the forms used by the milkmen and in the office, spending a day out on a round with one of the milkmen and talking to a wide range of staff at all levels. Ivy was keen that the payroll should be computerised, particularly if this would enable a bonus system to be introduced based on additional sales by the milkmen.

Holly felt that the computerisation of customers' accounts was an important priority. Computerisation would bring a closer control of record keeping, as well as increasing the accuracy of central records. The system as it stood involved each milkman being issued with milk at the beginning of a day and being required to produce the money from the customers to pay for it. This meant that each milkman kept his own account book in whatever way suited him. The lack of a centralised record, and the differences between systems caused a particular problem when milkmen were sick or on holiday. The amount of bookkeeping which each milkman had to do also limited the size of the rounds.

The milkmen themselves wanted to see a system which would reduce their workload on Thursdays and Fridays, when all the money had to be collected from customers. Money was collected from one half of the round each day, but sometimes the milkmen still did not finish until lunch-time.

From all his discussions, Mr Reed then drew up a report showing the benefits which could be expected from a computer system and a specification of the computer system requirements of Cowslip, which Ivy and her staff considered. This included new computer-readable forms which would be completed by the milkmen. The Board had no hesitation in giving its approval for the project to go ahead.

Mr Reed's endeavours were not completed, however, for he now drew up a set of criteria by which possible systems could be compared and he asked Ivy to discuss with him the importance which should be attached to each of them. He then received proposals of five possible systems and compared them according to the agreed list. Because of the range of software it supported and the capacity of the hard disc, it was decided to buy a Thistle system with both a daisywheel and a dot matrix printer. A simple optical character reader was purchased to read order forms.

Ivy and Holly felt the need to employ somebody to do the bulk of the work on the system. Mr Reed knew a young lady called Rose Thorn, who had recently completed a BTEC National Diploma in Computer Studies. Though they advertised the post at a reasonable starting salary and had a number of good applicants, it was clear at the interviews that Rose was well informed and had a clear idea of how to use a computer in a business setting. She had never used a Thistle before, but she said to Ivy that she was used to using a 'wide range of machines'. Rose was worried about possible problems when having to tell older colleagues what to do, but she was keen to gain experience, and so Cowslip took her on.

The changeover from a manual system to the computer was undertaken in stages, with one milkman's round per week being added to the records. The payroll was left until the end of the initial transition. Rose had her work cut out in the initial period in getting used to the new system and entering large amounts of data.

She had also to arrange for supplies to be ordered and delivered, though she used a database to help her in this. Rose showed other people how to use the system, though she was frustrated with some users of the system, particularly those who left discs out of their covers, those who smoked near the computer and some who left the forms incorrectly lined up on the printer. She also reorganised the room layout after a couple of weeks because of a number of near accidents.

Rose said that she felt that the screen layouts within the system left a lot to be desired and that more could have been achieved if they had used Cobol, though she was impressed by the use of colour.

Within a few months, Rose was recommending a word processing package and she used this to produce beautifully presented notes on how to use the computer system, which she would revise from time to time in the light of further developments and the comments of users. This convinced Holly of the need for word processing facilities in the general office. Rose was asked to choose another two computers and a word processing package and to train members of the office staff how to use it.

Mr Reed looked back on what he considered was a job well done.

QUESTIONS

1 Ivy Plant has read in magazines about things going wrong when firms get computers. Describe five or more ways, other than equipment failure, in which the process of computerisation could go wrong.
2 Name and describe the purpose of three fact recording documents which Mr Reed may have used when investigating the current system.
3 Outline the benefits that might be included in Mr Reed's report which Cowslip might gain from a computer system.
4 Do you think that it would have been better for Cowslip to have rented or leased a computer rather than buying one? Give your reasons.

5   Which of Mr Reed's activities would you consider to be part of the feasibility study? What were his aims in this, and what did he wish to show to the management?
6   What, in your opinion, should be included in the specification that Mr Reed drew up showing the requirements of Cowslip?
7   A shortlist was drawn up by Mr Reed in order to send the specifications of the computer system requirements to potential suppliers. State, in order of importance, five criteria upon which the selection of suppliers to include on the shortlist should be made. Suggest how these suppliers might be found.
8   List the ten most important criteria which you think Cowslip should consider when comparing computer systems.
9   What criteria should be used by Cowslip when choosing a printer for use by several people in a busy office?
10   In order to make a decision whether to go ahead with the implementation of a computer system, the members of the Board will have to be briefed about computers. What form of report should they be given, and what areas should it cover?
11   In order to budget for the running of the computer system, estimates must be made of the running costs. Write a list of the main headings under which expenditure will be made, giving examples of charges within each category.
12   Describe how Mr Reed might have gone about introducing the new equipment and system in ways which would cause the minimum disruption to the various members of staff.
13   Illustrating your answer with specific examples of the way that Cowslip went about computerisation, describe the ways in which Cowslip got individual staff and company policy to be positive towards thinking about computers.
14   Rose was asked to write a report about the uses of word processing that could be made at Cowslip. What do you think that the main recommendations of this report should be?
15   It has been suggested that a procedural database program could have been used for the necessary record keeping at Cowslip. What is your opinion of this statement?
16   With a fully functioning administrative system installed at Cowslip, it has been suggested that some use could be made of graphics packages. What would be possible, and would this be justified?
17   It has been suggested that Cowslip's administration might benefit from the use of a recently launched integrated package. There are some staff who are reluctant to consider switching to it. Outline reasons which staff might give for and against the introduction of such software.
18   It has been suggested that a network system could be considered by the company, as this would leave room for expansion for the future. What uses would you suggest a network could be put to by Cowslip?
19   When Rose is on holiday, she needs to be sure that the system will be run adequately. In particular, she has been asked to draw up a set of operating standards and a list of tasks which she would expect a trained user to be able to perform using the operating system. In order to monitor their performance, she has been asked to draw up a test of competence, consisting of about a dozen tasks to ensure that prospective users are capable of using the system on their own.

You are required to suggest such a list of tasks and to give reasons for their inclusion. Your questions should not be dependent upon a particular operating system, but should be generally applicable to any system.
20   When he heard about Cowslip's plans, another computer consultant said, 'I don't think that the accounts system will work, because of the amount of data to be entered and the accuracy of the information being fed in.' What is your opinion of this comment?

APPENDIX B SOME USEFUL ADDRESSES

Association of British Chambers of Commerce	212a Shaftesbury Avenue London WC2H 8EW	01-240 5831
Association of Professional Computer Consultants	109 Baker Street London W1	01-267 7144
British Computer Society	13 Mansfield Street London W1M 0BP	01-637 0471
British Institute of Management	Management House Parker Street London WC2B 5PT	01-405 3456
Co-operative Development Agency	20 Albert Embankment London SE1 7TJ	01-211 3351
Department of Trade and Industry	1–19 Victoria Street London SW1H 0ET	01-215 7877
Health and Safety Executive	Regina House Old Marylebone Road London NW1	01-229 3456
National Computing Centre	Oxford Road Manchester M1 7ED	061-228 6333
Small Firms Service	Ebury Bridge House Ebury Bridge Road London SW1W 8QD	01-730 8451 Freephone 2444

OUTLINE SOLUTIONS TO STUDY QUESTIONS

CHAPTER 2

1 Exception reports which include your details could include:

(a) a list produced of premises where it was not possible to gain access to read the meter,
(b) a list of consumers with unusually high or low consumption,
(c) a list of consumers who have not paid within 28 days of the reading being taken.

In each of these cases, action should be taken; omission from the list means no action need be taken.

Regular reports might include copies of bill details, which may have to be looked at in the accounts office for future enquiries. These are often produced in miniaturised form on microfilm to reduce storage space. Such reports are an additional guard against disastrous data loss.

On-demand reports might include:

(a) summaries produced, for example in evaluating the costs of all consumers purchasing central heating;
(b) details displayed or printed for an enquiry about the possibility of paying for electricity in monthly instalments.

The term 'on demand' can refer to reports produced with details of many customers (in a batch) or for an individual enquiry.

2 Four main problems in communicating are:

(a) what to communicate: deciding what facts are needed by whom;
(b) why communicate: there may be little motivation there to let others know; people may be unaware of the need to communicate;
(c) how to communicate: people lack skills and confidence in getting their message across;
(d) when to communicate: today may never be the right time to let people know things, because you might know more tomorrow.

3 Communication is a two-way process or it is nothing. The problems of communication start at both ends. The answer to question 3 is probably the same as the answer to question 2.

CHAPTER 3

1 Computer-based training should only be used where this is the best form of training. Early 'educational' programs were of a 'drill and practice' type, where the computer was used to take the teacher's place in setting questions in a fairly fixed format (for example arithmetic tests). This places the learner in the situation of being 'programmed' by the machine – the user interacts little and does not control the situation. This is bad educational practice. In the case of specific skills training, however, there is a fixed body of knowledge to be imparted and the programmed approach can work well when a user knows for what he or she is aiming.

2 Manuals are often written by the people who designed the software and so the manuals evolve as the software evolves. Those who are good at software writing are not necessarily good at writing texts. Once the software is completed, it is likely to be rushed on to a fiercely competitive market as soon as the documentation can be made presentable. Additionally, manuals are written primarily for reference and are often in alphabetical order of command rather than the order in which commands can best be learnt. Thus, text part way through a manual might depend on ideas both earlier and later in the manual. It is said that some manuals are ideal for teaching somebody who already knows how to use the package everything that there is to know about it.

CHAPTER 4

1 There is no one 'correct' answer to each of these problems. The following are suggested as likely explanations:
(a) There should be some checks within a program to ensure that zero bills are not printed – the systems analyst and the programmer should both have spotted this. However, just because the bill was produced, it does not mean that it has to be sent. Checking procedures should be included to ensure that such output is intercepted. If such procedures do not exist, ask the systems analyst. If they do, and were not carried out, see the operations manager.
(b) In this case, nobody is aware that the original error was made, or if they are, nothing was done about it. Similar checks to those in (a) should have eliminated this error, but there are also problems with the administrative staff if the error was spotted or reported by the customer and yet nothing has been done.
(c) Either the person using the software did not follow instructions in a manual or given by a program or there are no such instructions. In the first case, blame the user, in the other, it should be the systems analyst's job to make sure such instructions are available. The systems analyst has very little to do with ensuring that instructions are actually followed.
(d) There is clearly some (understandable) error in the program. Either this aspect of the program was incorrectly specified by the systems analyst, or it was incorrectly tested by the programmer and the analyst.

2 The costs of employing a systems analyst will include:
   (a) **Recruitment cost**: advertising expenses, interview expenses (travel, meals, accommodation);
   (b) **Revenue cost**: salary, employer's National Insurance, travelling expenses, office accommodation, secretarial support, materials and equipment.
3 Senior managers will have their roles changed to a greater or lesser extent by computerisation. They will have to act on the reports which the computer produces.
   Senior management and directors should be involved in identifying clearly why computerisation is to take place. They will then show more concern and involvement should the project go wrong or not live up to expectations.
   Shareholders or others who have a stake in or responsibility for the organisation will want to be consulted about something which may have a profound influence on the atmosphere and image.
   Some staff may well be redeployed to use the new computer system. The sooner they are involved in the process, the better.

CHAPTER 5

1 Staff might benefit from having less tedious copying of information from one sheet to another. There will also be a reduction in routine arithmetic and filing. The concentration of information at one source may well mean less searching around for information, so probably less physical activity.
   Staff might also gain some satisfaction from those benefits primarily seen as benefits to the organisation and so might like giving a better service to customers, might like taking a pride in the presentation of work and so on.
2 The main advantage which airlines have gained from their booking systems is that bookings can be made from a large number of sites based on up-to-the-minute information. Hence fewer alterations have to be made and there is less underbooking. (It is incredibly wasteful to fly with empty seats – the flight will cost the airline just the same whether the plane is full or half empty.)
3 (a) The sales clerk will need the greatest amount of detail, so that individual invoices can be prepared, sent to the right address, followed up and filed and so that statements can be prepared.
   (b) The sales manager will want to know things

like the range of products sold, the popularity of individual items, the size of orders and the frequency of orders. Much of this will be summarised from the information processed by the clerk.

(c) The company accountant will want to know things such as the profit margins, the total debt to the company, the scale of individual debts and the liability to tax. Much of this is again a further summary of the information needed by the sales manager.

CHAPTER 6

1   Management will view the benefits of a computer system in terms of the overall information needs of an organisation. This can include the introduction of new kinds of reports, the increased frequency of reports and so on.

Clerical staff will also have suggestions to make; these might be about the streamlining of individual processes, the speeding of throughput, questioning the usefulness of tasks which they carry out and so on. When it comes to implementing the system, they will have many practical suggestions to make, such as the siting of equipment, lighting and the use of printers.

Both kinds of suggestions can be valuable. A simple improvement to a frequent clerical process, for example, can save large amounts of time.

2   The supplier is more likely to have relevant experience on which the calculation of the sizing of a computer system can be based. If it is the supplier who decides the technical capacity needed for the business functions stated, then the supplier takes responsibility for those decisions. If the customer states what size the system should be, and this turns out to be inadequate, then there is no claim against the supplier. The customer will be disappointed, and the supplier will have produced a system which is not effective, through no fault of the supplier.

3   Names of suppliers can also be obtained at exhibitions (such as the 'Which Computer? Show'), through small firms advice agencies, through specialist trade associations (such as those for motor traders or builders) or through contacts in organisations like the British Institute of Management (BIM).

CHAPTER 7

1   New products are sometimes described as 'state of the art', whereas tried and tested products might be 'old hat'. New products, or newer versions of old products could at the same time be faster, cheaper and provide more facilities than was previously available. Sometimes new products can have fewer faults, though when older products have faults or shortcomings, people have usually designed a way round them.

2   A survey published in 1986 showed that the average annual costs for 'small' business users who responded were:

Discs	£331
Printer ribbons	£145
Paper	£291

In addition to this, a company will be spending something on cleaning (£100 is not unlikely), on hardware maintenance (contracts are charged at about 12% of the capital cost), on software maintenance and support (about 10%), and on electricity.

It is also reasonable to expect that expenditure will continue on minor enhancements to the equipment or upgrades to the software. Daisywheels wear out or staff want different typefaces; acoustic hoods or anti-glare screens might be requested after some use of the system; further or replacement manuals might be needed. It is useful to have a budget heading for such sundry items.

CHAPTER 8

1   Batch processing introduces delays into the processing, as nearly all transactions have to wait until a batch is ready to process. A possibility for error is introduced if two transactions for the same record are included in a batch. Thus, two members of staff, without knowing so might both attempt to solve a problem by, for example, issuing a credit note for returned goods. If this is not spotted by the system, two credit notes are sent and the system is in error; if it is spotted, one of the members of staff will have a transaction rejected. There could also be two different transactions on an account in the same batch which might conflict in some way.

Real-time processing requires a very sophisticated program or set of programs, which will be expensive to develop both in terms of computer time and personnel. Often a larger computer will be required than would be otherwise needed.

2   Possible stages of testing might be:

(a) test the normal cases with typical data, for which the results are known (as far as possible);
(b) test the exceptional cases, with data which should be rejected;
(c) test the program to the limits of unusual circumstances which should be processed normally;
(d) test the procedures to deal with unusual cases;
(e) having tested all the parts separately, test them together.

3   (a) Stock control in a shoe warehouse is a large-scale job. Perhaps the strongest argument for batch processing is that goods will be removed from the warehouse in batches for delivery. It is natural, therefore, for data entry to be in batches also. An on-line enquiry system to determine current stock levels would be useful, but this data might not necessarily be updated in real time.
(b)   Hire-purchase agreements do not have to be entered urgently. Batch processing will enable batch checking on data entry. Batch processing will also reduce the frequency with which special software and special stationery (to print payment slips, for example) will have to be loaded.
(c)   The entry of data from gas bills is a large-scale task which is carried out regularly. The actual processing is quite simple for the vast majority of accounts, in that all that has to be read in is the account number. This is an ideal application for batch processing.
(d)   The fire brigade would find a real-time retrieval system very useful. Data describing how to get to possible scenes of fires can be held centrally and can be sent to a number of locations if circumstances dictate.

4   (a)   It would be perfectly possible to computerise the stock control in a shoe warehouse gradually. As a large-scale job, much disruption would be caused by a direct changeover. There would be advantages and disadvantages in introducing a new scheme shop by shop or product by product.
(b)   A direct changeover could be used when changing the system for processing hire-purchase details, with all new agreements being entered into the new system, while old agreements work out their natural life on an old system. In this way, the amount of work done by the computer increases steadily. Staff would know that all agreements after a particular date would be in the computer system.
(c)   A gradual introduction of computerised gas bills would be helpful, as with such a large scheme there could be major teething troubles. With an accounting system, it is perhaps advisable to run the new system in parallel with the old one, as the results of problems can be particularly calamitous.
(d)   The new scheme of computerised instruction to get to the scene of a fire could be introduced gradually, with some districts and some fire stations being on line first. Even when the system is fully operational, of course, because of the immediacy of emergency work, there will have to be substantial back-up facilities in case of problems.

CHAPTER 9

1   A faults log book can form a common reference point for persons responsible for maintenance. A second person finding a fault can see that it has been reported. If several similar pieces of equipment begin to go wrong, this will be more obvious, which will enable something to be done sooner. A clear record of faults helps in diagnosing the latest problem (the equipment's 'medical history' can be traced). The principle of error log books could also be applied to faults apparent in software. In some cases, what is reported as a fault might, in fact, be a misunderstanding by the user. This is more likely to be followed up and corrected if it is in writing.

2   There are no hard and fast rules on the regularity of cleaning; much depends on level of use and the siting of equipment. The following are 'typical' figures.

The keyboard and screen could be cleaned about once a fortnight. The inside of a printer might be cleaned monthly, as should all the daisywheels and the roller. The outside of a printer might be dusted down fortnightly. A disc drive could be dusted fortnightly and cleaned internally in the proper manner about every month. All casing should be cleaned thoroughly about twice a year.

CHAPTER 10

1   If the package uses discs, do you have disc drives? If the package uses a printer, do you have one? (And if it requires a matrix printer, for

example, for graphics, have you one of them?) Does the use of the package depend on colour? If so, do you have an appropriate monitor? Do you have, or could you get the appropriate operating system to run the package? Have you the correct version? Is the memory capacity of your computer sufficient?

2   Are error messages self-explanatory? Is it clear at each point what you are expected to do next (through a menu or some other means)? Are 'help' facilities provided, allowing you to get detailed descriptions of facilities whilst the program is operational? Can the program be 'crashed'? If this can be done deliberately, it can also be done accidentally. Does the program ensure that a user finishes 'cleanly', that is, all data from one run is saved on exit ready for the next run? This is usually provided by only allowing one exit point. No facility will legislate against somebody deliberately turning off the computer when a program is operational.

3   Programs from a 'family' will have a similarity in style, for example in the use of the same name for commands. They will also have a similar screen presentation, so that the user knows where to look for things. Utility software (such as print utilities) may be common to a family.

The most popular or most suitable package for each particular situation, however, might not be from the same family, so that a second-best might have to be chosen in several cases. The quality of different packages in the same family can vary considerably, as later products might be rushed on to the market to follow a successful product. The purchase of a complete suite of programs from one source will mean that the purchaser is very committed to one company. This can cause difficulties, most obviously if the supplier ceases to trade.

CHAPTER 11

1   A tutorial guide will step a user through from the basics to the most sophisticated features. Once a user is fully trained to use the package, then he or she is most likely to remember that a particular operation can be done and only needs to look up how – hence the different emphasis of reference manuals.

2   Although codes for the printing of characters are agreed as a standard, many of the codes used for control features, including those for special effects, differ from manufacturer to manufacturer, as they have been added on since the standard codes were agreed.

3   The text might now refer to 'custhomasers'! So, be warned about unattended replacement. Such mistakes are difficult to spot and tedious to undo. (Many programs would ignore upper- and lower-case in exchanges.)

CHAPTER 12

1   In the simplest file handling programs, records are related by being physically in order. A more flexible approach is to use what is called a pointer, which holds the address of another record. Thus records can be related in order by associating a pointer with each data item. This then means that a new record can be added by being placed physically after all the other records, but by amending pointers, it has the appropriate logical relationship with other records.

Similar arrangements can be made for associating fields together, which is particularly vital when the length or number of fields can be altered.

2   The name that a field is given within the screen display should be the best title that can be given so that the meaning is clear to the whole range of possible users. The name by which the field is referred to within the data manipulation language is used by far fewer people and so is chosen to be meaningful, but should be short enough for inclusion in formulae which might be fairly complex. Such formulae are usually easier to understand when fields are referred to by name than when they are referred to by number. The general user will not see such formulae and so need not be worried by them.

3   When storage space has been allocated for a variable length record and then the data is altered, the new data will often not fit exactly into the space released by erasing the old data. If the new data is shorter, some space may not be re-used. If the new data is longer it will not fit. It is clearly not practicable to move all the subsequent records to re-use space or create space. Often such flexibility is implemented using pointers.

4   Files will have to be reorganised from time to time because with continued amendment, records will be related by more and more pointers. Retrieval of data can become quite slow if a chain of pointers has to be followed through. It is not always possible for the pointers to be reorganised efficiently while the data is in use. What may be required is for the complete file to be copied to a new disc, putting records in the most efficient order.

CHAPTER 13

1   The first use of the term window is the feature allowing the user to look at part of the whole sheet, which cannot be displayed at one time. The area on display can be moved in four directions, up, down, left and right, to view the appropriate part.

The second development of the meaning of windows is the provision to view more than one part of the worksheet on the screen. In this way, parts which are widely separated and could not normally be viewed together can be shown.

2   The entries within a worksheet will fill the memory of a computer well before all the cells are all used. A typical maximum might be 63 columns and 255 rows, which gives a little over 16 000 cell addresses. If each cell contained a formula of 20 characters (which is not exceptional), this would amount to over 320 000 bytes for data alone.

The following exercise can be used to determine the sophistication with which a sparse worksheet is held:

  (a) A worksheet which is completely blank except for one entry on a high numbered row in a column well to the right is entered.
  (b) The effect on the amount of memory space remaining is measured.

3   Possible applications include:

  (a) estimation of running costs,
  (b) tabulation and comparison of tenders,
  (c) the use of weighted ranking for the comparison of options,
  (d) estimations of volumes of processing.

CHAPTER 14

1   Analytical software provides graphics as the end result of what might be a long set of calculations, such as might occur in a spreadsheet or database. The software is then additionally used to present the results calculated in a form which is readily understandable. This will often necessitate fairly straightforward forms of presentation of numerical data, though there might be a wide range of possibilities, such as bar charts, pie charts, scatter graphs and so on. Presentation software, on the other hand, can be used to present data which might not be numerical and might not have been computer generated. The emphasis is on a better presentation of already accumulated facts, whereas analytical software presents facts which have been generated as part of the processing.

2   Pie charts are particularly suitable when the intention is to give an idea of the relative sizes of data items to the whole. There should not be too many slices in the pie; seven is a recommended maximum for the reader to take in. Pie charts show what slice of the pie is in each category, but do not always say how big the pie is!

3   The lines joining up points are used to emphasise the points; they do not represent actual values. They are based on the approximation that the change of values between the two points which were measured was steady. This may or may not be a realistic assumption. Thus if sales have grown from £3000 one month to £4000 the next month, intermediate values have no meaning (which month do they represent?), but it is realistic to assume that the rate of selling has steadily increased between the two dates shown.

4   The ink blot method of shading an area depends on a painstaking check on each cell of the picture to see whether the edge of the shape has been reached. Shading might have to go back on itself in order for the ink blot to spread in both directions and round corners in an unusual or irregular shape.

5   The CPU hardware determines the size of a screen cell and so this is not generally under the control of the program. Thus the writers of graphics packages are limited in their on-screen manipulation. When the plotter is being driven, the computer will have to send signals to the plotter to give a speed of horizontal and vertical movement within the page. The smoothness of the curve is then only limited by the units in which each of these speeds can be set. This is being done with increasing accuracy as hardware technology develops. The curves on plotters can be much smoother than curves on the screen but are still made up in a discrete, digital way.

CHAPTER 15

1   Of course, it is impossible to say whether an integrated package will fulfil all an organisation's requirements without knowing individual circumstances. And why does it matter whether it is all-powerful anyway? A software tool should be evaluated on its own merits and, as long as its usefulness is worth its cost, the purchaser should be satisfied.

What is often true about integrated software is that it is a very good starting point for first-time users. It is approachable enough to get new users going and at the same time begins to show off the potential power of a computerised system. After a number of months, or even years, a user might then have enough knowledge and experience to evaluate critically packages at the top of the range in each application area, opening up many new features.

2   The problem of compatibility has a lot to do with which came first. Thus, older, well-established and possibly more-popular packages were written before some of the newer ones. Newer packages have the advantage then that they can be designed to read a number of file formats from existing popular packages. The reverse is not true, because the newer packages had not been released, or even designed when the older ones came out!

Some manufacturers of established packages have been fighting back, however, and newer versions of 'old favourites' are including code which will read file formats from packages which were not around when the first versions were released.

CHAPTER 16

1   A computerised system is one of the best ways in which to ensure that all staff involved in the accounting side of the work are using the same standards. Providing that the system is not being used to its absolute maximum capacity (which it should not be, to allow for mistakes and breakdowns), then a computer can cope more easily with a fluctuation in the volume of work and can handle work peaks more easily. Following on from this, a computer is likely to stabilise administrative costs. Unlike humans, a computer does not make more arithmetic or procedural mistakes when working under pressure. If the workload increases, however, the actual time for manual input will rise in proportion. Thus, if staffing has been adjusted to the new level needed, then some flexibility might be lost.

2   When an invoice from another firm is received, the details of the firm and the amount must be entered, so that a purchase is registered against the appropriate account. The details of the account might be entered as a number for simplicity of data entry. If purchases are to be analysed by categories other than the source of the purchase, then a code or codes will have to be entered to denote the type of purchase. All this data will be entered into the purchases ledger. The corresponding amount will be entered into the nominal ledger as part of a figure analysed in whatever way purchases data is to be used in that ledger.

3   It would be possible to total all transactions in the trial balance, showing for instance that a customer had received a total of £150 worth of goods, but only paid £100. These two figures would appear on opposite sides of the balance sheet. The trial balance shows the state of affairs of a company at a particular time, not the sum of transactions that have brought that state of affairs about. In the example, what should appear in the trial balance is merely the fact that the customer owes £50.

CHAPTER 17

1   When a computer manufacturer provides an operating system unique to a model or range of models, this enables it to exploit the hardware features to the optimum. It also means that customers are provided with support for hardware and software from the same company. Disadvantages include the necessity for applications software to run under the particular operating system. From the purchaser's point of view, these factors make switching between manufacturers an expensive business. From the individual computer practitioner's point of view, his or her skills are less transferable, as detailed knowledge on one operating system is of little use without retraining for another system.

2   If other manufacturers are able to design add-on features to an operating system, this can mean that a number of specialist companies could provide features not developed in the original product. If these are good, this can increase commitment of users to the particular operating system. There are, of course, more problems if the add-ons are not very good. Increased public awareness of the operating system design might lead to more creative thinking about additional features, but also paves the way for easier imitation of the whole operating system and brings in difficult areas of copyright law.

3   If several users request printout at approximately the same time, the first document to be produced must be completed before the second starts to be printed. Similarly, the second must be completed before the third starts. Otherwise, if users had direct control over the printer, printouts might consist of a line of A s printout, followed by a line of B s, then a line of A s, then of C s, then of B s and so on. This would not be welcomed by A, B or C!

CHAPTER 18

1   You certainly do not have to be a touch-typist to use a computer effectively. Clearly there are advantages to be gained by being able to type without looking down at the keyboard all the time. The typing speed which you feel you need is very much a matter of individual taste. If you can type about as fast as you can compose a sentence in your mind, then you can produce typed text at about the same speed that you can write it neatly.

   Training in the use of a keyboard can be achieved by joining a typing class or by reading a book about it (and working through the exercises) or by using one of the computer programs which are now available for keyboard training.

2   Much has been said in the past few years about computer literacy. Many schools aim to produce people who are computer-literate. Part of a person's ability to use a computer is based on overcoming his or her fear of the unknown. Games can often form a good motivation to learning and users can quickly become familiar with ideas like loading a file and operating the keyboard if they want to get on with a game. Perhaps what we should be encouraging, though, in the development of the technology is the building of people-literate computers!

INDEX

Acceptance testing   *65, 71, 72*
Accounting period   *160*
Accounts,
  balance forward   *157*
  open item   *157*
Accuracy   *17*
Acknowledgements   *5*
Agenda   *13*
Appearance of a report   *6*
Appendices   *5*
Application package, see Package
Audio-visual aid   *27*
Audit,
  external   *86, 161*
  internal   *86, 161*
  trail   *86*
Authorisation   *20*
Awareness of computers   *26*

Balance forward accounts, see Accounts
Balance sheet   *157*
Bar chart,
  description   *139*
  stacked   *140*
Batch processing   *44, 69*
BCS, see British Computer Society
Benchmarking   *61*
Benefits of computerisation   *41–42*
Bibliography   *5*
BIM, see British Institute of Management
Boilerplating   *107*
Books   *27*
Brainstorming   *14*
British Computer Society (BCS)   *40, 200*
British Institute of Management (BIM)   *40, 200*

Browse   *115*
Buffering   *181*
Bus   *185*
Business information   *16*

Calculated field   *119*
Cell   *126*
Changing to a new computer system   *73*
Cleaning equipment   *83*
Clerical document description   *49, 50*
Clerical procedure   *68*
Colour   *142*
Command summary   *94*
Command-driven programs   *96, 120*
Committee   *13*
Communication,
  electronic   *148*
  information   *1*
  skills   *23*
Comparing solutions   *36, 45*
Compiler   *89, 123*
Computer document description   *49, 51*
Computer error   *33*
Computer-aided training   *27*
Consultant   *38*
Control code   *105*
Converting files   *72*
Cost-benefit analysis   *41*
Costing   *42*
Costs,
  capital   *43*
  revenue   *43*
Courses   *27*
Cursor   *101*
Custom-written software   *91*

Daisywheel *178*
Damage *79*
Data *16*
Data description language *114*
Data manipulation language *114*
Data processing *16*
Data Protection Act *192*
Data Protection Registrar *192*
Database,
  description *112*
  flat record *120*
  procedural *120*
  transactional *119*
Decision making *16*
Decisions,
  long-term *19*
  short-term *19*
Dedicated word processor *110*
Defining a new system *48*
Demonstrations *30*
Design *35*
Designing the system *47–58*
Detail, level of *17*
Dialogue *96–98*
Direct changeover *73*
Directory of disc contents *169*
Disc,
  copying *80*
  directory *169*
  drive cleaning *83*
  floppy *79, 183–184*
  formatting *169*
  hard *184*
  laser *27*
  verifying *169*
Discipline,
  using a printer *78*
  using discs *80*
Discount *62*
Discounted cash flow *64*
Distributed processing *22*
Document flowchart *49*
Documentation *93, 95*
Double entry (bookkeeping) *154*
Drawing package *138*
Dump *170*
Duplication of data *113*

Electrical hazard *82*
Emacs *104*

Embedded command *104*
Environment *70*
Equipment cleaning *83*
Ergonomics *193*
Error, see Computer error
Evaluation of a package *95*
Executive *13*
Expert *23*
Exploded pie chart *140*
External audit, see Audit

Facsimile transmission *188*
Fact finding *47*
Facts *1*
Fault logging *79*
Fax, see Facsimile transmission
Fear of computers *44*
Feasibility study *35, 41–46*
Field *112, 114*
Field type *114, 115*
File *112*
File conversion *72*
File specification *49, 54*
Finance *63–65*
Findings *4*
Fire *81*
Flood *82*
Floppy disc *79, 183–184*
Font *100*
Footer *103*
Formatting discs *169*
Forms, standard *49*
Friction feed *181*

Gantt chart *67, 68*
Generations *21*
Glossary *5*
Goal seeking *134*
Gradual changeover *74*
Graphics,
  for analysis *137*
  for drawing *138*
  for presentation *138–139*

Hard disc *184*
Hardware *22*
Hazards *81*
Header *103*

Health and Safety at Work Act   *193*
Help facility   *94*
Hidden line   *141*
Histogram   *139*
Housekeeping   *171*
Human aspects   *43*

Icon   *98, 99, 173*
Illustration   *8*
Impact printer   *178*
Implementation   *67*
Index   *5, 110*
Information   *16–19*
Information flow   *17*
Information technology   *188*
Ink-jet printer   *180*
Insurance   *85*
Installation guide   *93*
Intangible benefit   *64*
Integrated accounts   *163*
Integrated package   *146–152*
Integration   *18*
Integrity   *23, 191*
Interface   *181*
Internal audit, see Audit
Interview   *48*
Invoicing   *162*

Jargon   *34*
Job description   *70*
Journal   *155, 156*
Justification, see Right justification

Keyboard,
  cleaning   *83*
  layout   *76, 181–182*

LAN, see Local Area Network
Language compiler, see Compiler
Laser disc   *27*
Laser printer   *180*
Learning the lessons of computerisation   *36*
Ledger   *154–155*
Line graph   *140*
Live, going   *36*
Liveware   *24*
Loan repayment   *128*

Local Area Network (LAN)   *185*
Locking files   *170, 187*
Locking records   *187*
Log book   *79*
Logical file structure   *113*

Macro   *107*
Mailing   *109*
Maintenance contract   *84*
Manual   *29*
Mathematical functions of a spreadsheet   *131–132*
Mathematics   *22*
Matrix printer   *178*
Meeting   *12–14*
Menu-driven program   *96, 106, 120*
Merging files   *169*
Minutes   *13*
Modem   *186*
Modular package   *149*
Monitor   *176*
Monolithic program   *149*
Mouse   *173, 182*
Multiplexor   *186*
Multitasking   *173*
Multi-user system   *121, 186*
Myths   *22–23*

National Computing Centre (NCC)   *40, 49–55, 200*
Needs of an organisation   *47*
Nellie, sitting by   *24*
Net Present Value (NPV)   *64*
Network   *185–186*
Nominal ledger   *154, 155*
Normalisation   *113*
NPV, see Net Present Value

Observation   *48*
On-line system   *70*
Open-item accounts, see Accounts
Operating system   *89, 167*
Operator   *24, 25*
Opinion   *1*
Order processing   *162*

Package   *89–94, 167*
Page layout   *107*

Parallel running *73*
Payroll *163*
Performance guarantees *63*
Performance targets *60*
Perspective *141*
Physical file structure *113*
Pictogram *140*
Pie chart,
   description *140*
   exploded *140*
   solid *140*
Pirating *174*
Planning change *67*
Polytechnics *26*
Power,
   problems *81*
   sockets *77*
   supply *77*
Print pitches *181*
Printer output document *52*
Printer,
   cleaning *84*
   daisywheel *178*
   facilities *77, 176*
   friction feed *181*
   impact *176, 178*
   matrix *178*
   modes *78*
   non-impact *180*
   tractor feed *181*
Privacy *191*
Procedural databases *120*
Procedure *4*
Program,
   command driven *96, 120*
   menu driven *96, 106, 120*
   monolithic *149*
   tutorial *101*
   utility *89, 169*
Program generator *90*
Progammability,
   databases *120*
   integrated packages *151*
Programming *21, 22*
Proportional spacing *181*
Proposals, call for, see Tender document
Proposals, comparing,
   objective criteria *60*
   subjective criteria *60*
   weighted ranking *61–62*
Purchases journal *156*

Purchases ledger *154–155*

Quantitative surveys *48*
Questionnaires *48*
Quick reference guide *29*

Ragged right text *103*
Real-time system *44, 70*
Recommendations *4*
Record *112, 114*
Record specification *49, 55*
Reference manual *94*
References *5*
Report,
   example *2–10*
   exception *20*
   on-demand *21*
   regular *20–21*
   types of *7, 20*
Right justification *103*
Ring *185*
Running a system *36*

Safe *81*
Sales journal *156*
Sales ledger *154–155*
Scale of a project *34*
Scatter graph *140*
Screen cleaning *83*
Screen input/output documents *49, 53*
Scrolling *102*
Search *116*
Security *191*
Slide production *138–139*
Small Firms Service *40, 200*
Software,
   applications *91*
   custom-written *91*
   evaluation *95*
   systems *91*
   vertical market *90*
Sorting *115*
Spelling checker *109*
Spooling *118, 171*
Spreadsheet *126–135*
Stacked bar chart *140*
Staff attitudes *44*
Star *185*

Stationery *78*
Statistics *148*
Stock control *162*
String replacement *102*
Summary *5*
Suppliers *30, 58, 62–63*
Switching on and off *77*
Systems analysis *34*
Systems analyst *36–39*
Systems flowchart *56*
Systems outline *49, 56*
Systems review *74*

Talks *11*
Targeting *17*
Task,
   active *19*
   reactive *19*
Teamwork *14–15, 23*
Technical colleges *26*
Technical feasibility *35*
Technical vocabulary *34*
Tender document *56–57*
Terms of reference *3*
Testing, see Acceptance testing
Text,
   formatting *103*
   presentation *103*
Theft *82*
Thesaurus *110*
Three-dimensional drawing *141*
Time management *148*
Timeslicing *173*
Timing *17*
Topology of networks *185*
Trace *170*
Tractor feed *181*
Training,
   computer skills *26*
   initial *25*
   materials *27–29*
   needs *24*
   off-site *31*
   ongoing *25*
   on-site *31*
   training agencies *30*
Transaction-driven system *70*
Trial balance *156, 160*
Tutorial guide *94*
Tutorial program *101*

User friendly *22, 96*
Users *25*
Utility software *89, 169*

Validation *115*
VAT inspector *161*
Verifying a disc *169*
Vertical market software *90*
Viewdata *187*
Visual aids *14*

Warranties *84*
Weighted ranking *61–62*
What if? analysis *128*
WIMPs *173*
Window *106, 127, 150, 173*
Wire-frame *141*
Word processor, dedicated *110*
Word wrapping *102*
Work scheduling *82–83*
Working party *13*
Write-protect *79*
WYSIWYG *104*

Younger Committee *192*